Behind Sach:
The Huntz Hall Story

by Jim Manago

Behind Sach: The Huntz Hall Story

© 2015 Jim Manago. All Rights Reserved.

All illustrations are copyright of their respective owners, and are also reproduced here in the spirit of publicity. Whilst we have made every effort to acknowledge specific credits whenever possible, we apologize for any omissions, and will undertake every effort to make any appropriate changes in future editions of this book if necessary.

No part of this book may be reproduced in any form or by any means, electronic, mechanical, digital, photocopying or recording, except for the inclusion in a review, without permission in writing from the publisher.

Published in the USA by:

BearManor Media

P O Box 71426

Albany, Georgia 31708

www.bearmanormedia.com

ISBN   978-1-59393-772-0 (paperback)
         978-1-59393-773-7 (hard cover)

Printed in the United States of America.

Book & cover design by Darlene and Dan Swanson of Van-garde Imagery, Inc.

Front cover pictured: Huntz Hall and Darlene Fields in publicity still from Allied Artists' *Spook Chasers* (1957)

Table of Contents:

Preface v

Acknowledgements ix

Dedication xi

Introduction xiii

Part One: Huntz Hall's Life

Chapter One: American Chaplin? 3

Chapter Two: From Dead End, A Career Is Born 9

Chapter Three: Developing His Comedy 31

Chapter Four: Here Comes Sach:
       "Ohp! Ohp! Ohp!" 51

Chapter Five: Not Running Scared for Jobs 67

Chapter Six: A Sad Farewell 95

Part Two: The Bowery Boys Films

Chapter Seven: Sach's Comedy, 1946–1949 107

Chapter Eight: Sach's Comedy, 1950–1953 143

Chapter Nine: Sach's Comedy, 1954–1958 191

APPENDIX:

Interview transcript of 1963 television appearance 257

Endnotes 263

Selected Bibliography 269

Award 275

Credits 277

Index 365

Preface:
by Gary Hall

Huntz Hall, my father, died fifteen years ago–on January 30, 1999. A decade and a half after his death, he remains an enigma to all who knew him. He was at once hilariously funny and deeply serious, open-hearted and vindictive, generous and selfish. He could be sweet and thoughtful one moment, possessed by unreasonable rage the next. He was at times supremely confident in his abilities as a comic actor and at others plagued by terrible insecurity. All this means he was a complicated person to have for a father. Much of what I know and believe as an adult comes from what I learned from my father as a child. He always empathized with the poor, the oppressed, and those who were up against it. His friendships crossed lines of race, class, and religion. Though he was alienated from institutional Christianity early in life, he had a lifelong faith in a God whose goodness and justice reside in the human heart.

On the other hand, because he was absent (my mother and I lived in Los Angeles, he in New York) for most of my adolescence, I did not receive much mentoring from him. I knew my father in one way as a small child, in another way as an adult. But the middle part of our relationship is simply missing.

Carl Jung said, "The greatest burden a child faces is the unlived life of the parent." My father wanted to be a priest but was turned off by the judgmental aspects of Roman Catholicism in the 1930s. He also wished he had received a formal education. So here I am, a priest with a graduate degree in English. Go figure.

If you love the character Sach, you have an idea of how much fun it would be to have a man with Sach's best qualities for a father. My earliest childhood memories are of a man who was fun-loving and generous. I spent some part of every summer from ages 4 to 8 on the stages of the *Bowery Boys* movies at Monogram (then Allied Artists) Studio. There was constant laughter and good feeling on the set.

When I got to college age, I developed a different kind of relationship with my father. In the summers and on weekends we would sit up and watch "The Late Show" movies on the New York CBS affiliate, and every time an actor came on screen I would be regaled with some backstage story about the person: their sexual preferences, political opinions, physical oddities. One example: watching a Preston Sturges movie, my father suddenly spotted Brian Donlevy and announced, "Brian Donlevy has short arms!" It was true. His arms were incredibly short for a man his size. His suits were specially tailored so you wouldn't notice, but once you are on to the short arm problem you'll never see Brian Donlevy the same way again. Extrapolate from that one instance some anecdote or fun fact about every star of Hollywood's Golden Age. I can hardly watch an old movie without hearing my father's voice in my head.

In 1987, the two of us took a cross-country drive to visit my wife Kathy's family in Ohio. We drove the modern version of the old Route 66 as far as we could, and he told me several stories about traveling this road with the Dead End Kids and his act with Gabriel Dell. That was the year the evangelist Oral Roberts was sequestered in his tower high atop his university asking God to give him guidance about the future of his ministry. As we drove by that building, my father rolled down his window, yelling, "Jump, Oral, jump!" On that trip I learned about every nightclub and theater between Los Angeles and Toledo.

Many people think my father stopped working when the *Bowery Boys* series ended in 1958. In fact, he worked pretty consistently up until his wife Lee died, five years before he did. If he made one big career mistake in the late 50s it was misjudging the importance of television. While he did have several ongoing appearances on *The Milton Berle Show, The Red Buttons Show,* and *The Eddie Fisher Show,* my father thought of himself as a movie and not a TV actor. He turned down several sitcom roles after the movies ended, and he simply missed the boat in terms of what they call TVQ--an actor's television recognizability. His longtime fans came to know him principally through the movies when they ran first in the theaters and then for years on Saturday morning television.

It is hard even at this remove to assess Huntz Hall's achievement as a movie actor. The early *Dead End Kids* movies are undoubtedly cinema classics. The later *East Side Kids* movies, while not great films as such, have wonderful comic moments. The *Bowery Boys* series showed Leo Gorcey and Huntz Hall to be a great comedic team. The movies suffer today because of the melodramatic nature of their plots. The Three Stooges have survived largely because their gags are encased in movies that have no story to get in the way. (Stooges go to society soiree: food fight ensues.) The best way to watch a Bowery Boys movie is to fast forward through the story and look for the comic moments. Taken in isolation, the scenes between Slip and Sach are as good as film comedy gets.

I'm grateful to Jim Manago for the care and dedication that went in to writing the story of my father's life. Because my father was a complicated man, you will read here some stories that will make you love him more, some that will challenge your affection for him. All in all, he was not the father I would have asked for, but he was the father I got and much of what I do as an Episcopal priest is grounded in the values I took from him in early childhood. My father loved people, he loved life, and he loved to laugh. He was even funnier off screen than on. I love and miss him still, and I'm thankful for this book and the opportunity to remember him in all the complexity of who he was.

The Very Reverend Gary R. Hall
is Dean of Washington National Cathedral.

Acknowledgements:

I offer special thanks to the Very Rev. Gary R. Hall. As Gary freely answered my many questions, he shared with me priceless information about his father, much of it revealed here for the first time and quoted just as he wrote it.

As a biographer and writer, I am most comfortable with information that can be verified as truthful; or, at the very least, has sources that can be quoted. Too often biographers make assertions and tell stories without having a source that can be named. I have been compelled to avoid this style of writing.

I am thankful for Gary's honesty in telling me of his father's imperfections, and not choosing to hide or whitewash them. His assistance by offering direct quotes has made this endeavor most comforting to me.

In addition, I am especially indebted to Phil R. Gries, Archival Television Audio, for giving this first biography special value by providing a transcript of the rare and earliest surviving interview with Huntz Hall from back in 1963.

My book would not be complete without the contributions provided by Randy Bonneville. He compiled the superb credits in the

Appendix by using many sources to make it as complete and accurate as possible. I am most indebted to him for offering his services gratis.

Ben Ohmart, my publisher and friend, is to be especially commended for unhesitatingly agreeing to publish this book when I first proposed it to him back in April of 2013.

I offer many thanks to all those individuals offering assistance to this project that wished to remain unnamed. Of particular importance to the success of my work is the research and help offered to me by my partner, Donna. She watched the films with me, offering pertinent comments; besides, reviewing everything contained herein.

Special thanks to Joe Franklin for inspiring my life-long study of movies.

As always, this authorship is a pure labor of love. The supreme reward to me will come when I receive the opinions, complimentary and critical, from you the reader. Therefore, I would be remiss not to thank you in advance for purchasing this book. I hope it will be as memorable an experience for you as it has been for me.

I thank Huntz Hall posthumously for benefiting humanity by giving us so many laughs throughout his motion pictures. This book is offered respectfully in the hope that readers can appreciate and learn from his life–an assortment of trials and tribulations as well as aspirations and achievements.

Readers wishing to contact me should do so by visiting my blog dedicated to Huntz Hall at http://huntzhall.blogspot.com

Dedication:

I dedicate this book to the memory of my Mom and Dad, as well as to all those individuals that made these productions possible; from producers, directors, writers, supporting cast, technical support, to Hall's Chief on screen, Leo Gorcey.

Introduction:

"Now wait a minute young fellow. I might be dumb, stupid and idiotic. But give me a chance to talk and prove it! Will you?"

Smugglers' Cove, Monogram Pictures
Sach (Huntz Hall) speaking to Slip (Leo Gorcey)

Someone may think it is dumb of me to author this book. I hope that when they read it, they will think otherwise. As my third book, the subject is different from my first two, as they focused on Shirley Booth, the critically acclaimed actress of stage, screen, radio and television

Here I offer the first book-length biography of Huntz Hall, a popular motion picture actor from the 1930s thru the 1950s. He played almost the same character as a Dead End Kid, an East Side Kid, and a Bowery Boy in nearly ninety motion pictures. Unarguably, Hall's best-remembered work remains as the Bowery Boy Horace Debussy "Sach" Jones, which gave moviegoers so much pleasure.

However, Huntz Hall did not receive much critical recognition then, due to the fact that he spent much of his career at a "Poverty Row" studio, primarily playing the seemingly dumb, rubber-faced goofball, the naïve patsy. Hall superbly played the foil to Leo Gorcey's street tough, known for a speech humorously littered with malapropisms.

With the choice of writing another book on anyone I wanted to, you may ask: "why write a book on an actor known best for offering lowbrow physical comedy solely in B-movies?"

I spent many years watching and studying the motion pictures of true masters of filmmaking who made their successes at major studios with excellent production values, complex and extraordinarily planned productions, and reasonably large sums of money. I also spent considerable time studying the "B" movies–often embarrassingly shoddy and cheaply made genre productions, including formula serials, westerns, and comedies.

Unlike major studio stars, Hall acted in a slew of low budget, quickly made, and often flawed motion pictures that usually do not hold up well to any critical scrutiny. The plots are limited–even at times melodramatic, and the characters are almost never psychologically complex, not at all like the motion pictures made by the top talents.

In addition, unlike the critically and commercially acclaimed performers, such as Shirley Booth, Huntz Hall never received his due in terms of accolades or awards. Although he proved he had the potential to do more than he did, his range became considerably limited.

Even on the Hollywood Walk of Fame, the Dead End Kids have a star at 7080 Hollywood Boulevard, which is at the corner of LaBrea and Hollywood Boulevards. However, Huntz Hall was never honored with an individual star (as was Shirley Booth). In short, he is an under-appreciated performer.

I asked myself, "Why am I drawn to study Hall?" He does not receive even a footnote in film history books.[1] Could the fact that his pictures were designed for the juvenile audience account for the disdain of critics? Would my associates find my choice of Hall as not worthy of a book-length study?

As I pondered these and other questions concerning the relevancy of this book, I went back to watch, re-watch and study all forty-eight of the motion pictures from the *Bowery Boys* series, as well as most of his earlier movies. Soon the answer became quite evident. I came to see that though they vary considerably in quality, Hall, when given the chance, made these pictures better than they would have been without him.

What I re-discovered is that the funny comedy business of Hall resulting from his slapstick and comedic mannerisms sets him apart as truly worthy of a book-length study.

I fondly remember seeing Hall's antics on New York television during the 1970s. I spent many weekends choosing between timeless classics. Years before VCR's were invented, I had the difficult choice of deciding what to watch. Should I see one of Leo Gorcey and Huntz Hall's movies or one of Bud Abbott & Lou Costello's movies? Unfortunately for me and countless other youths, these movies often were broadcast on television at the same time, especially on Sundays.[2]

Undoubtedly, I can never forget the intense pleasure I got from watching these slapstick masters; and I cannot stop remembering all of the ridiculous comic bits that were forever imprinted in my mind.

Over a half a century has passed since Huntz Hall last starred in the final entry of the *Bowery Boys* series, and fifteen years since he departed us. There have been several studies of these pictures, offering basic plot summaries and biographical descriptions of all of the players. However, there is so little behind-the-scenes information about these pictures from those responsible for them.

Unfortunately, those actors, writers, directors, producers and others connected with these motion pictures have died. No longer is it possible to thoroughly chronicle these productions and the talent via first person accounts from those participants.

However, more importantly, no book-length study has focused its complete attention on Huntz Hall. To remedy this, I offer this biographical study of him, with considerable attention given to chronicle many of his comedic moments found in the *Bowery Boys* series from the 1940s through the 1950s.

I committed to pursuing this endeavor because I realized that a book-length study of Huntz Hall is necessary to fill a gaping hole in film history by recognizing one of the forgotten talents who kept a studio in business.

Hall's comedy on film grew as he continued to make more of them. His talent came to fruition through a gradual evolution of his comic persona in each separate series of motion pictures. Eventually his diligence would pay off and his career would reach its pinnacle with the creation of the character of Sach in his final series.

I am offering this modest publication to stimulate a critical appreciation of the comedy brilliance of Huntz Hall. He often played a character of limited intelligence. Yet, I discovered in examining his life that although his schooling was insufficient by today's standards, and his behavior was not always faultless; nevertheless, the real man was a performer of intelligence.

In the first six chapters that follow, the focus is on the facts and truths of Hall's life presented as fairly and balanced as humanly possible. By no means is this part of this book intended to be an exposé or psychological study. As you will see, it describes an individual, just like the average person, who had many assets as well as shortcomings. The last three chapters examine and assess his comedy moments in all of the *Bowery Boys* movies.

First, my hope is that this book will provide a much deserved tribute; second, provide never-before revealed information so readers can better understand the man behind his characters; and third, enhance the viewing of his motion pictures.

Of the four series of films, my favorite character who funnyman Huntz Hall played was, and will always be, Sach. He is endlessly fascinating to watch. There are many facets to Sach. For instance, when he met up with a pretty woman, he made those distinctively silly lip gyrations known as motorlips. At other times, he would dash into a room and interrupt whatever was happening by waving his arms and nonsensically uttering: "Ohp! Ohp! Ohp!"

Nevertheless, whether he played Dippy, Pig, Glimpy, or Sach, Huntz Hall's characters were more than just dopey sidekicks. Hall's comedy persona is unpredictable, quirky, and original. You never know what to expect from him. That is, in a sense, he can stupidly step into crap one moment, but then just as unknowingly find gold in the next.

No matter what any of Hall's characters are doing in any of the motion pictures, I know I will be laughing! I beg your indulgence as I hereby invite you to join me in viewing and reveling in the zany, wacky, crazy, insane world of Sach, and learning only the truth about the man behind Sach–Huntz Hall.

May the following pages keep you laughing!

Jim Manago

November 2014

Part One:
Huntz Hall's Life

Chapter 1:
American Chaplin?

"Your father is the American Chaplin."

Groucho Marx to Gary Hall

Huntz Hall most emphatically left an indelible mark in the annals of B-movie filmdom. He got his start as one of the juvenile delinquents in a socially conscious Broadway play. He reached his peak when he appeared in 48 motion pictures as quirky "Sach." Through it all, Hall has given fans many laughs. What few people know is that between the beloved and zany character who Hall created, and the real person, lay a gulf.

His son, the Very Rev. Gary Hall, summed it up best: "Huntz Hall was a complicated person: extremely generous and loving on the one hand, scarily angry and violent on the other."

I listened to one of the sermons that Rev. Gary (hereafter referred to as Gary) delivered at the National Cathedral. Gary told an anecdote about a musician, Townes Van Zandt. He noted: "As you can imagine, this man's children bear many of the scars left by their father's behavior. As one of his children says, 'As a father he had a lot of unforgivable shortcomings that can't be excused by his music.'"

When I heard that, I surmised that this is true of so many people, including Huntz Hall. Gary confirmed my thinking: "You are right to hear in that a coded reference to my own experience. I have a priest friend who says you can't really grow up until you forgive your parents.

"As I get older I understand my father much better–he was emotionally deprived as a kid, and then he was unprepared for fame and money when they arrived in his teenage years. So he didn't have the skills to be a parent. He did the best he could with the emotional equipment he had. I have a lot of good memories of him as well, so it's not quite as bleak as the Van Zandt story."

Gary explained: "I think the hardest thing for me was the absolute disappearance [of him] from my life as a father beginning in the 6th grade and lasting until I got out of high school. My father was very proud of me over the years, but I was essentially raised by my mother."

The title of this opening chapter came via a memory provided by Gary. One day long remembered, when he was a teenager, Gary met up with Groucho Marx on a street in Beverly Hills. He introduced himself as Huntz Hall's son, and Groucho simply and emphatically told him: "Your father is 'The American Chaplin.'"

Yes, that is quite a complimentary title coming from a comedy master. To affix to Huntz Hall a title such as "The American Chaplin" is to elevate him to such a supreme level, and give him a recognition that he never received during his lifetime.

It might seem a bit of a stretch, when considering that Hall was very much <u>unlike</u> Chaplin in many ways, so the comparison may seem unexpected.

First, Chaplin not only starred in his motion pictures, but also he directed, produced and wrote them. In addition, Chaplin ended up making highly celebrated independent features that received mainstream audience viewing. In sharp contrast to Chaplin, Hall did little more than act in his movies, Also, with the exception of character parts in two productions (*A Walk in the Sun* and *Valentino*), he never got much beyond starring in low-budget and bottom-of-the-bill movies that reached mostly young or juvenile audiences.

Second, Chaplin became a figure of much controversy due to his possibly subversive political views and alleged moral improprieties. He decided not to return to the United States when he learned that he would have to appear before Immigration and be subject to deportation. Hall, though a supporter of left-wing causes (as Chaplin), never got mired in any substantial controversies or political issues, with the exception of several minor non-political arrests.

Third, Chaplin's character became a universal symbol of the downtrodden. Chaplin himself was liked, as well as despised, for being a social satirist and critic. On the contrary, Hall's Sach did not reach the lofty heights of representing something universally, nor was Hall acting as a satirist or critic.

However, in the sense of being an originator of a unique comic persona, Groucho's attribution of Hall as the "American Chaplin" makes sense. For that alone, I will agree, Hall deserves the accolade.

As Chaplin expressed his Little Tramp character in successive motion pictures, so too, Hall did with his Sach character. Both are garbed in an easily identifiable manner; Chaplin with his baggy trousers, Sach with his upturned baseball cap. You can see the gradual progression of each comic's character from film to film. Hall's Sach character grew in complexity and was refined in successive motion pictures, just as Chaplin's Little Tramp blossomed. In the best movies of both men, one will find the fullest and most complex manifestation of their respective characters.

Both comics had the ability to inspire comedic moments with props. Chaplin managed to get us to laugh at his handling of some rather ordinary objects, as when he makes his dinner rolls dance, or when he eats his shoes in his 1925 classic *The Gold Rush*. Similarly, some of the funniest moments occur when Sach goes into a room all by himself, talks to himself, and handles ordinary objects, poking at, and simply discovering things in a uniquely comedic way that makes us laugh.

Just as Chaplin accrued a sizeable fortune from being among the top moneymakers of his era, Hall (along with Leo Gorcey) also received a large financial reward when he reached his peak, although not accruing anything near Chaplin's riches. Unlike Chaplin, neither did Hall reach the same height in worldwide fame and recognition.

Gary offered his opinion, as he summed up his father's importance: "I think if the pictures had been better–they have got horribly melodramatic plots–more people would have seen his comedy. So I think he should be remembered as a pioneer of screen comedy who gave birth to a whole type of comic actor."

Both Groucho Marx and Gary acknowledge Hall's film persona provided an important, influential, and fresh approach to comic acting. Though it may be difficult to prove it, one may see the truth of that instinctively after watching Hall in enough of his movies to see how readily he can draw you into his comic world.

Perhaps, in the best of all possible worlds, the day will come when Hall will receive his due, be taken seriously, and be credited as the originator of a unique persona and lauded as surely as much a comic genius as Chaplin. Indeed at the very least, Hall deserves the same serious critical appreciation as has been bestowed upon Chaplin.

Besides his movies, there is another aspect to Hall's contribution to comedy. This is something that few, if any, ever speak about when Hall is mentioned by fans. It is, as Gary noted, "the thing that hasn't survived is the improvisational comic work he did with Gabe Dell in their nightclub act. Their act was way ahead of its time, and when I was in college they would do bits from it for me. Their comedy was influential on a generation of comics like Lenny Bruce, and it's too bad the act broke up before it could be recorded."

Gary said a writer friend told him that "most New York-style comics do 'early Huntz Hall.' One of his father's great joys later in life was the way younger comedians would seek him out to tell him how much his improvisational style of wild comedy had influenced them."

Unfortunately, because no recordings are known to exist of Hall's improvisational comedy on stage, it has not been possible to study this aspect of his career. Instead, the focus here must remain on the biography of Hall as regards his film career.

As regards his comedy on stage, here is another similarity to Chaplin. Hall did live comedy stage work, as Chaplin did. The difference is that Chaplin started out as an English music hall performer for Fred Karno before he made his movies; Hall did his stage act with Gabe Dell later, after many of his movies were already released.

Nevertheless, by the fact that he was a comedy originator, Huntz Hall must be credited just as Groucho Marx declared. Huntz Hall was and is the "American Chaplin."

Chapter 2

From Dead End, A Career Is Born

"I Stood in Line for Love"
Huntz Hall's title for a proposed autobiography.

Family life for Huntz Hall had an unsettling aspect to it as regards its large size. Hall's mother was the former Mary Ellen Mullen. His father, Joseph Hall, worked as an air conditioning engineer. Mary Ellen and Joseph gave birth to sixteen children. In short, besides Huntz, the couple raised twelve boys and three girls.

The details of his family life were never offered in print in his heyday. From Hall's son Gary, we know a few facts about his family since all are dead now. Danny was his oldest sibling. His brother Richie accompanied him to Hollywood from New York. Paddy was estranged from the rest of the family.

In addition, Catherine, Mary, Huntz, Mickey and Vallie are among the eight who lived to adulthood; eight died as children. Two of the eight who died before reaching adulthood were his favorite siblings; Martha, died from complications from bad sunburn; and Frankie died from peritonitis.

Hall's modest beginning occurred on August 15, 1920. His parents named him Henry Richard Hall. Huntz entered the world as the fourteenth of sixteen children. In his last years, when Hall thought of writing his autobiography, he was going to acknowledge his quite rear position among his siblings by entitling his book: "I Stood In Line For Love."

The experience of being born so late in the family tree gave him reason to consider that a perfect title. Besides, the fifteenth and sixteenth of the family got more attention over him. That is, everybody swooned over his two youngest siblings, the twins Michael and Valentine.

Gary: "He always felt that people were tired of the endless procession of babies until the twins came, so he felt under-appreciated as a kid. I think the acceptance he got from acting compensated for a kind of parental neglect all the brothers and sisters seemed to feel."

Henry Richard became more frequently known as "Huntz" later, when he began making radio shows in the early 1930s. It has been said that he was given that name by one of his brothers due to his Germanic features. Notwithstanding that attribution, Hall explained it this way: "I got my name 'Huntz' because my godfather was German and a 'Huntzie' in German is [a] puppy, which is what I looked like as a baby." Actually, the German word for dog is "Hund," and puppy dog is "Hündchen." It is not much of a stretch to pronounce "Hündchen" as "Huntz."

Gary: "Everybody called him Huntz. That was a family nickname and only became his professional name when the SAG [Screen Actors Guild] rules required that he use another name than Henry. Two actors cannot have the same name. Tim Conway's real name is Tom, but he changed it because there already was a Tom Conway (similar with Henry and Harry Morgan). There was a Henry Hall before my father got into pictures."

As a youngster, Hall lived on East 30th Street between 1st and 2nd Avenues in New York City. Down the block from where he lived became *the* place where he indulged in one of his regular pastimes. Hall recounted tales of the crazy fun that came from standing outside below the windows of Bellevue where he would taunt the mental patients. Hall would bring a blanket to catch the items that the patients would throw out the windows–alarm clocks, clothes, shoes, etc.

The limited information on his childhood that circulated in all the published references unfortunately tells us so little.

One story that has been often reported regards Hall's supposed first performance in the play *Thunder on the Left* at the tender age of one is problematic. This claim is clearly false since the first publication of the play's inspiration, a novel by Christopher Morley, did not come out until 1925 (Hall would have been five years old). Then the story was adapted as a play by Jean Ferguson Black in 1928 (Hall was then eight years old).

The Hoboken Theatrical Company, formed by the author with two others, planned to run *Thunder on the Left* at the Rialto Theatre in 1929. However, another play, which was held over, kept *Thunder* from ever running at the Rialto. When it did have a run, it was at the Hedgerow Theatre in Rose Valley, Pennsylvania in 1929 (Hall was then nine years old). After going to London, it returned for a short-lived run on Broadway on October 31, 1933 (Huntz was then 13 years old). The run ended in November of 1933 after 33 performances.

In short, for Hall to have appeared in *Thunder on the Left,* he had to be at least eight years old, based on the dates when the play was performed. Therefore, it is incorrect to say he was an infant performer in that play. Nevertheless, no credited record of his appearance in this show exists.

Just before I finished reading through several hundred articles about Huntz Hall in the *Chicago Tribune,* the *Los Angeles Times,* the *New York Times* and the *Washington Post,* I found clarification that Hall acknowledged that he did appear on stage as an infant–but the question remained "which show?" In an interview with Hall, Pat H. Broeske said: "Just 3 months old when he made his Broadway debut (he can't recall the play's title), Hall spent his childhood in vaudeville and radio."[3] Perhaps Hall appeared in a different play as an infant. Where or why *Thunder on the Left* is attributed to him is unknown.

Hall attended St. Stephen's, a Catholic grammar school. Although he would not finish high school, he went for training at the Professional Children's School in New York City.

He would sing as a soprano with Madison Square Quintette. The details of his youth membership in this singing group are sketchy. What we know is that Huntz and his younger brother Mickey were both members of the Madison Square Boys Club. The singing group performed at New York's Roxy Theatre, and he was heard on the radio in New York City. It is claimed that he damaged his beautiful singing voice one time by hawking peanuts at a circus.

Gary offered an interesting connection in his young father's life. Milton Berle's mother and Huntz Hall's mother were friends, as they both worked in radio. A teenaged Milton is said to have babysat Huntz. With that being true, it would not be difficult to see that Huntz would at some point find some work as a youngster on radio.

Unfortunately, the full scope of Hall's early credits, particularly his work on radio, is unknown. For instance, how often he was heard in a supporting role on *The Bobby Benson Show* during the early 1930s could not be determined since the seasons with Hall seem to no longer exist. Most interesting about the show is that Hall first worked with the lead character played by Billy Halop. Later, Hall and Halop would be together as Dead End Kids on stage and screen.

Hall's other known radio appearances are scant. The most notable included his guest appearance with Freddie Bartholomew on the *Fleis-*

chmann's Yeast Hour starring Rudy Vallee. The NBC show, broadcast on March 5, 1936, offered Hall a dramatic sketch called "Rich Kid." The story, written by Arch Oboler, depicted a wealthy youngster learning for the first time the horror and misery of want.

The May 26, 1938 episode of *Elza Schallert Interviews* featured Hall as one of The Dead End Kids (Billy Halop, Leo Gorcey, Huntz Hall, Bobby Jordan, Gabriel Dell, and Bernard Punsley). Later that year, *The Kate Smith Hour* broadcast on CBS on October 20, 1938 has the Dead End Kids performing in an original drama.

In a television interview for *Tomorrow with Tom Snyder*, alongside his co-star and pal Gabe Dell (who reportedly with other friends called him "Harry"), Hall said that he knew and worked with Milton Cross (1897–1975), radio announcer and "Dean of American Classical Music." Cross had a number of shows at the time, such as *Information Please*, *The Magic Key of RCA*, and *The Metropolitan Opera Broadcasts*, but the one that Hall connects himself to was *Coast to Coast on a Bus*.

That Sunday morning show featured host Cross as "The Conductor," who introduced talented children performers each week. Unfortunately, there is no complete log of this show to confirm which episodes Hall appeared on. However, the show had a long run starting in 1924 on WJZ in New York. The show moved to NBC Blue in 1927 thru 1940, and to NBC from 1940 thru 1948. More than likely, Hall was heard on the show when he was part of the Madison Square Quintette, since Cross's show featured plenty of songs and instrumental music, primarily classical.

Though his acting career began on radio, Hall's real break came when he was hired to appear as a street youth in a Broadway theatrical production.

Huntz Hall's career took shape in the autumn of 1935, when he acted on the Broadway stage at 15 years old. His renown in future productions would be rooted in a variation and development of a Broadway role. That role would be his livelihood and life, as well as his claim to fame, for the next twenty-three years.

The role he found himself in was as one of the delinquent teens in the socially conscious and dramatic production on Broadway called *Dead End*. Hall's life became defined by Sidney Kingsley's stage production, which opened on October 28, 1935. Hall shared the stage, and that ensemble acting included other "juvenile delinquent" youngsters; nicknamed the "Dead End Kids."

From the very beginning, Hall would seem to be generally cast as a second banana character, providing comic relief wherever and whenever possible. Although he would be associated with being part of an assemblage of actors as a group, he would eventually achieve his greatest success as the sidekick of a duo.

Hall liked to explain how he got his first break. This happened simply because he did a better imitation of the sound of a machine gun firing. According to his account in his interview with Tom Snyder, he initially auditioned for the leading juvenile part of Spit in the play, but he was turned down.

He was encouraged to re-apply when he met up with actor/director Martin Gabel (1912-1986). Hall said this happened one day when his class from Professional Children's School was heading to Recess Hall.

Gabel asked: "You've been down to tryout?" Hall replied: "I lost it–forget it." Gabel advised: "Come back down." He gave Hall a buck to take the cab up to the theater for another audition. The enterprising young Hall took the subway for a nickel and kept the other 95 cents.

He arrived at the theater to try out again. Everyone was in the green room. Hall and Gabel proceeded to walk into the entrance to the rehearsal. One of the hopeful kid actors was not getting across what director Sidney Kingsley was expecting.

Hall told Snyder that the kid weakly read the line: "Hey look at me fellows, I got a machine gun–kitty, kitty, kitty." Kingsley forcefully prodded the youngster to correctly read the line, by demanding that he: "Do that line again!" However, he could not offer the sound of a machine gun.

Kingsley turned to Hall, who was standing in the doorway with Gabel, and asked him, "Can you do a machine gun?" Hall responded: "Look at me fellows, I got a machine gun." Then Hall feigned the sound effect of a machine gun: "Ahhhh! Ahhhh! Ahhhh!" Hall: "That's how I got in *Dead End*."

Hall remained amazed that with all the training he had (the tap dancing, singing lessons, etc.), none of that mattered in getting his career off and running. Unbelievably, it was so simple for him to win the part of Dippy in a major Broadway stage production.

The show successfully ran for two years, keeping Hall steadily working as a teenage performer. Then the Kids were offered to make the Hollywood film version. They screen tested for it at the old Fox studios on 54th Street in New York City. Hall explained that at first the producers tried out everyone they could on the West Coast before they realized the Broadway Kids would be the only ones that could deliver what the roles called for.

Hall: "I fell asleep during it––I was tired." After the audition, Hall explained that they were asked if they would like to go to Hollywood. Once Leo agreed, "Yeah, I guess we'd like to go to Hollywood," they were signed.

It has been reported that when the play closed on June 12, 1937, Hall and the rest of the Kids, the so-called street urchins of *Dead End*, headed out to the West Coast with a contract to do the film adaptation for Samuel Goldwyn Studios. Actually, the Kids headed to Hollywood nearly two months before the show's demise, and presumably stand-ins played their stage parts.

An April 21, 1937 clip noted: "The six youngsters from the local company of *Dead End,* who were engaged last winter by Samuel Goldwyn for his film adaptation of the Sidney Kingsley play, will leave for the West Coast on Sunday. One of their number, Huntz Hall, will be guest of the East Side Boys Club at a farewell party this afternoon at the Madison Square Boys Club."[4]

A month after going to Hollywood, Hall would be quoted as saying: "I think I'll stick to the movies. It's easy. You sit around and don't do nothing and get paid."[5]

His reference to all the "easy" and lucrative work would indicate that the making of the picture already began within that first month when the Kids moved out to the West Coast.

The film version retained the poker game that Kingsley put in the play. George Shaffer explained: "He wrote in the scene as a sort of protest against a society that lets little boys gamble and fight and swear. He wanted to show how the slum boys live in the hope that society would do something about it."[6]

Hall's part of Dippy is important as his ignorance of the game brings the comic relief to the scene. During the draw, Dippy asks for five cards. Shaffer: "Leo looks at Huntz in disgust. 'For years,' he says, 'we've been telling him he can't take five. And five he says.' 'I'll take four,' says Huntz. 'You can take only three,' says Bobby. Huntz looks at his hand again. 'Give me one,' he says." Shaffer concludes: "perhaps the lesson in draw may do some good, that it may prevent unskilled players from demanding more than three cards."

The Kids would appear in motion pictures starting in 1937 with *Dead End*. In 1965, nearly 30 years after the film's release, Richard Lamparski interviewed Hall. Lamparski, best known for his book and radio series (*Whatever Became Of?*) asked Hall his opinion of the film that started his motion picture career. Hall, an easy-going conversationalist, tended to drop names or details without always speaking in fully formed sentences.

Hall: "Well, not that I was in the picture, [but] that to me was one of the greatest pieces of work ever done." However, Hall expressed his displeasure that the film is just put on *The Late Late Show*–he believed that it deserved better treatment.

Hall continued: "It was a great story–the story is so good, and picture–it's a real piece of art. It's what the technicians did. The acting was there from in the show, you know. Basically, with the kids, you know, the kids were the whole, they were the Greek chorus really of everybody. But as an overall picture, it was a great piece of work. First time I saw it, I was frightened.

"The intrigue of it–it's an artistic piece of work. Some of the camera angles. Shots going through it. Bobby Jordan, when the gangster calls us over and gives us instructions regarding the knife, he's shooting from the shoe box up into my face and Gabe Dell... But it was like [a] painting, just not like shooting film. It was like everything was done great, it was put into its position."

Dead End, the Sam Goldwyn film, with William Wyler directing, did not win a single Academy Award. It was nominated in four categories––Best Picture (Samuel Goldwyn Productions), Best Supporting Actress (Claire Trevor), Best Cinematography (Gregg Toland), and Best Art Direction (Richard Day).

However, Hall seemed to believe otherwise in his explanation to Lamparski. Hall: "[Goldwyn] never belonged to the Academy at that time. [The film] wasn't even in the running–you have to belong to the Academy of Arts and Sciences." Hall incorrectly believed that *Dead End* did not win any Oscars because he did not remember that it was indeed nominated. He believed that this all had something to do with Goldwyn not joining the Academy. Unfortunately, Lamparski did not realize that Hall's statement was erroneous.

The stories of the havoc caused by the shenanigans of the actors playing the *Dead End Kids* have been told many times. There were a number of outrageous and costly pranks, including the setting off studio sprinklers, which flooded the sets and shut down production.

Hall recalled to the gossip columnist Hedda Hopper: "At Warners' we had to do something to sustain our reputation. Once we wrecked a set; another time we tested the sprinkler system by putting a blow torch against a jet. It worked.

"The Kids arrived here with a ready-made reputation for toughness, so we tried to act the part and succeeded. We couldn't step out of character when the whistle blew. Our stage characters were too well known. Everywhere we went genuine tough guys would choose us, so we had to fight back. I have been slugged at least 25 times, the last time only two weeks ago, by guys who wanted to find out if I am as tough as I make out. I have had more black eyes than a prize fighter, and the experience of the others has been the same."[7]

Actress Ann Sheridan explained, in rallying to their defense with the studio bosses, the Kids were acting out their "teenager angst." As the story goes, the boys were sure to tamper with Sheridan's automobile the following day just to show everybody that they played no favorites.

The *Los Angeles Times* reported: "The haggard look that Humphrey Bogart occasionally wears around the Warner Brothers lot has been diagnosed as 'Dead End' trouble." In short, Bogart, who appeared alongside the Kids in *Dead End* and *Crime School*, did not escape the Kids's pranks. The Kids "used him as the butt of their practical jokes–including such old favorites as leaking water glasses, exploding rolls and suddenly appearing frogs in a scene in which he has been required to eat before the camera."[8]

Simply stated, Samuel Goldwyn had his fill of their antics after shooting *Dead End*. Hall: "What would have been ordinary mischief in any group of kids our age was always blown up into super-toughness, like the time all six of us got aboard Willie Wyler's motorcycle and raced all over the Goldwyn lot, causing Mr. Goldwyn a slight case of heart trouble, as we were right in the middle of a picture."

Critic Douglas W. Churchill: "They appear to treat the great of the cinema with a lack of reverence that is discouraging and the purity code of the Hays office means nothing at all to them. They insist on discarding the cleansed lines of the picture script and either substituting their own version or quoting some of the more torrid passages from the play."[9]

In his autobiography, Leo Gorcey described several times when Hall acted up. One time when they attended the studio school, Hall glued all the students' IQ test papers together before the teacher graded them. Gorcey noted: "The other kids had their difficulties with the Highway Patrol, but Huntz probably got in the most trouble; he never could understand why you were allowed to buy liquor in a store on your way home, but were arrested just because you drank it before you got there."[10]

When they were done shooting *Dead End*, they purchased a 1930 roadster. They paid a down deposit of $20 for the $125 due for a three-day trial concession. Gabe Dell obtained an operator's license. Thomas H. Pryor explained what happened next: "Huntz Hall immediately wanted to take the wheel, but was voted down on the ground that he had no license. However, Huntz was not the fellow to be dissuaded easily, and when the boys parked the car to do some shopping he volunteered to stay behind and keep an eye on it.

"When they returned to the spot where the machine was parked,

Huntz was standing there but the car was gone. To make a long story short, Huntz decided to take a drive and ran into a tree. It cost them $35 to have the car repaired. Then they drove down to Tijuana, Mexico, to Lake Arrowhead and toured Los Angeles, after which the car was returned to the dealer with the explanation that they were not satisfied with its performance."[11]

The film version of *Dead End* impressed the reviewers. It "adheres with remarkable fidelity to the spirit and scene of the original work. A few minor alterations have been made, to be sure, but they are relatively unimportant.

"The play's enlivening realism, however, springs primarily from the amazingly natural performances of the ragged urchins who make the docks a breeding place of petty crime–Billy Halop, Huntz Hall, Bobby Jordan, Leo B. Gorcey, Gabriel Dell and Bernard Punsley. These lads, borrowed from Norman Bel Geddes' New York stage production, make "Tommy," "Dippy," "Angel," "Spit," "T.B.," and "Milty" as precious a gang of young cutthroats as one would care to run up an alley to evade."[12]

The January 5, 1937 contract of employment that Hall had with Samuel Goldwyn, Inc., Ltd. was transferred to Warner Bros. Pictures on July 29, 1937 and amended on August 6, 1937.

With said contract, Hall stayed in Hollywood to make additional motion pictures as one of the *Dead End Kids*. In no time, the play and motion picture had spawned a whole series of movies at Warner Bros. Studios. Though Hall played Dippy in *Dead End*, he became Goofy in *Crime School* (1938). In *Angels with Dirty Faces* (1938) he played Crab.

The friendship that developed between Hall and co-star Gabriel Dell had its vicissitudes. For instance, reporter Read Kendall gave an account of one of those difficulties in which Dell lost a tooth and Hall sustained bruises and a black eye.

Kendall: "Though they're the best of pals, two of the brilliant youngsters who gained so much fame for their work in *Dead End* came to blows yesterday.

"The fight began when, during the playing of a tenement scene for *Crime School,* Dell didn't like the way Hall acted his part–a way he thought was calculated to steal the spotlight from himself. He grabbed a head of cabbage from a near-by stand and almost floored Hall with it. That proved the spark to ignite the anger in both of them and fists began to fly.

"The other four boys joined in [Gorcey, Halop, Jordan, and Punsley]." Bogart broke up the fight, and got Hall and Dell to shake hands. Kendall: "A dentist was hurriedly summoned to put a new tooth in Dell's mouth, and the makeup department covered over Hall's black optic."[13]

Eight months later, things were different. This time Dell helped resolve Hall's encounter with the police. The situation is like a scene from one of their movies. "They tried to move a car and open up a parking space for their vehicle on Hollywood Boulevard during the Santa Claus Parade.

"Dell stopped his car on the boulevard while Hall got out and got into another car to release the emergency brake so he could move it back a few feet. He found himself looking into the face of the officer. 'So you're the kids who broke into this car this morning,' the officer said. 'Come on.' Hall explained who he was and Dell came to his rescue."[14]

Hall revealed his friendship to fellow Dead Ender Bobby Jordan when he tried to help him get the part to be Bonita Granville's boyfriend for a movie in the Nancy Drew series. UPI published a letter that Hall sent to Jack Warner after Warner Bros. studio announced that one of the Dead End Kids would be picked to be Granville's co-star.[15] The press noted: "with modesty worthy of John Alden himself," Hall wrote:

> "Dear Mr. Warner... I would take the job in a minute but I got a girl already and she might not think I was acting because Bonita is a swell babe.
>
> "Besides, maybe I'm too manly to play a sixteen-year-old kid. You know I smoke a pipe already. But Bobby Jordan would be perfect for the part. He isn't much more than sixteen and besides he played with Bonita in *My Bill*. He likes her an awful lot and would certainly give as her boy friend."

Hall concluded the note by saying, "He won't be acting the part. He will be right in his glory. Respectfully, Huntz Hall."

In 1939, Hall made four more movies. He was back as Dippy in *They Made Me a Criminal*. A reviewer noted: "Billy Halop as Tommy and Huntz Hall as Dippy outshine the other kids."[16] In addition, the movie was shown accompanied by *Swingtime in the Movies*. This short subject featured an appearance by the Dead End Kids portraying 'Crime School Kids,' a "pretentious Technicolor short."[17]

In addition, in 1939, Hall played Ace in *Hell's Kitchen*. Then Hall managed to use his own first name in *The Angels Wash Their Faces*, when he played Huntz Gartman. Finally, he played Cadet Johnny Cabot in the last Warner Bros. film, *On Dress Parade*.

Although the part that Hall played in each of the Dead End Kids series is minor, he said at the time that his ambition was to be a producer. The *Los Angeles Times* reported: "Huntz Hall won't be satisfied with anything less than a producer's berth."

Fortunately for him, the innumerable movies he acted in did keep his face before audiences and it gave him much-needed experience. It would benefit him most when he was called to play a major part in his last series of movies. As far as the Dead End Kids series, his contribution is minimal.

What is quite intriguing in looking back at the press reports from the time after Hall made the *Dead End Kids* movies. Hall, at his most outspoken, told of how he definitely regretted earning money from the productions. The title of Hedda Hopper's column said it all: "A Former 'Dead End Kid' Regrets Every Penny He Made from the Play's Hollywood Career." [18]

Hopper: "Hall... believes that the 'Dead End Kids' pictures not only touched off a wave of juvenile delinquency whose reverberations are still distressing the Nation, but he has just learned how the Nazis converted the series into anti-American propaganda.

"Skillfully edited by experts under Dr. Paul Joseph Goebbels, the pictures were presented not as dramatizations of social evils which were the exceptions rather than the rule, but as documentations showing the degradation of youth in the 'decadent democracies,' especially America....

"Old enough now to know better, and with a keener sense of social responsibility, Hall voices the contrite conviction that the 'Dead End Kids' on the screen created among American youth a horde of bullies, exhibitionists, vulgarians, and just plain brats. Even now when he passes a group of junior commandos at play, he hears some of the expressions the Dead-Enders put into circulation:

'Wanna breathe thru a broken nose?'

'Lookin' for a fat lip?'

'I'm gonna spit in your eye and charge you for an eye wash.'

'I'll hit you on the head so hard you'll be looking out your stomach.'

'I'll dig your eyes out–you wanna sell pencils?' "

Hall did not find any fault with his first film, *Dead End*. Hopper even reported that Hall was proud of that film for it brought much attention to the evils of slum life, eventually spurring the end of slums and improvements to housing. It happened that Hall became unhappy with the Dead End Kids' characterization after *Angels with Dirty Faces* was released. "[It was then] he began receiving letters from teen-age boys who wanted to join him in a racket, a bank stickup, and various other illegal enterprises."

Simply put, Hall held some real hope that his upcoming movies would change to improve his reputation. Hall: "Maybe I can make amends by making some pictures that will counteract the 'Dead End Kids.'"

So his disillusionment with the pictures came when Hall had received letters from boys asking him to be part of their plans for breaking the law. Hall felt that the Dead End Kids could and should have been depicted differently to make them a positive force. Eventually, this hope would find some fulfillment later when Hall saw the movies turn from social delinquent melodramas to become slapstick comedies with Hall playing his best comic character, Sach.

Hall suggested to Hopper how the Kids could have been depicted. She quotes Hall as saying: "The public went for the kids' personalities. They were all vital–with the same kind of intense interest that Cagney and Robinson created in *Five Star Final, Little Caesar*, etc. Each Dead-Ender was a character. They could have been shown as a typical gang of good American boys–rough, ready, adventurous, but basically sound, and certainly not vicious."

The pressure was high, but Warner Bros. would pull the plug on the series, and not admit it had anything to do with the negative image the Kids were generating. It all had to do with them being too old to play Kids anymore. The gossip columnists were not buying that studio spin.

Six months earlier to Hall's remarks to Hopper, gossip columnist Louella O. Parsons wrote: "The 'Dead End' kids have outgrown their

Warner Bros. contract—and for that reason they are not being renewed. I thought at first, when I heard the news, that it might be because the Hays office received so many letters from parents protesting that the boys' antics have had a deleterious effect on the youth of the country.

"But Warners deny that, saying it is too difficult to get material for young men who hardly fit the description 'kids' any more. However they plan to go on a personal appearance tour for the next six weeks—all but Billy Halop, who will remain here and try his luck as an independent actor. The rest, Huntz Hall, Bobby Jordan, Leo (Bridegroom) Gorcey, Gabriel Dell and Bernard Punsley will meet their public face to face."[19]

The issue of the negative influence of the Kids remained and was reiterated four years later. Hopper: "The Dead End Kids have played their parts so well they've been a bad influence on youth of the nation. Huntz Hall got a fan letter from a young man who wrote the Dead End kid that he was hitchhiking to California where he'd like to get together with Huntz and rob a bank! Huntz returned the note with a personal aside that 'crime doesn't pay' and I'll bet that 12-year-old adventurer's parents will take his dead-end out in the family woodshed."[20]

Then, forty years later, in his interview with Tom Snyder, Hall seems to have made peace with the criticisms leveled at their series. He explained that he remembered why the Dead End Kids were considered bad. Simply put, the Kids did not say that they accepted that Rocky Sullivan turned yellow at his execution in *Angels with Dirty Faces*.

Hall: "We got a lot of pressure, being censured and saying that they should be put out of pictures, they're teaching bad things. But that was the time, that was the era. Every kid was growing up to be a gangster, you know. That was what was happening at that time. If they didn't have a war, there would have been like machine guns all over the streets."

Though Hall was not singled out for praise, some of the reviews of the *Dead End Kids'* productions nonetheless show the appreciation given to them, despite the controversy over their negative influence:

On *Angels with Dirty Faces*:

"In his dealings with these robust and rebellious young actors known as the 'Dead End' kids...Cagney meets them on their own ground and outguesses them at every turn, with results that frequently are intensely amusing."[21]

A year earlier on *Crime School*:

"These lusty young men...Each is an actor born, as well as a comedian who can impart humor to the grimmest of speeches. Their talents, individually and collectively, are given freely and considerable 'punch' in *Crime School*."[22]

"This is a strangely gifted gang of youngsters. In addition to being a competent actor in the play's moments of melodramatic intensity, each is a comedian of many parts. Each, also, is an individualist in style. No two lads are in the least alike; no two follow the same groove in method or pace. These six kids form an amazingly effective combination of variegated personalities and talents."[23]

". . . lusty young hellions...They are six of the toughest and most natural young actors who ever found their way before the cameras–something that probably never would have happened had they not previously found their way behind the footlights in Norman Bel Geddes' original stage production of the Sidney Kingsley melodrama that gave them their pseudonym.[24]

Twenty-year-old Hall would exaggerate his prowess as any young man would with the luck to become a Hollywood commodity. Hall declared: "Take me, now. I've become a kind of Romeo with the girls. They write me mushy letters. Jeez, I get more fan letters than Errol Flynn. How many? Well, put me down for sixteen thou' a month, will you?"

Punsley corrects Hall: "You don't mean Errol Flynn. You mean Francis X. Bushman." Hall challenges Punsley: "But who's the guy who dates up all these Follies girls? Tell him. Go ahead."[25]

The article went on to say that the press agent disagreed with Hall's boasting, saying that the entire group of Kids might get a total of 2,000 letters a month. Hall had been in last or second from last place in regard to the most letters received by any of the Kids. If anything, Hall's response is an admission that he was simply girl crazy.

"Huntz Hall confided that his current *Weltanschauung* [German for 'philosophy of life'] is built around an appreciation of the aesthetic–'dames, cars, and pictures.' He virtually haunts the art galleries, he vows." He continued: "Looking at pictures is restful to the eye and to the mind."

Louella O. Parsons followed Hall's dating life in her column, "Close-ups and Long Shots of the Motion Picture Scene." Here is a sample:

> "Huntz Hall, one of the Dead End Kids, is spending all his time with Ruth Skinner who recently separated from Nick Stuart. They've been at the La Conga every night for a week."[26]

> "Huntz Hall ('Dead End' kid) and Elsie Anderson, N.T.G. girl, talking elopement at La Conga."[27]

> "Elsie Anderson, Florentine Garden cutie, and Huntz Hall, 'Dead End' kid, have set the date."[28]

> Huntz Hall and his best girl, Elsie Anderson, eloped and

were wed in Yuma Sunday. Last night they were celebrating at La Conga."[29]

Hall, at 20 years old, married the 18-year-old dancer on September 9, 1940. This first marriage lasted for less than four years before it ended in a divorce. The *Los Angeles Times* reported on May 9, 1944 that Hall was sued for divorce on May 8: "Henry Richard Hall, known as 'Huntz Hall' in the 'Dead End Kids' in motion pictures, yesterday was made defendant in a suit filed by his wife, Mrs. Elsie May Anderson Hall. The wife charges cruelty and asserts a property settlement has been made.

Hopper reported: "Huntz Hall, ex-Dead-Ender, and ex-wife Elsie Anderson have ended the 'ex,' and are reconciled."[30] This was not true for long, as the divorce would be finalized. Though not verifiable, Hall's apparent penchant for woman chasing is presumed to have contributed to the marital woes. Gary: "I don't really know much about his romantic life, but when he was single he was always going out with women. He really liked women and they liked him. But we never talked in any detail about that stuff."

One of his female co-stars, Evelyn Ankers, had her own memorable experience with Hall while he was married to Elsie. She had co-starred in *Hit the Road*, the *Dead End Kids and Little Tough Guys* film from 1941. Ankers: "On one occasion after a day's shooting I thought I was the last one to leave but on my way out I bumped into Huntz Hall (acne and all). He put his arms around me and tried to force me to kiss him. I responded as my daddy taught me to–I let him have it with my knee right between his legs."

As already reported in 1940, and now again in 1944, Hopper reiterated that Hall's ultimate ambition was to return to Broadway and follow that with becoming a film producer. Hopper: "There should be a crack in here somewhere–from a Dead Ender to a colossal producer."

Hopper concluded: "No one knew better than Huntz that it's easier to get a bad reputation than it is to clean it up and make it good–that there's so much bad in the best of us and so much good in the worst of us that it ill behooves any of us to talk about the rest of us."[31]

In short, after two years on the stage, Hall made *Dead End*, his first film for Samuel Goldwyn. Then there were a series of six *Dead End Kids* motion pictures for Warner Bros. What followed at the same time is that the Kids regrouped and reappeared at several studios; first, a series called *The Dead End Kids and Little Tough Guys* for Universal Pictures. This partially overlapped another series, this one made at Monogram Studios called the *East Side Kids*. Then finally another reworking at that same studio referred to as the *Bowery Boys* series.

Chapter 3:
Developing His Comedy

"I quit the club! I'm going home! You're not my leader anymore. I give my life for you. But being a girl is out of the question! I tell you, I quit!"
Glimpy, *Clancy Street Boys* (1943)

With the enormous success of The *Dead End Kids* series at Warner Bros., things got quite busy now for Hall. He would be working at more than one studio with an overlapping series of movies. For a time, while he had *Dead End Kids* movies coming out at Warners, he was also appearing in a series of movies at Universal, a series that ran from 1938 thru 1943.

Leo Gorcey and Bobby Jordan stayed at Warners after making their second *Dead End Kids* film, *Crime School*. Universal offered a series modeled after the Warners series, called *The Little Tough Guys*. On January 28, 1938, Universal signed Huntz Hall and Billy Halop, adding them to that series, and calling it a combination group title of "*The Dead End Kids and the Little Tough Guys*."

Hall did the same shifting back and forth at film studios when his work at Universal for the last three years would overlap his work for Monogram Studios. It is at Monogram where he would appear as the character named Glimpy in the *East Side Kids* series from 1940–1945. In addition, he made a few movies not connected to any series during these years.

There would be two *Dead End Kids and Little Tough Guys* motion pictures released by Universal for each year for 1938, 1942 and 1943; and three of them released each year in 1939, 1940, and 1941; the series had twelve movies and three serials.

In the first entry, entitled *Little Tough Guy,* four of the Dead End Kids appeared, Hall, Halop, Dell, and Punsley. Hall played a tough gang leader named "Pig."

Hall's first appearance as Pig has him demanding some stolen sausages from one of his gang members. Pig: "What's you're hiding?" Gang member: "Nothing, nothing." Pig hits the member's hand and snatches the sausages. Pig: "Nothing, nothing huh? What's the idea of holding out? I'll fight ya all over the joint, and that goes for the rest of you!"

Johnny (Halop), another gang leader, moved in to Pig's territory. Pig (while eating a sausage): "…you're new around here. So don't put anything over on us. Mind your own business and you won't get hurt." Pig and Johnny have a fight over Pig's demands for Johnny to give him money earned from his paper route. Pig comes to respect Johnny after the latter wins the fight by knocking Pig hard to the ground.

Pig: "Why didn't you tell me you could fight?"

Johnny: "I'd figure you'd find out. Hey, am I gonna have a shiner?"

Pig: "Maybe a little one. Ya know a mouse."

Johnny is put in detention at Juvenile Hall after throwing a brick in a car window of a judge. When he gets out, he joins in a crime spree with Pig and the rest of the gang. Eventually, the police corners Pig and Johnny. The latter does not want to give up, as Pig's paranoia makes him want to listen to the police and surrender. Pig: "I ain't staying, I'm giving myself up." Johnny: "If you do, I'll plug you full of holes before you get to the backdoor." Pig: "You kill me, you'll end up just like your old man. You wouldn't like that, would ya?" Impulsive Johnny acts like he's gonna shoot Pig as Pig begs forgiveness. Pig: "Johnny, I didn't mean it. You know I didn't. I'll do anything you say. Please don't shoot! Johnny, let me go!" Johnny lets Pig leave, but then a policeman fires a shot killing Pig instantly.

Little Tough Guy sets the mold of the series with Billy Halop becoming the lead of every film. Halop seemed to play the youth who always has the story bent around him. At times, the stories are a bit stretched as far as credibility. *Little Tough Guy* has Halop's character Johnny do quite a number of illegal acts; including being involved in a crime spree, carrying a gun, threatening his pal Pig at gunpoint, resisting arrest, and causing a police officer to be wounded. In addition, Johnny's stubbornness in refusing to surrender contributes to Pig to be killed by the police.

The finale is unfair since Pig does not get a chance to surrender, and Johnny receives a ridiculously soft sentence. The judge commits Johnny to a military academy to correct his bad behavior based on the thought that the boy's family believes he will come back a good kid.

A reviewer noted: "Huntz Hall as 'Pig' is splendid and so are all the other 'Dead End'-ers...The film was directed with sympathy and understanding and has several extremely dramatic and moving sequences."[32] Indeed, Hall stands out in *Little Tough Guy*, and he proved he had the ability to play a very tough gang leader in competition with Halop for top honors.

Though Hall's character of Pig was killed here, it was only temporarily. Of course, the continuity in the series was not considered at all since Hall appears in future movies alive and well. More importantly, Hall's tough guy persona would be a casualty, and this was more permanent.

Unfortunately, with the exception of the last film of this series and some isolated scenes scattered throughout this and two other series made at Monogram, Hall was never again given the advantage of being the tough gang leader or co-leader. Halop would be scripted instead as taking charge in the rest of this series.

With Halop as lead, Hall changed from playing tough guy with serious overtones to playing comic foil. This slow progression to taking on more broad physical comedy, readily evident in later movies, is apparent as starting with their next entry.

The three motion pictures after *Little Tough Guy*; namely, *Little Tough Guys in Society, Newsboys Home*, and *Code of the Streets*, would not have any of the Kids.

The Dead End Kids's second appearance, although the fifth film of the series, would be in *Call a Messenger* (1939). The credits read: "Billy Halop and Huntz Hall of The 'Dead End Kids' in Call a Messenger." The cast is listed followed with "and Little Tough Guys." Halop is shown smacking Hall behind the title credits.

From the start, Hall quickly and clearly excels at playing the submissive goofy character in the remaining movies in the series. This character from his work starting at Warners, and now at Universal, then continues to be Hall's forté in the two series produced by Monogram.

Interestingly, the credits in *You're Not So Tough* (1940), the Dead End Kids's third appearance (sixth film in the series), no longer billed Halop and Hall before the 'Dead End' Kids moniker. The credits simply offer their group name "The 'Dead End' Kids and The Little Tough Guys."

In August of 1940, the *Dead End Kids* and the *Little Tough Guys* would be seen in their first of three serials at Universal. The first one, *Junior G-Men*, gave Hall (playing Gyp) sixth billing after Billy Halop, Gene Reynolds, Lionel Atwill, Frank Albertson, and Richard Lane.

Developing His Comedy

Typically, Hall offered comic relief, and seemed to always be getting hurt somehow. For instance in Chapter 4 of the serial, after a car crash, Hall was revived with a whiff of ammonia. Hall: "Hey, what is that stuff?" Man: "Ammonia." Hall: "Ohh! That's stuff really got a kick. Give me some more of that." Man: "No, you got enough."

Hall was back as Pig in the next two movies; *Give Us Wings* (1940), and *Hit the Road* (1941). Hall's growing talent for comedy got acknowledged simply: "Huntz Hall amuses as Pig."[33]

In the second serial, *Sea Raiders,* Hall played Toby Nelson. Next up, Hall played Pig again in *Mob Town* (1941). He then played "Bolts" Larson in the third and final serial for the Kids, *Junior G-Men of the Air* (1942). Bobby Jordan would not appear in any of the three serials.

Hall's character of Pig would return in *Tough as They Come* (1942), *Mug Town* (1943), and finally in the last film of the *Dead End Kids and Little Tough Guys* series, *Keep 'em Slugging* (1943). Hall is given top billing here for the first and only time, as Billy Halop was absent. However, Hall is not the leader–Bobby Jordan is.

Shemp Howard shows up in several of these Universal movies with Hall. At the time, he was not playing one of The Three Stooges. Although he was part of the original Three Stooges act in vaudeville in the 1920s, he had left in 1932 to pursue a solo career. By then, he had appeared in only one film as a Stooge, *From Soup to Nuts.*

Eventually Shemp would be connected to Huntz Hall. The credit goes to Shemp for apparently helping Hall refine his comedy. Several sources tell of a close friendship that existed between them.

The strong admiration that Hall had for Shemp developed when they were both under contract at Universal. It has been reported that they both would visit each other at their respective sets. Of course, Shemp's solo career would include being seen in movies with Abbott & Costello, as well as appearing with Hall in three of the *Dead End Kids and Little Tough Guys* movies: *Give Us Wings*, *Hit the Road*, and *Keep 'em Slugging*.

Most notably, the youthful and aspiring twenty-year-old Hall lacked something Shemp's years had given him; namely, extensive vaudeville experience. Shemp most certainly had a deeper well of gags to draw upon than Hall. Therefore, Shemp could offer valuable pointers to Hall on timing, and other aspects to comedy performance.

The friendship between Shemp Howard and Huntz Hall, and the great influence the former had on the latter, may not be apparent from watching their motion pictures. It would be interesting to know what specific influence that Hall's admiration and association with Shemp Howard had on Hall's career, but this cannot be determined.

The best proof of the connection between them comes from Hall's son. Gary remembered: "My father thought Shemp was the funniest man who ever lived. The Howards lived near us in Toluca Lake, and though Shemp died when I was five, I remember him well. They considered Shemp (and his wife Babe) to be my godparents. I do remember my father saying that he was on the set when they were shooting the W. C. Fields' movie *The Bank Dick*. Shemp did many hilarious scenes that Fields cut out because they were too funny and therefore competition for Fields."

In 1947, Shemp returned to Columbia Pictures to be just a temporary replacement for his ailing brother Curly. However, he then became a regular part of The Three Stooges comedy team for his own endearing contribution to the two-reel shorts.

Hall's non-series motion pictures at various studios were all brief appearances made while he was busy with the respective film series at Warner Bros., Universal and Monogram. In 1939, he was seen alongside Humphrey Bogart in Warner Bros.' *The Return of Doctor X*, in which he played a character named Pink.

What apparently was Count Basie and his orchestra's first visit to Los Angeles, Hall, along with Dead Enders Gorcey, Dell and Punsley, appeared with them at the Paramount Theater. The Kids "precede the orchestra in a so-so comedy skit with Sam (Schlepperman) Hearn. Some of their material is pretty 'blue.'"[34]

In *Zis Boom Bah,* also known as *College Sweethearts* (Monogram 1941), Hall is billed in fourth place after Grace Hayes, Mary Healy, and Peter Lind Hayes. As the character of Skeets Skillhorn, Hall rides in a car carrying racks of clothing in the back.

He offers his card to two women (one is Grace Hayes visiting her son) at the campus.

Suits Cleaned and Pressed   Sick Friends Sat Up With
Shoes Soled and Healed   Jitterbug Lessons
Dogs Walked   Swedish Massage
Babies Minded

Skeets Skill Horn
At your service

Phone Janitor's Entrance, Midwick College

One woman reads the card, and asks the other: "Is this a college or a Sanitarium?"

Again, Hall's character is offering some comic relief. Halfway through the film he asks: "Is my credit good?" After being refused, he then admits: "Nobody can pay–so I'm out of the cleaning business." He declares: "I do imitations. Once I did an imitation of Washington crossing the Delaware so well that my hands got frost-bitten."

He wisecracks at a restaurant table about a woman: "The best thing she does is she carries a torch." After his female companion responds to his comment by smacking his face, he quizzically asks her: "What did I do now?" Later he reacts to something by declaring to her: "Great guns, little pistols and swords!" He proceeds to smack himself, and then asks himself: "What did I do now?"

The high point, albeit brief, of *Zis Boom Bah* for Hall is the floorshow at the restaurant club in which he dances and sings. Peter Lind Hayes sings "Annabella" to a blonde woman seated at a table. After the number, the woman exits, and Hayes expects her to return seconds later to dance with him. Instead, Hall surprises him when he appears in drag wearing a blonde wig and evening gown. His wild dance with Hayes segues into Hall singing.

The two songs he sings are by Johnny Lange and Lew Porter; only one is a complete number, "It Makes No Difference When You're in the Army." The second song is a disappointingly brief twelve seconds of "Annabella" in the finale. Hall sings to a girl on the stage: "Annabella, if you'd get a job, I'd be your steady fellow, Annabella, say that you are mine." Hall would plainly sing in other movies as well (see the credits list in the Appendix).

The reviewer of *Zis Boom Bah* noted: "Benny Rubin helps the comedy most effectively, while Huntz Hall, Skeets Gallagher, and Frank Elliot give other commendable performances."[35]

A newspaper clipping revealed Hall's involvement in a charitable social event at the time. Hall joined Gabe Dell, Eddie Foy Jr., Billy Halop, Rags Ragland, and Bob Ratford, to serve as busboys to a dinner feast on Christmas Day in 1941 for 300 orphans at Leone's. The New York tradition, which included entertainment, went back for 35 years.[36]

In *Private Buckaroo* (Universal, 1942), Hall made a brief appearance as Corporal Anemic, who ironically is seen teaching the great trumpeter

Harry James how to play the trumpet.

Junior Army (1942) was a loan-out for Columbia in which he played a most despicable gang leader named Bushy Thomas. Hall appears early on when he fights and almost kills Billy Halop's character (Jimmie Fletcher) by pushing him off a cliff. Freddie Bartholomew's character (Freddie Hewlett) saves the day. By the finale Hall reappears again, this time he is supposedly wanted for murder and is hiding out with a Nazi saboteur. Hall is not at all a likeable character here.

Unfortunately, Hall's appearance in this film, as with many of his other non-series movies, gave him little opportunity to do much. *Junior Army* is really a showcase for Halop and Bartholomew's talents.

Don't Kill Your Friends, the 1943 United States Navy training film, has Hall playing the bumbling Ensign Dilbert. This serious and episodic short of almost fourteen minutes tells viewers "Don't Be a Dilbert!" It has Dilbert repeatedly causing calamity because he ignores procedures and makes up his own rules. Hall's Dilbert admits that he's "got a million disguises," and "we're good for a lot of laughs." The narrator warns: "Even a dummy certainly could cause a tragedy."

His incompetence does not allow him to think he is doing anything wrong. He walks around misunderstanding things. He mumbles to himself and wonders why he has to do certain things. He blames his mistakes on someone else. Further, he always apologizes for his mistakes. "He's always sorry, always extremely sorry." This does not help much afterwards.

In one example, his anxiousness to call his girlfriend means he does not "park his plane in proper position for safety. He also forgets to tell his ordinance man something is wrong with the armaments." This leads to ammunition being fired, which causes the deaths of others nearby. We are told that they are killed just as much as if the enemy got them.

Dilbert also forgets to notify the control tower when he is landing short. The narrator warns how simple this can cause personnel on the ground to be decapitated by the line and sleeve. The short concludes by explaining that the life of your mates really means that you stick to the rules. "Make safety a habit. Don't be a Dilbert. Don't kill your friends."

Over at Paramount, he played a sailor in *Bring on the Girls* (1945). This Eddie Bracken film had Hall being used differently. Hall explained: "[In] *Bring on the Girls* at Paramount…my voice was offstage. Well, you know I worked in some scenes with a comic, and so everything you heard offstage wasn't in the camera range too much."

For Goldwyn/United Artists, Hall briefly plays a sailor named Mike in a scene from *Wonder Man* (1945). Mike sits down on a park bench with his girl (Virginia Gilmore) where twin brothers Edwin Dingle and the ghost of Buzzy Bellew (both played by Danny Kaye) are conversing. After Buzzy was murdered, his ghost wanted Edwin to get justice. Only Edwin can hear Buzzy talking to him.

Consequently, sailor Mike and his girlfriend think that Edwin is talking to himself. The girlfriend says: "Let's get out of here." Mike: "Ahh! Brooklyn's full of them." Mike makes out with his girl, until the ghost does something that makes the girlfriend smack the sailor. His response is typical for any of the characters Hall played in this period of his career. Mike: "What did you hit me for? I didn't do nothing." He then walks off.

When Edwin talks to his brother Buzzy's ghost, the girl thinks he is talking to her and things get uncomfortable. She calls Mike back saying: "This guy is getting fresh with me." Edwin responds to his ghost brother: "Let's settle this alone, come up to my room like you used to." Both Mike and his girlfriend are surprised, asking: "What?"

Hall's tough guy persona surfaces as he plays Mike, demanding that Edwin take off his glasses. Mike then punches Edwin in the face. Edwin mimics Mike saying: "You see honey, you can't trust nobody these days, except for sailors."

Hall's most noted non-series role, though with only three scenes, came from the 1945 film released by 20th Century Fox, *A Walk in the Sun*. Here, Hall played a soldier named Private Carraway. His first lines of dialogue occur over a half-hour into the film:

Soldier: "*Saturday Evening Post* has the best covers. That guy, what's his name? Norman Rockwell. He can draw covers that beat all. He has some covers about the army."

Carraway: "Yeah, I'll take a camera picture any day. Drawings okay, but it ain't real. I like things to be real."

Soldier: "This guy Rockwell made it look just like a picture. I used to look at them–it's looks just like a picture. I used to say: 'You'd never know it's a painting.' "

Carraway: "You should've took a picture–it saves time."

Soldier: "No, you can't get the touch in a picture."

Carraway: "Drawings alright when they didn't have cameras. So now they got cameras so you don't have to."

Soldier: "That's screwy."

Carraway: "Why's that screwy?"

Soldier: "You might just as well say that now they got moving pictures, there's no sense in taking regular pictures. You might just as well have a movie on the cover of a magazine."

Carraway: "Someday they'll have it. Maybe"(shrugs).

Soldier: "Yeah they will. Maybe someday, they'll have movies that smell though. Maybe the scene will be in a garden or something and you can smell the flowers."

Carraway: "I'd like to see one made in a brewery so I can smell the beer. If a guy came up to me right now and said, what'ya give me for this schooner of beer? I'd give 'em my GI rifle, my GI bayonet, and even my GI pants" (he spits).

Although Hall's speaking scenes in *A Walk in the Sun* are limited, there is the oft-referred and memorable scene in which he converses with another soldier about the complexity of a leaf versus a human:

Soldier: "Just look at this leaf."

Carraway: "What about it?"

Soldier: "Look at the complications. Think of all the trouble it took to make this leaf. You never saw nothing as complicated as thus."

Carraway: "I'm as complicated as that. The human body is the most complicated thing in the world."

Soldier: "It ain't no more complicated as that."

Carraway: "Sure it is. That leaf's just a little thing. The human body is a lot bigger."

Soldier: "That's what I mean. It's got a lot more to be complicated about. This leaf ain't got nothing to be complicated about when you get right down to it.'

Carraway: "What's so fancy about it?"

Soldier: "Look at the veins, for instance."

Carraway: "You gonna tell me the leaves' veins are more important than human veins?"

Soldier: "I didn't say that, I only said look at it."

Carraway: (he takes leaf, stares at it, sighs) "Alright, I'm looking, so what?"

Soldier: (takes leaf back) "You're fancy."

The critical reception for *A Walk in the Sun* recognized Hall's fine acting. The New York Theatre Critics Circle acknowledged his achievement by awarding him their Blue Ribbon Award. One critic has been quoted as saying: "Huntz Hall of *East Side Kids* fame is particularly good in a scene wherein he argues over whether the human body or the leaf is the most complicated structure."

If his serious appearance in the dramatic film *A Walk in the Sun* did not prove his acting ability, then his comedy acting would draw praise from cast members. Even the less significant minor character actors observed first-hand Hall's acting skill. For instance, Robert Nichols, a cast member from his later *Bowery Boys* film *Hold That Line*, told Tom Weaver: "Well, Huntz Hall was a good actor–Huntz was really *quite* a good actor."[37]

Hall was considered for a part in the film *Stage Door Canteen*. Hopper: "Huntz Hall will do a role in that picture if director Frank Borzage can get him to change that Brooklyn accent to a New Jersey one."[38] Apparently, Hall balked, and he did not play the part.

Next Hall enlisted in the Army, but it has been said that his poor eyesight led to an honorable medical discharge. However, Hall's second wife, Leslie Wright, though not married to Hall at that time, told their son Gary that his father was discharged for nervousness and anxiety issues.

Hall's screen partner, Leo Gorcey, got a 4-F classification, and so stayed home during World War II. Hopper reported about the rest of the gang: "Halop is a sergeant in the Signal Corps, Dell a lieutenant (j.g.) in the Navy, Punsley's in the Army Medical Corps, plans to be a doctor; Jordan is an infantry private."[39]

The most memorable achievement for Hall in the early 1940s happened over at Monogram Studios, where the Kids would make some twenty-two *East Side Kids* motion pictures, featuring Hall in seventeen of them.

Unlike a major studio such as Warner Bros., the low-budget movies that Monogram released were made to fill the bottom of a double bill. They were offered for release to theaters at a fixed flat rate, rather than as a percentage split. With guaranteed distribution, the risk was small.

This would account for why the movies would be made quickly (usually in less than two weeks), and at the least cost. Nevertheless, the small profit they generated would be sure. The downside of this arrangement meant major studios would not make bottom-of-the-bill movies since the profit was so small indeed.

The so-called "Poverty Row" studios, such as Monogram, made these B-films with a running time of about an hour. Unfairly though somewhat understandably, Monogram's motion pictures have been labeled as "trash."[40]

Hall did not come into the series right away. He did not appear until after the first five *East Side Kids* movies; namely, *East Side Kids, Boys of the City, That Gang of Mine, Pride of the Bowery,* and *Flying Wild*.

Generally, Hall's character, named Glimpy (except in his first outing when he was Limpy), blended in with the other Kids. In the *East Side Kids* movies, there are brief moments which exhibit the development and increased comedic importance that Hall's character would take on in the later *Bowery Boys* series.

Hall makes his first appearance in *Bowery Blitzkrieg*, the sixth film of the series. His name is credited as "Introducing Huntz Hall." His scenes and lines of dialogue are few. After Muggs (Leo Gorcey) slaps a guy, Hall's first line as (here named) Limpy seems patronizing as he exclaims: "Ain't Muggs a generous individual?" Here wearing a top hat, Limpy's role is as Muggs' fight manager. Limpy: "I'm the brains of the outfit!"

Limpy's impulsive nature is obvious when it comes to food. He takes a sandwich made for Muggs. Limpy: "Quiet, a man's got to have his calories." More importantly, he quickly shows his knack for annoying wisecracks. Limpy: "Boy, sure like to see Dick Tracy and Superman in a good fight." Muggs turns toward him in disapproval as if he was going to hit him with the newspaper. Muggs: "Ah, shut up you stupid lug."

When Muggs uses the phrasing: "Friends, Romans, and Countryman," Limpy fires back: "You know we're only city kids." Now Sach gets his first slap in his face from Muggs' hand.

The review of this movie acknowledged: "Huntz Hall is new to the organization, and contributes an excellent characterization as the beanpole stooge of the leader..."[41]

In *Spooks Run Wild*, Hall's second entry, Hall, renamed Glimpy, now is billed in fourth place after Bela Lugosi, Gorcey, and Halop. The stale "old as the hills" jokes found elsewhere pop up from time to time in the *East Side Kids* series as follow-up or throwaway lines. For instance, here Bobby says to Glimpy: "How can you read in the dark?" Glimpy: "I went to night school." When Glimpy sees inside the dreary house, he remarks: "The maid service in this house is terrible."

There is also Glimpy's misuse or misunderstanding of language that is also based on old standard jokes, or such as thinking a word and its definition are two different choices, or the same thing is described with two different expressions. For example, Glimpy orders, not realizing he is ordering the same thing twice: "I'll have a Demitasse and a large cup of black coffee."

Other times Glimpy will use a word correctly, but another character, including Muggs (a real Mr. Know-it-All), will get it wrong. Here Glimpy tells scared Scruno (played by black actor Sammy "Sunshine" Morrison): "You're yellow." Scruno misunderstands the phrase and says, "If I'm yellow, you're colorblind."

Muggs sometimes would say something just as nonsensical as Glimpy or speak with malapropisms. In *Mr. Wise Guy*, while waiting for a female crook to return Glimpy says: "Let me talk to her, because when it comes to women, I'm a connoisseur." Muggs responds: "That's just where you belong, in a sewer."

Glimpy says a silly or stupid remark that would offer viewers some comic relief. That line or action that Glimpy said would give Muggs an opportunity to poke fun at it. In *Let's Get Tough,* Glimpy is practicing at a violin lesson and Muggs asks: "What's he learning, barnyard imitations?" Scruno interjects: "It's sure not Boogie Woogie, if you ask me." Then when Glimpy is done, Muggs says: "That's the most murderous interpretation of music I have ever heard."

In *'Neath Brooklyn Bridge,* Glimpy collects a load of food for the Kids by acting like a bully. Perhaps, he does this because Muggs does it to him. Here he aggravates a pushcart fruit seller, so that the merchant throws fruit at him. He pesters two men who wind up dumping their soup in his hat. However, he smartly had a bowl inside the hat in order to catch the soup. In addition, he takes a sailor's ice cream cone.

Glimpy sometimes will ask a simple and fair question but receives a slap on his face. He asks Muggs about a girl Muggs is taking care of: "Why take her to my house?" Muggs offers the obvious answer: "Cause the food is better at your house." That question motivates Muggs to slap Glimpy, and insult him: "You moron!"

Later, Glimpy challenges Muggs recurrent physical response when Muggs hits him over the head with a book. Glimpy: "Cut it out will you, you want to make me silly?" Muggs continues the insult: "I never interfere with nature."

As will often be the case, when a fight ensues, Glimpy will stay in the background, and stand away from the fighting. At other times, Glimpy just plays along with the gang and fulfills the role of background gang member. However, sometimes he gives Muggs ideas.

Muggs credits Glimpy but still finds a way to bamboozle him. Muggs: "You know that's the first idea you ever given me since I ever known you?" Glimpy feels sorry for himself. Glimpy: "Yeah the trouble with you is you don't appreciate me." Muggs: "Sure I appreciate you, Glimpy. You know what I'm gonna do? I'm gonna make you Vice President of Miscellaneous Stuff." Glimpy: "Is that a commissioned officer?" Muggs: "No, but you can work your way up."

Mostly, Glimpy stays in Muggs' corner, seemingly intimidated or impressed by Muggs' leadership. For instance, in *Kid Dynamite*, Muggs is bothered every single time Danny (Bobby Jordan) is successful at something. Glimpy automatically assumes Danny is wrong because Muggs says so. Perhaps Glimpy would have been better named Wimpy. Interestingly, by the time of this movie, Hall's billing in the credits moved to second place after Gorcey.

In addition, in *Kid Dynamite*, when the Boys get in trouble for disturbing the peace with a ruckus, they appear before a woman judge. She asks: "I don't suppose any of you boys have a job?" Glimpy: "A job. I worked once, I was a pin-setter." Judge: "What?" Glimpy: "They knock 'em them down, I set 'em up. Gee Judge, ain't you never bowled?" The annoyed Judge demands: "Stop that!"

One of the most notable and prolonged displays in the *East Side Kids* movies of Hall's comedic talents is in *Clancy Street Boys*. In that production, Glimpy eventually gives in to pressure to dress up as a girl at Muggs' insistence. Upon initially hearing of Muggs' plan, Glimpy's refusal is fierce and adamant: "I quit the club! I'm going home! You're not my leader anymore. I give my life for you. But being a girl is out of the question! I tell you, I quit!"

The next scene shows Glimpy convincingly dressed up as a girl, complete with skirt and stockings, blonde hair and lipstick. Nevertheless, he still resists the idea as ludicrous. Muggs is not accepting the excuses. He tells Glimpy: "Jack Benny got away with it in *Charley's Aunt*."

Furthermore, if Glimpy does not go along with the idea, Muggs threatens to mess up his lipstick. Later, Muggs reminds Glimpy that he should be sure to remember: "Keep your skirts down and your voice up."

Clancy Street Boys is not Hall's first, nor will it be his last, foray into cross-dressing and a funny high-pitched voice. A little more than a year earlier, in *Mr. Wise Guy*, Hall briefly appears in drag impersonating Muggs' mother to avoid being arrested for supposedly breaking a store window. The rest of the boys walk out with mannequins in front of them. However, Glimpy dons female clothes and cries, even asking the Officer: "Would you unhook me?"

At times, Glimpy annoys Muggs with his behavior and remarks. For example, that is the case in *Bowery Champs,* the twentieth *East Side Kids* movie. In one scene, when Muggs is questioning a girl to investigate a murder, Glimpy, uncharacteristically and without provocation, hits Muggs. The latter surprisingly asks: "What are you doing?" Glimpy answers: "I don't know, I lost my mind."

Again later, Muggs is questioning a woman seeking a divorce. In demanding her securities from her husband, she aims a gun at him. An unseen gunman fires a fatal shot from outside the window. The woman explains her confusion: "Everything went blank." Glimpy interrupts. He thinks she's referring to a blank bullet, and humorously remarks: "No blank honey, you killed the guy." Muggs responds: "Will you please keep your Zeppelin nose out of this!" These annoyances will be the main fodder for much of the slapstick of their next series, *The Bowery Boys*.

Bowery Champs also foreshadows the usual finale in the *Bowery Boys* series. The final scene becomes a typical Gorcey-Hall slapstick ending. Here club secretary Glimpy failed to take notes at their meeting. Muggs calls Glimpy back into the room, and asks him where he was. Glimpy explains that he found a big button that his mother will love. Muggs then pays back Glimpy for his absence by pushing a pie in his face. By contrast, the finale to the *Bowery Boys* movies often had Slip repeatedly slapping Sach's head with his hat.

In a Johnny Carson show appearance from December of 1967, Hall recalled some memories of his Monogram days. Hall: "My idol in those days was Bela Lugosi, who had a part in one of our pictures. He came on the set with his servant–a dwarf–who was wearing a big black hat and a cape. It cracked me up. I really loved Bela, but when he was around, I always carried a wooden stake with me.

"We used to make those Monogram pictures for $32,000 (Leo and I got top money). They were produced by Sam Katzman–Yeah that's right–Psychedelic Sam–he does all those pictures now about the hippies. One time, in one scene I was supposed to fall down a flight of stairs on a fire escape, but Katzman wouldn't pay for a stunt man. I told him I wasn't going to do it, and went off to lunch in the Monogram commissary (which was so small, we had to go outside to chew). I came back from lunch, and there on the fire escape, wearing a baseball cap and sweatshirt, was Sam Katzman, waiting to take the fall.

"We used to do 36 pages of script a day, if you can believe it. One night we had done only 18 pages and it already was 11 o'clock. At midnight, Sam announced, 'All right we'll leave out the rest.' Everyone naturally was startled, and someone asked. 'What about the plot, Sam?' He said, 'Never mind–the audience'll never remember it anyway.' "[42]

Eventually Katzman's reign over the Boys would end. A time for change came, as a new producer would take charge. With that, the most developed work in Hall's career would be made in still one more series–the second and final one he did for Monogram. This allowed Hall the opportunity to develop his ability as a comedy master to its fullest in an amazing output. Leaving Glimpy behind, in walked Hall as "Sach," the idiotic but lovable character who brought viewers Hall's most enduring and funniest comedy ever.

The success of Hall's movies drew lines of fans adoring the characters who he and Leo created. This assured Hall that he would be loved. Indeed, unlike his early years growing up, Hall would no longer be standing in line for love from his parents. No, things would be different now. Countless fans would love standing in line to see his movies and give their approval. Huntz Hall achieved fame and fortune.

Later, there would be the awareness by some that there is something unfortunate or less satisfying about Hall not breaking into major stardom or A-movies. An example of this insult reached the public via the press. Vernon Scott: "AIP [American-International Pictures] is to 20th Century Fox as Huntz Hall is to John Wayne." [43]

Chapter 4:

Here Comes Sach: 'Ohp! Ohp! Ohp!'

"This might sound like I'm an egomaniac, but I think Sach is one of a kind."
Huntz Hall, *Entertainment Weekly* interview, 1994.

Soon Hall's greatest achievement would become apparent. The continued teaming of Leo Gorcey and Huntz Hall seemed more than ever to be made in heaven with the next series at Monogram, named the *Bowery Boys*. Their consistently excellent quality of output exceeded all expectations, and they really got into their characters. Undoubtedly, lead Leo Gorcey and second banana Huntz Hall play off each other extremely well as a team.

When he appeared on the *Tonight Show Starring Johnny Carson* in 1967, Hall said he loved playing Sach, "although Leo would hit me too much–especially after he'd have a fight with his wife."

In a recorded interview Gorcey observed: "[We] never were as friendly as most people might think we were. Had little arguments with actors who work together, whether it's Abbott & Costello, Martin & Lewis. Had a few little beefs–once in a while. If one got a broken nose, it meant they didn't duck fast enough."

In short, Gorcey and Hall never seemed to have any serious disagreements, as with other comedy duos. That would have stopped the team from continuing to make more motion pictures before they ran their course with audiences.

Among the urchins, Hall's character had some brief moments of comedy in the *Dead End Kids* and the *East Side Kids* series. However, he seemed to fully break away from the tough kid in order to evolve into a well-developed buffoon-like member in the *Bowery Boys* series. Hall's comical character developed over time. With each passing production, a little more goofiness would be exhibited in his interactions with the other characters.

In retrospect, an important turning point in Hall's career came when in 1941 he signed up to have Jan Grippo of the Jan Grippo-Flo Brown talent agency represent him. Grippo had been Gorcey's agent, and now Hall would benefit when he helped him secure more roles, such as the non-series work he did for several studios.

By 1946, Grippo became Hall & Gorcey's producer of a new series that evolved when Gorcey was unhappy with the pay arrangement for the *East Side Kids*. Gorcey apparently asked for double his current salary to go on making more movies. When Sam Katzman turned him down, Gorcey worked out a deal with Grippo to make a series called the *Bowery Boys*. The duo would have creative influence; besides, the pay would be much more generous. Reportedly, Bobby Jordan thought up the idea of Hall and Gorcey going off on this new series.

Now Hall's greatest contribution to comedy is reached with his creation of Sach. The wacky character in all of his lunacy is endearing and likable. Sach always brings laughter with his wide-eyed look. He wears an upturned baseball cap, and unleashes a whole array of comic business, including an unusual and funny cheek and lips flutter (or motorlips) on

Here Comes Sach: 'Ohp! Ohp! Ohp!'

the left side of his face, and his impulsive and unpredictable behavior.

Hall evolved his character of Sach in successive *Bowery Boys* productions. Gary explained to me what his father said to him: "He told me he based the character on a newsstand guy he knew in New York." Leonard Getz disagreed: "He based his character Sach on a shoeshine who worked in the theater district of New York."[44] Gary responded that perhaps it was a shoeshine and not a newsstand guy, "that's all I remember." Gary: "I would describe Sach as embodying my father's best qualities– generous, trusting, empathetic. The more you watch the movies the more you realize that Sach isn't really 'stupid.' I think he's evolved a way to survive/outwit Slip."

Some of the funniest Sach moments in the *Bowery Boys* series are when he goes off on his own. Slip seems to stifle Sach's wackiness. However, whenever Sach is alone, he has his moments of innocence and fun. It is only then that he has the opportunity to explore the objects in his surroundings. It is then that we come to see in that moment, the stream-of-consciousness of Sach's zany mind.

As Slip, Gorcey is at his best, and he is a better actor than most viewers give him credit for. He had his character worked out early on. It seems that his greatest gift is the naturalness of his tough guy persona. Repeatedly, Gorcey's Slip Mahoney character is unsentimental but endearing. He is always putting Sach in his place. He really does not know any more than Sach. He is not well mannered, and he does not know all the social rules of etiquette. The way he talks–part of him wants to be smart, even using words like he is some sort of literary giant. He tries to sound intelligent, but instead mangles his speech.

Slip likes to be the leader, and he appoints himself in charge of every situation. Slip will tell Sach what to do, as if Sach does not know his ass from his elbow. Slip is bent on always watching Sach or getting someone else to watch him so that Sach does not do something stupid. Slip succeeds with others by making himself come across with a swagger that he believes he's smart. He bluffs his way through situations. If he has any doubt about his abilities, he covers it up. Yes, he is street smart, always picking up the angles.

As the study of their movies will reveal, neither Gorcey nor Hall lack comedic or dramatic talent or abilities, although at times they both could have used some further training and polish. It is more likely that their lack of discipline early on tainted their chance at having a much more successful career later.

It is unfortunate that the bad reputation that the Dead End Kids earned with their misbehavior as teenagers may have affected and limited the demand for their talents by major studios. It is likely that their immaturity prevented the major studios from wanting them since they could not trust them.

Undoubtedly, a study of his movies shows Hall should be remembered right up on top with other comedy greats. However, his primary association and success with "Poverty Row" productions kept him from a real opportunity with the "Majors."

Though he was not lauded with the universal acclaim he deserved, Hall did make a mixed impression on some of his co-stars. As an example, Teala Loring (1922–2007), co-star of *Hard Boiled Mahoney* and *Blonde Bombshell*, told Tom Weaver: "[Huntz Hall] was the craziest of them all [the Bowery Boys]. When asked whether she meant "crazy in a nice way?" Loring explained: "Oh yes. He wanted to take every girl out, and if you didn't say yes, he didn't *like* you very well. He asked me a few times and I said no. But he was fun to work with." Tom Weaver: "And no problem with him after you said no?" Loring: "No, he just didn't really talk to you very much after that."[45]

A more critical Loring later contradicted that quote concerning Hall asking her for a date. Loring insultingly said: "Huntz Hall thought he was God's gift to women and the world. He apparently never looked in the mirror (laughs). He asked for a date, and of course, I said 'No.' He said, 'I'll ask you again,' but fortunately, he never did."[46]

Two things of significance happened in 1948, two years into the *Bowery Boys* series. Hall made the news for being arrested in October. In addition, while awaiting trial, Hall broke his 2-year engagement to a showgirl. In December, he eloped to Mexico City with another showgirl. A few months later, he would have a formal wedding.

His second marriage occurred four years after his first divorce. This marriage to Leslie Wright lasted for five years, and it gave Hall his only child, before it ended in his second of three divorces.

The *New York Times* reported his arrest on October 30, 1948. The headline read: "HUNTZ HALL ARRESTED Former 'Dead End Kid' Accused in Marijuana Case."

The article noted that "Hollywood, Calif., Oct. 29–Los Angeles police, pursuing their campaign against the traffic in marijuana, last night arrested Huntz Hall, 28...."

"[He] was the second film figure taken into custody in the drive, his arrest following by just two months that of Robert Mitchum.

"Narcotics squad detectives said they found Mr. Hall and a friend, Ben Melzer, 34, a theatrical producer, digging under a tree in the yard of Mr. Hall's home at 1775 North Sycamore Street to retrieve a cache of four tobacco cans of marijuana valued at $200.

"The men were charged with suspicion of violation of the state narcotics law. Declining to comment on the charge, they were released on writs of *habeas corpus* under bond of $1,000 for hearing in Superior Court Nov. 4."

Gary: "Ben Melzer was a boxer who became my father's and Gabe's manager. A lovely guy. He was from San Jose, California. He, my father, and Gabe stayed friends all their lives."

Three months later, *The Washington Post* reported on February 27, 1949: "Huntz Hall, 28-year-old former Dead End kid, must stand retrial of charges of possessing marijuana."

Nearly six months after the charges were first filed, *New York Times,* April 19, 1949: "Huntz Hall was cleared of drug charges on April 18, 1949. The clip stated: "On the recommendation of the district attorney's office, Superior Court Judge Frederick Houser dismissed today a charge of narcotics possession against Huntz Hall, 28 years old, stage and screen actor. Mr. Hall was arrested Oct. 28 after some marijuana cigarettes were found buried under a tree behind his Hollywood home."

Gary clarified how this came about since reports at the time gave no reason why the charges were dropped. Gary: "He essentially beat the charge on procedural issues. So he was hiding it in the yard, but was cleared because of entrapment."

Interestingly, eight years before the arrest, Hall referred to Gabe Dell and marijuana ("janes"). Dell: "I collect pipes and jade," Mr. Dell announced, proudly. 'Jade,' exclaimed Mr. Hall, from behind a swirl of cigar smoke. 'Don't you mean janes?' "[47]

Hall's 1948 arrest was for possession of marijuana, and though he was acquitted, there is the revelation that there was more to this matter than the public ever knew all the years since then. What is intriguing is that the public never learned the full truth about Hall and his use of marijuana, in any of the years since the charges were brought and dropped.

Gary acknowledged that Huntz Hall was a longtime pot smoker.

With that as a given, some may wonder if his use of marijuana had any influence on the development of any of his comic characters? One can speculate on that.

A further fact that connects here is that those close friends and associates of Hall knew that he was a lot more fun to be with when he was 'stoned' rather than when he was drunk.

Gary revealed: "He smoked marijuana pretty regularly, but it only made him mellow. He didn't act disoriented or [what one would consider as] stoned. I don't know about any occasional use of other drugs. Pot was his lifelong mainstay, and he was a lot nicer stoned than when he was drunk. Nobody close to him worried about the marijuana use."

The revelation of Hall's life long use of marijuana, as well as the common knowledge of him being an alcoholic (up until he was 62 years old), may seem more surprising. However, his son explained that his father suffered all his life as being a high-strung and anxious man. Gary: "I believe he turned to marijuana because it allowed him to self-medicate in less dangerous ways."

Gary: "Alcohol was another matter. He went through extended dry periods and then he would drink, especially in my high school years (1960s). When he was drinking, he was truly horrible–angry, argumentative, and violent. When he was stoned, he was like a calm version of himself. Anyone who ever knew him would much rather have been around him [when he was] stoned than drunk."

Gary: "[My Dad] went through long sober periods when he was working, and had a different relationship to alcohol than Leo had, as Leo was almost always drunk in later years. The later police events (1955 and 1959) were fights he got into when drinking. He was a terrible, aggressive, mean drunk. The reverse of the Sach persona."

On September 22, 1949, less than a half-year after being cleared of the drug charges, his wife Leslie gave birth to his first and only son, originally named Leslie Richard.

Over at Monogram, from 1946 thru 1958 (renamed Allied Artists in 1952), Hall would appear in four motion pictures a year. As time went on, the *Bowery Boys* movies increasingly relied on slapstick to propel them. This is especially noticeable in those *Bowery Boys* movies directed and written by Edward Bernds, with the assistance of Elwood Ullman. Bernds' prior association was working with The Three Stooges. One would think that with the same creative talent responsible for the Stooges shorts that the movies would be just as memorable, since they typically have moments remarkably similar.

Gary: "The Three Stooges have stayed in the public imagination longer, I think, because they made shorts which were not burdened by plots. The *Bowery Boys* movies have moments of comedy every bit as great as in the Stooges films, but you have to wade through melodramatic stories to get to them. So with a few exceptions, I don't think the movies hold up very well, but I do think that particular scenes and bits do."

One of Hall's last radio appearances occurred on November 8, 1951. Hall was heard as a celebrity panelist on a CBS radio show called *How To*. Art Linkletter and Anita Martell were part of the panel. The show, hosted by Roger Price, Martell's husband, dealt with contestants asking members of the panel their advice on how to cope with a variety of problems. In the episode that has Hall appearing, a dentist in Hollywood wanted to know how he could eliminate patients' fear of a dental visit.

Price's experience included script writing for Bob Hope. *How To* had its critics because it did rely on remarks that were scripted and rehearsed. Price: "These remarks are about as ad lib as a presidential address and, in some cases, no sillier…This show has been on the air for only a month, and already it has attracted thousands of enemies. Here's a letter from a reader. 'I've been following your health hints and they have made a real he-man out of me. I'm suing you for $100,000 because six months ago I was a girl.' "[48]

Columnist Hedda Hopper expressed the reality that Hall and Gorcey's success had to do really with theater locations where their movies played. Hopper: "I was amazed to discover that the *Bowery Boys* movie series...are top moneymakers for small-town exhibitors. The pictures get very little play here."[49] She noted that Hall and Dell were going to go to Europe with their vaudeville act. First, they would film *Jalopy* and *Clipped Wings*.

Four days after Hopper's column, Hall appeared on the televised Saints and Sinners 24-hour Milkathon on KHJ-TV Los Angeles. Jackie Coogan directed the fund drive that had a host of guests, including Rose Marie, and famed cornetist Ziggy Elman.[50]

Of more consequence than his few radio and TV appearances at this time, Hall and Gabe Dell started a nightclub act, they named "Hall and Dell." This began sometime in the early 1950s; perhaps even as early as 1950, but the date is uncertain. The act had been drawn partly from vaudeville routines. Hall played foil to Dell's straight man. They sang and they danced. Press clippings indicate that they headlined stage shows around the country with their act.

For instance, a caption of an article read: "The Bowery Boys Top Stage Show at Regal Theater." They were described as: "The Bowery Boys–Huntz "Sach" Hall and Gabe Dell–well known to motion picture fans."[51] In short, they kept busy with their act throughout the year whenever they were not in the studio at Monogram making the contractually agreed four movies per year.

Gary: "I got to know Gabe Dell quite well when I was in college, and Gabe studied acting very seriously. But he always felt that my father was more of an instinctive comic than he was, and he envied my father's ability to do things without a lot of over-thinking. When I was in a play once, I had my father come to a rehearsal and watch. His criticisms were extremely sharp and helpful. So I believe he thought more carefully than people gave him credit for."

Walter Winchell's column made mention of one of Hall's passing remarks that was overheard. Winchell: "Mickey, the Jelk, got 3 to 6 for procuring, and Huntz Hall cracks: 'Sounds like his working hours.' "[52]

Apparently, it was reported at the time that Hall and Dell's nightclub act became a pivotal boiling point issue in their respective marriages. Both Hall and Dell got so absorbed in their stage show activity that their wives felt that their husbands' act was far more important to their husbands than their marriages were.

The headline on May 15, 1953 read: "Wives Team Up, Divorce Former 'Dead End Kids.'" The caption under the photo of the wives noted: "Love on the Rocks. They said their actor husbands don't love them any more." Mrs. Dell took the witness stand and gave her testimony. Mrs. Hall corroborated Mrs. Dell's story.

Then Mrs. Hall testified how her marriage started unhappy. Mrs. Hall: "[Huntz] took delight in being argumentative…He had an 'Oh! shut up!' attitude. He was snide and insulting to me in front of other people." Mrs. Dell corroborated Mrs. Hall's allegations.

From this newspaper report, one might think that Hall was abusive, but this is not so. Gary: "I'm not sure 'abusive' is the right word. In those days in California, you had to prove 'mental cruelty' as a ground for divorce. While my father could be an angry and sometimes violent drunk, I don't recall him ever being physically violent with my mother and she never complained of that.

"From my mother's point of view, the time my father and Gabe spent on the road with their act was an abandonment. In those days, they made four *Bowery Boys* movies a year, so that meant about two months in L.A.

shooting. The rest of the time my father and Gabe were on the road with their act. My mother and Gabe's wife got sick of living that way and filed for divorce and set the trial date so they could testify for each other about 'mental cruelty,' [as I said] the cause you needed in those days."

Judge Kincaid approved property settlements; Gabe Dell paying his wife $250 a month for alimony, Huntz Hall paying $700 per month total support for his wife and their 3-year old son ($100 a month of that amount is child support). In addition, Hall agreed to pay five percent of his gross income that exceeded $25,000.

As can be expected, their son Leslie was adversely affected by the break-up. It became necessary for the divorced couple to change their son's name from Leslie to Gary at this time. Gary revealed: "When I was 3 and they got divorced, I started throwing tantrums. A child psychiatrist told my mother that boys have enough problems with their mothers without having the same name. So they read me a list of names and I chose Gary."

This is the second time Hall would be divorced. Gary: "What was complicated was that they were divorced when I was three and then my father moved back in for a year or so when I was seven. They didn't get back [together] to live with us; he just moved into the guest room because he was between houses and ended up staying. That was very confusing to [me], an 8 year old."

Though they were divorced and did not remarry, Hall and Leslie's apparent reconciliation in 1957/58 was not explained to the public. Photo piece in the *Chicago Daily Tribune*, September 3, 1957 noted: "Huntz Hall, former child star of 'The Bowery Boys' fame, and wife at benefit party for Motion Picture Country home in Calabasas, Cal."

Gary: "My mother had custody of me, and she went to work in television, first as a set decorator at CBS in the days of live TV. Then [she worked] as a motion picture costumer, eventually becoming one of the most prominent in the business (*Bewitched, Get Smart, Mary Tyler Moore Show*). She's still alive, and is in the Motion Picture Home."

Hall would remarry two more times after this, and get divorced once more. His son Gary said it became especially difficult after his father moved to New York when he was 11 or 12. Gary: "I'd say the hardest part of my growing up was my father's absence in my junior high and high school years. I went to New York every summer to see him, but I keenly felt his absence. My mother was married two more times, so altogether my father had 4 wives and my mother 3 husbands. [It was certainly] not the most stable upbringing, which probably explains why I gravitated to both church and academic life."

In 1954, Hall reportedly lived in Los Angeles at 8818 Appian Way. Columnist Dorothy Kilgallen offered one of the few press items from this time. Kilgallen observed: "End of an era: Huntz Hall, the original Dead End Kid now wears a homburg."[53]

Hall would appear as a guest panelist on "Musical Chairs" for KRCA-Channel 4 Los Angeles on the January 18, 1955 show. The program, hosted by Bill Leyden, included panelists Mel Blanc, Johnny Mercer and Bobby Troup being tested on musical matters from questions submitted by home viewers.

On April 1, 1955, Hall would be arrested for a second time. This time his trouble with the law involved a noise dispute at a party he was attending in Los Angeles. Hall apparently was upset when the apartment occupants were told by the manager to stop making noise.

On July 14, 1955, the *Los Angeles Times* reported that Hall: "pleaded guilty to a charge of disturbing the peace and was fined $250 or 25 days. However, Beverly Hills Municipal Judge Henry H. Draeger suspended $200 of the fine and 20 days of the jail term. Hall paid $50 and was placed on one year's probation. Originally, Hall was charged with assault and battery and disturbance of the peace, growing out of an apartment row last April 1.

"H. H. Stoner, manager of the apartment at 1111 Larabee Street complained that when he tried to quiet a noisy party he was 'roughed up' by Hall."[54]

Between this arrest and sentencing, Hall saw his thirty-seventh *Bowery Boys* film released on April 17, 1955. One of the most unusual stories to connect to the *Bowery Boys* is the Academy Award nomination for Best Original Story for that movie, *High Society*.

Apparently, the nomination was intended really for the MGM release using the same title that year for the movie starring Bing Crosby, Grace Kelly, Frank Sinatra, Louis Armstrong, among others. Hall gave his account of the mistaken nomination to Lamparski.

Hall: "Well, MGM wanted the title. I don't know what deal it was for. Allied Artists gave them permission to keep the title "High Society." We owned it, our *Bowery Boys* was our title. They, I don't know what money exchanged hands or what, so forth. But they took it. So when they took it, they used it on "High Society," which was originally "The Philadelphia Story." So when they took it, you know they called it ("The Philadelphia Story") "High Society." When it came out, they voted the Best Original Story and then voted "High Society."

"Well, it wasn't because "High Society" was "Philadelphia Story," which was the original story. "High Society" was the screenplay. So we were voted the Best Original Story–Bowery Boys' *High Society*."

In short, what Hall explained seems to mean that the nominating committee for the Academy of Motion Picture Arts and Sciences must have thought that since MGM purchased the title "High Society" from

Allied Artists (formerly Monogram Studios), they were purchasing the story as well. They probably thought that MGM had adapted a screenplay from the Bowery Boys' story and/or movie *High Society*, so the Best Original Story award for the MGM adaptation *High Society* would have to go to the *Bowery Boys* story.

Lamparski remembered: "And there was a terrible commotion." Hall: "Yeah so it was a big deal, uh, about such a mistake was made. They didn't know and everything. So the writers all jumped on us. They thought it was idiotic. They didn't know what was original and which isn't." Lamparski: "The writers on your picture?" Hall: "No, all writers. So they said, 'We'll go along with it. We're gonna vote the Bowery Boys in *High Society*' (laughs). So here goes, a Bowery Boys picture is gonna get an Academy Award. So from nowhere I understand because I used to scream, 'this is the greatest thing, get *Life* magazine, get so and so.' This we win. You kidding? It's like the greatest publicity that can happen to people. And everybody got shocked, ya know. What, you kidding? You can't do this. "So what happened I think, the writers of our picture had to withdraw from the nomination."

Lamparski: "They asked you to?"

Hall: "No, somebody got to the writers and they said, 'you better withdraw or, know like a Charlie ah, you won't be working you know. So this is one of my opinions or else like if I were the writers and, a, they'd never get me to withdraw. I don't care what happens, it's going through."

Lamparski: "You might have an Oscar today."

Hall: "Yeah it'll be fine. It would be the greatest if they had won the Oscar. It would'a been."

Also in 1955, Hall contributed his time to the Thalians when they put on a show at Ciros. They "put on a takeoff of 'Love Me or Leave Me' with Gary Crosby and Huntz Hall doing the burlesque which Bob Wells wrote."⁵⁵ The show was for the benefit of the mental health fund.

More importantly in 1955, the brilliant partnership of Gorcey and Hall would end as a result of the death of Gorcey's father, Bernard Gorcey. The latter actor, who played the Sweet Shop owner Louie, would die after being injured in a car crash.

The tragic loss exacerbated Leo's erratic behavior on the movie sets. Of course, this was fueled even more so by his heavy boozing now. After 40 movies as a Bowery Boy, Gorcey could no longer competently perform as evidenced in his first production without his father. His forty-first movie in the series, *Crashing Las Vegas*, undoubtedly proved that Gorcey's drunkenness spoiled his comic timing. It would be his last *Bowery Boys* movie.

Gary: "My father used to tell me that Leo was drunk all day long and found the last pictures with Leo very difficult. I was very young (8 years old) when the *Bowery Boys* movies ended, and my trips to the set were not made with a critical eye. But I can say that though he and Leo improvised a lot, they did plan what they did pretty carefully. As to improvisation–there is a lot in the movies [my father made]. They made these things in two weeks with only a little bit of rehearsal time."

Hall would go on to make the last seven *Bowery Boys* pictures without his comic partner. In stepped Stanley Clements to fulfill the role left vacant by Gorcey. Although these movies that were made are mostly Hall's least effective comedic output, they are oddly appealing since Hall got star billing above the title for the first and only time in his career. The final film, *In the Money*, closed the series of forty-eight movies in 1958.

When the *Bowery Boys* series is weighed against the other series (the *Dead End Kids*, the *Little Tough Guys and Dead End Kids*, and the *East Side Kids*), it stands supreme in overall quality. Gary revealed his father's personal favorites: "Of the *Bowery Boys* movies, he loved *Blues Busters*,

Clipped Wings and *No Holds Barred.*"

Before the series ended, Hall continued to participate in various activities that kept him among his loving fans. On July 25, 1956 he, along with his new *Bowery Boys* co-star Stanley Clements, Chill Wills, and military brass, made an appearance preceding the world film premiere of *Hold Back the Night* in Oceanside, California. The movie, produced by Hayes Goetz and Allan Dwan, starred John Payne, Mona Freeman, Chuck Connors, Peter Graves, and Audrey Dalton. The story offered a salute to the Marines during the Korean War. The press reported: "Appropriately, considering the nearness of the Marines base, the picture, *Hold Back the Night*, dealt with the courage of that branch of the service and also was unusual in stressing ideals of humanity."[56]

By this time, Leo Gorcey had been gone from the Bowery Boys for a year. Although the disastrous negative effects from the loss of Gorcey could not be fully comprehended yet, Hall had immersed himself in the productions with his new co-star. In addition, he still had his friendship with Gabe Dell. Gary: "Gabe Dell was the closest relationship my father ever had. They were pals during the Dead End Kids all the way up to Gabe's death in 1988, with the exception, of course, of periodic feuds. They were both smart and had similar senses of humor.

"My father also kept Gabe working in the *Bowery Boys* movies–he was always the guy who had left the gang and made good. When their act broke up, Gabe went to New York and studied at the Actors Studio. My father admired Gabe as an actor but also took his leaving as rejection."

Chapter 5:
Not Running Scared for Jobs

"Acting can get out of hand, you know. Some of these guys killing themselves 16 hours a day on the set.
For what?"

Huntz Hall, 1971 interview

Not only did Huntz Hall feel rejected by Gabe Dell, but Hall found himself receiving some negative press coverage for the third time. The coverage on February 17, 1959 concerned an apparent driving while intoxicated (DWI) incident:

> ### Held
> Huntz Hall, 38, above, a former "Dead End Kid" of films, was being held in Malibu, Calif., yesterday on suspicion of driving while intoxicated. Police said Hall was belligerent when police stopped him on the Pacific Coast Highway.

This arrest occurred four years after his last reported encounter with the authorities. Obviously, Hall's alcoholism caused him problems with the law every so often. Gary: "He was an angry and abusive drunk. He never hit me, but he could be incredibly cruel verbally when drunk and got into fights easily with others. So I would say that he was abusive when drunk."

Gary explained that his father was not one to avoid being open. He also did not know of his father having any secrets or something that would make someone abhor him. There was only one thing that people that knew Hall definitely did not like about him. It was a lifelong issue that accounts for the extreme opposing opinions of people who had met or known him.

Gary detailed: "I think [his] temper was probably his most negative characteristic. It would flare up out of nowhere." In addition, Hall shared with his father Joseph a temper, which "apparently got [his father] into fights with some regularity."

His mother Mary Ellen was very unlike Hall's father as she was a devout churchgoer; what many would consider "a formidable Irish Catholic woman." Gary explained: "When my father began making serious money, he sent it home and discovered that Mary Ellen had given it to the church (St. Stephen's) for a new altar.

"My father's bad luck was to give a lot of people their starts–Leonard Stern being a prime example–who turned their back on him when they became successful. Part of Lenny's issue was his trying to cover up having written *Bowery Boys* movies (under the pseudonym of 'Max Adams'); part of it was my dad's temper."

"[My father] especially loved the old-Hollywood types and had a harder time with younger people who had no idea who he was. He was especially happy when the SCTV group (Martin Short, John Candy) came to Hollywood and looked him up as they all loved the *Bowery Boys* movies. But he was pretty contemptuous of the incestuous Hollywood system whereby people without a lot of talent keep each other working."

Cecil Smith later reported that Hall remarked: "[Would] do a lot of these Hollywood actors a lot of good if they had to get out and work at it again, fight the street for it again. They ought to take all their money away from 'em and let them fight for it again. You find out who you are."[57]

Besides a few negative press reports, Hall would get an occasional mention in the papers. As an example, "Radio TV Gag Bag," culled by Larry Wolters, offered this joke: "Huntz Hall knows a Texas rancher so rich from oil that he no longer brands his cattle: he has them engraved."[58]

Reportedly, Hall claimed that he invested in offshore oil and gas, and did quite well. This is a story that has circulated for many years. It turns out to be untrue, and his son confirmed it. Gary: "He made that up."

What is true is that he (and Leo) were top earners at their peak, earning a staggering $10,000 a week while shooting the Bowery Boys movies. However, that income would be only for the weeks each picture was being made. It totaled about $80,000 a year; since they made four pictures per year, and he would be paid for two weeks per film.

Hall married his third wife, television actress Colleen Vico. The *Los Angeles Times* reported on September 6, 1960: "Huntz Hall, 40, one of the 'Dead End Kids,' is wed to Colleen Vico, 32, in Las Vegas." Another press report noted that it was a midnight ceremony on September 3rd in the office of the justice of the peace. The best man was Kingsley Abrams, and the matron of honor was actress Sherry Vanfelt.

The couple lived with her friend Augusta (and daughter Cher of "Sonny and Cher" fame) in a large house. Gary reported that he was three years younger than Cher, and that he would see her often at his Dad's house. Apparently, little else is known about this marriage, except that it also ended in a divorce settlement in a short time. Vico died sometime in the 1980s. Colleen had a daughter from another marriage named Paulette who tragically died of cancer as a pre-teen.

The public saw little of Hall again until around 1963. Then on February 5, 1963, he appeared as a guest on the first season of a lost episode (#50) of *The Tonight Show Starring Johnny Carson*. Fortunately a complete transcript of Hall's interview, culled from the only existing audiotape recorded by Phil Gries, appears in this book's Appendix.

What is most revealing about this interview is that Hall described his failed attempt to branch out into another business; namely, public relations for a construction business.

Hall: "I wanted to go into business. I said, I had my acting and everything. So I wanted to become a business man. Some friend of mine came to me and says, I have a friend who's in the construction business. Go in and talk to him. So, I went in and he said, 'Look Huntz, we want you in the organization. And what we're gonna do…You go out and plug our product and we're gonna go on television with it, and you'll be the sponsor.'

"It was putting up siding on houses. Alright, I thought, I was going to do television. He said you'll have to go around and look at the pictures. So I said, 'Great.' He took me into a house…the first house we went to. 'And, Mr. Hall's going to be with the advertising end of the business. He's going to be on television.' We are going to take your house and we are going to show it before and after. And, all of a sudden, from nowhere…you know Al come from a family of 16 kids: 13 boys, 3 girls."

Carson: "You do?"

Hall: "Yeah. 16 children in my family. I saw eight kids.[59] I saw food being taken out of their mouths. And this guy was going with a pitch and everything. He had him. And here he is and he's gonna do this. And, he had the man for like $7,200 for the deal. And I flipped. And, I screamed. I got up and said 'You're kidding.' I looked at the guy and said, 'He's robbing you out and out. He's a thief.'"

Carson: "This is your partner."

Hall: "He's a crook. You pick up a phone. Call SEARS. You get it for $12! I walked out. He sold the deal!

Carson: "And that was the end of your business affiliation?"

Hall: "I said I can't take it. I got deathly ill."

Carson: "They had a lot of pretty good rackets going on out there in California."

Hall: "Oh yeah. Suede shoe boys. I couldn't wear suede shoes. That's why I got out of it."

Carson began the interview by asking Hall: "How did you get away with that nutty stuff? That's funny stuff though. I mean the old slapstick type of humor. You're still playing all over television in the *Bowery Boys* series."

Hall: "Yeah. We have 48 of them now on television, just released. Allied Artists Television Corporation just released them."

Carson: "Do you guys get anything out of the television or is that in somebody else's hands? It's none of my business, but…"

Hall: "We get a piece."

Carson: "Oh you do."

Hall: "Most actors get a pension; a pension plan. How much money you make a year. That's the Screen Actors Guild."

Carson: "So you get a certain amount out of it."

Hall: "Well, when you're 65 they give you a pension."

Carson: "Well, it's like I was reading earlier in the show. Retire at 50 if you got $495 a month, and you can retire."

Hall's response managed to make the audience laugh from this dull issue of remuneration. Hall: "I told them, I'll shoot them double or nothing."

The following year, a reader wrote to a TV Mailbag asking "Is Huntz Hall still living? If so, please tell me about him.–S.B." The paper answered: "Huntz is still alive. Just because he was once a Dead End Kid, doesn't mean he's really dead. He makes occasional movie and television appearances, but when he had his 40th birthday, producers thought he was a little too old to play juvenile delinquents any more."[60]

In 1965, Hall told Lamparski that he had a hard time shaking the image of *Bowery Boys* and the *Dead End Kids*. Hall: "You still have a hard time, can never get away from it." Lamparski got specific: "Do you have problems when you're up for a picture?"

Hall: "Always have. You become an image to people. It's like you know, forget it, let me get a little abstract, let me look at Rembrandt, let me change."

Nevertheless, Hall did not regret making the movies. Hall: "I'm not sorry, I loved it! But I'm just sorry they got a handle on it. It's pretty hard not to, like a gang or a group. These kids are basically good actors. Association doesn't help. It comes to a point that people don't believe you can do anything else. They get you so typed."

Lamparski: "By people you must mean casting directors? I don't think the general public."

Hall: "Not the public! No the public will accept if you're good in anything. They're afraid the public will go (*whew* sound, making sound of brushing you off). They really don't know the public."

When asked by Lamparski: "Whatever happened to the Dead End Kids? And Huntz Hall?" Hall facetiously admitted he had been making quick bucks doing work that required little time or effort. Hall answered: "Stealing right now."

Lamparski: "Do you want to tell us what you are stealing?"

Hall: "Well I just came from an ad agency. I might do a commercial, so I call it 'I'm stealing.'"

Lamparski: "A television commercial? Will that be a first?"

Hall: "No, I done one, a few more. But that's stealing to me. You work for one day, and it's beautiful. You get your residuals."

Hall had planned a movie with Gorcey called "Space Nut," to be filmed in Puerto Rico. It is unknown why the plans were cancelled. Hall told Lamparski: "We're right in the middle of putting the deal together." Lamparski asked: "Won't be a Bowery Boy or Dead End Kid." Hall: "No, no, no Bowery Boys, no handles, no Bowery Boys."

As noted in Clifford Terry's "Dead End Kid Dippy Didn't Sing, He Almost Didn't Talk,"[61] Hall had supposedly made another appearance on *The Tonight Show Starring Johnny Carson*, four years after his first. The exact date of the appearance is uncertain due to incomplete logs of the show from that year, but it is known that Hall did not get as much time as some wished he had.

The show in question had this promotion: "Huntz Hall... who has a featured role in the forthcoming Ivan Tors production, *Gentle Giant*, will make his debut as a singer on the Tonight Show Friday...." The film was coming out that week in theaters across the country. So the Carson show in question had to be on the week or so before the Terry article appeared.

Terry explained how it always seems to happen that "along comes some loudmouth who proceeds to monopolize the whole deal.... The thing is, it always seems to happen to those you want to see the most. Like Huntz Hall, truly one of the all-time greats.... Singing debut? Huntz barely made his talking debut...." The loudmouth who stole the show that night was comedian Buddy Hackett.

Hall came on fifteen minutes before the show ended, and he did offer details about his career at Monogram. However, Terry seemed disappointed that Hall's "gigantic 7 or 8-minute allotment" got curtailed by Hackett.

Terry: "Huntz was starting to get warmed up now, but it was also nearing midnight on the *Tonight Show*, and Johnny Carson, like Sam Katzman, was about to cut into Hall's material. Buddy Hackett, of course, couldn't remain silent any longer, and with Carson breaking up on his every syllable, managed to get in the last few hundred words." Terry concluded with this street talk: "Dippy, you should have belted him one in the mout.'"

The talk show appearances that Hall made could only remind millions of viewers across the country of Hall's celebrity status. There has been the assertion that his fame necessitated some need to frequently change addresses over the years. Supposedly, he was forced to move often for his safety, every couple of months at one point, because of the annoying fan attention.

No one, including his son, could find any truth to this rumor. Gary: "I've never heard about that, though I do know that in the 1930s the Dead End Kids were like the Beatles and were mobbed by teenage fans. I do remember being out in public when guys would recognize him and want to hit him the way Leo did in the pictures. That didn't go down too well."

In an article entitled "Huntz Hall Thankful the Bowery Boys Dead," [62] Hall expressed regrets. Hall: "I sold my interest in the Bowery Boys in 1958. Now I get no residuals at all. But somewhere around the country that series is still strong. I knew it would click on TV.

"But the greatest thing that happened to me was when the Bowery Boys died. I'd been doing the same character all those years. Now when the cameras go on I become Dippy or Glimpy or Sach. I gotta fight that and act. Now I play myself.

"I look at my career mostly as slapstick...It's a lost art. But we're bringing it back in 'The Chicago Teddy Bears.' I know about slapstick just like I learned a lot about baseball caps–by getting hit in the face with it."

Hall connected his fame with the Beatles in a lengthy interview with Ken Michaels entitled "Say, Isn't that Huntz Hall over there?" Hall: "We were the first hippies. Beatles? Forget it. Remember Bobby Jordan's hair? It was way down to his shoulders 'way back then."[63]

Most may not recall that Hall had been immortalized among the 87 images on the 1967 LP cover of The Beatles' "Sgt. Peppers Lonely Hearts Club Band." Leo Gorcey's image was going to be there until he refused to grant permission without receiving a fee. Gorcey's image was to be found in the space between Hall and the Varga girl–but it was airbrushed out. Shortly thereafter, Gorcey died on June 4, 1969.

Hall had occasion to meet up with at least one mob boss. Tom Folsom, in his book on Joey Gallo (who Bob Dylan called "King of the Streets") recalled when Gallo introduced Hall to his associates. Folsom: "Few had forgotten the summer day a decade before when Joey showed up with none other than Huntz Hall. To the Mod Squad, Joey's nickname for the bell-bottomed hippies in the Gallo gang, Huntz stood two spots to the left from Dylan on the cover of *Sgt. Pepper's Lonely Hearts Club Band*. To the old folks, Huntz was Dippy, one of the Dead End Kids, a pack of street urchins who ran amok in Hollywood's golden years, starring in juvenile delinquent hits like *You're Not So Tough*."[64]

Hall told Michaels: "You know, gangs of tough kids challenged us wherever we went. Thought we were from the tough part of New York in real life. We'd come out the stage door to go walking around a city– say Chicago–and waiting for us in the alley, like behind the State-Lake somewhere, would be a gang of the toughest punks you ever saw, and they'd come up tough and make a pitch."

"We could have called for help and brought out bodyguards with guns and everything, but we'd just stand off, tell the kids we were just actors doing a job and not looking for any trouble but if they wanted to push, we'd fight. Mostly they'd come off it and get friendly, then they'd latch on behind us and follow us–this big gang of tough kids following us place to place all over town."

"About the bodyguards: It'd surprise you, but every town we went to, all kinds of guys–adult, tough men with guns and clubs–would offer their services to protect us for nothing. Hundreds of them, every place.

"Leo's dead. So is Bobby Jordan. Billy Halop, I don't know––back East someplace. Gabe Dell I see. My best pal. See him everyday, practically. We've worked together a long time–from the start in *Dead End*, then up thru Bowery Boys and East Side Kids. We used to race thru those pictures–budgets called for only a couple weeks' shooting. Everything was improvised. Keep going no matter what. It was fun. You got to be a professional in a hurry.

"We did 28 *Dead End* pictures, 48 *Bowery Boys*, 26 *East Side Kids*. We owned Monogram. That was the deal. Nobody else got in. After that Gabe and myself worked comedy routines moving from town to town, sometimes doing good, sometimes a flop. That's the way it's been. As far as money, I'm doing all right. No worry. Maybe I don't work a while, maybe I just travel around, read books. It doesn't matter. I don't let myself get hooked in this Hollywood syndrome. Sure, when something comes along, I go in and do a professional job for a day or two and maybe get $5,000."

Hall stands corrected here, as he did not always get the numbers right. Although he was right about the *Bowery Boys* movies with Hall appearing in all of them, the numbers quoted for the other series is incorrect. There were 22 *East Side Kids* movies, Hall appeared in 17 of them. There were 22 movies in the *Dead End Kids* series (including three serials). Hall appeared in 19 of them (Combining the *Dead End Kids* films at Samuel Goldwyn (1), at Warners (6), and at Universal (15) gives a total of 22 films.

Michaels concludes his interview with Hall: "That's it. Like a Bowery Boy, Huntz judges with a comedy face what's left in his beer bottle, then with another *Dead End* comedy face gulps it down, and we get up and get out. He wraps his blue-and-white Yale muffler that his son gave him around his neck a couple of times, and goes shuffling happy and depressed at the same time down the street."

Hall's second of three appearances on *The Merv Griffin Show* [65] in 1968 gave television viewers a chance to see some of Hall and Dell's improvisational work. Gary: "They recreated (with my writing help) a bit they used to do about a Hindi swami who was a fake. We updated it to have Gabe interviewing my Dad who was dressed in a sheet like the Maharishi. That's the only bit I remember."

By 1971, Hall did not feel burdened by the Dead End kid image. Hall: "Not anymore. For a long time, I couldn't shake it, but now things have opened up completely. I go on as a professional actor, that's it. Did an Alka-Seltzer commercial recently, the fan mail came pouring in–not for the product, not for me as a Dead Ender, but for myself as myself. Agency guy was unhappy. He says he doesn't think the sponsor will like the viewers remembering the actor instead of the product. What the hell do I care? I loved it.

"What I want to tell you about is this new TV show coming up–it might develop into a series. It might hit. It's about the occult. You know, magic, ESP and all that. About a Houdini-like guy who owns a bar where magician kind of people hang out. I'm not the Houdini; I'm the bachelor. It's a nice role. You're there all the time but don't have all the lines. Christopher George is in it. And Avery Schrieber. Both real pros. It's going to be a good show. On ABC. First one's an hour long, called *Escape*. And another thing. I just hooked a role in the *Chicago Teddy Bears*. It'll be on TV in the Fall.

"So that's what's up with me. Not running scared for jobs. Don't need it. I'm finally where I know how to relax and just live my life. Spend time with my wife and people I want to spend it with. Acting can get out of hand, you know. Some of these guys killing themselves 16 hours a day on the set. For what?"

Hall would marry for the fourth and final time to Leah (Lee) Stevens. This last marriage was briefly reported in Jack O'Brian's column on December 28, 1966: "Former Dead End Huntz Hall was lively enough to wed long-time gal pal Lee Stevens."

Some reports said that he converted to Judaism at this time. Gary (in his eulogy to his father) observed: "…as crazy and high-strung as it was, that marriage seemed to be a great blessing to both of them." Leonard Getz reported that Hall participated in Jewish rituals; including attending services for Yom Kippur and Passover, and when Lee died, he sat shiva.

Gary: "My father used to say he was Jewish after the wedding. [He would say]: 'I've got the glass in my foot to prove it.' But he never actually converted. He was pretty much a non-practicing Catholic all his life. He and Lee did attend the Synagogue for the Performing Arts, but that was more a high holy thing. The rabbi there, Jerry Cutler, was also an agent."

Hall said in 1992 that his psychiatrist told him: "Sach was the part of me that I didn't like, the happy guy. Sach was the dreamer. He was the good Huntz Hall."[66]

When asked whether he was a troublemaker like Sach? Hall: "I was nuts. [My parents] wanted to lock me up. There were 16 kids in my family and I was the 14th, so I had to get some recognition. Actually, I got into worse trouble than Sach. I was locked up plenty of times, once for marijuana, but I got out of it. The cops would say to me, 'We don't want to lock you up, Huntz. You lock yourself up.' I'm lucky that I made it this far."

Hall continued: "We were the hippest kids there were. We were the first kids to come to Hollywood who wouldn't let anyone put us down. *The Bowery Boys* were the original hippies, showing people that a 15- or 16-year-old kid had a right to say something."

When asked why is Sach a popular character? Hall explained: "People liked the cuteness of the guy. He was the underdog: Leo was hitting him; everybody was blaming him for things. Everyone thought he was the f---up—but he wasn't. Without Slip, though, Sach wouldn't have made it. Leo and I had a chemistry that was great. I didn't have it with anyone else. We really loved one another."

Nevertheless, Hall kept working as an actor long after his *Bowery Boys* series ended. Unfortunately, most of the roles were insignificant and not worthy of his skill. He did not play in a regular series again, and often the parts were inferior, some geared for juvenile audiences. He also found additional acting work with roles in dinner theater.

Beginning in the early 1960s, he could be seen on television in various programs. On February 16, 1962, two weeks after his appearance on Carson's show, Hall appeared on another popular comedy show, *The Jerry Lester Show*.

He played a poacher named Barney in a two-part episode of the 1966 TV show *Flipper*.

The 1966 feature *Second Fiddle to a Steel Guitar* offered a series of performances by a number of country music legends. The segments were introduced and tied together by some silly and lame routines by Hall with his old co-star Gorcey playing stagehands.

"Huntz Hall will have a key role in Ivan Tors *Gentle Ben*, now filming in Florida under the direction of James Neilson."[67] Actually, he was in the film *Gentle Giant*, which spawned the TV series *Gentle Ben*.

In January of 1967, Hall opened in a production of Neil Simon's

The Odd Couple with a Southern road company.⁶⁸ The Florida circuit production included E. G. Marshall and Dennis O'Keefe.

The following year a reader asked about Hall. Robert Goldsborough responded: "Hall, now 47, lives in North Miami, Florida, with his third wife. He is still active in movies, and also does television work, both as an actor and in commercials. In a two-part episode of the *Flipper* series over NBC-TV this season, he played the part of a grizzled old alligator poacher. He is also in the new Paramount motion picture *Gentle Giant*, in which he plays a stumble-bum fisherman [named Dink Smith]." ⁶⁹ A reviewer called Hall: "the one-time Dead End-Bowery Boy extraordinaire."⁷⁰

In 1968, Milton Berle gave to Friars Roast honoree Joey Bishop: "a full-length motion picture starring Huntz Hall, produced by Sam aKtzman–just this morning."⁷¹ Either the newspaper made a typographical error or the Roast intentionally misspelled the name of producer Sam Katzman.

Hall's next appearance occurred in 1970 when he had a cameo in *The Phynx*. The only reference to it appeared in an article about "intolerably bad" movies: "*The Phynx* was released in Indianapolis for two weeks and was not seen again. It featured Joan Blondell, Dorothy Lamour, Johnny Weissmuller, Maureen O'Sullivan, Leo Gorcey and Huntz Hall among others."⁷²

Also in 1970, Hall was seen in an episode of the TV series *Barefoot in the Park* called "Disorder in the Court."

A TV listing in the Fall of that year indicated that Hall would appear on the game show *Lohman & Barkley's Name Droppers*. "Huntz Hall, Teresa Graves, Harvey Lembeck, and Peter Boyle join Lohman & Barkley midnight on channel 4."⁷³ Lohman & Barkley had the top-rated morning line on KFI Los Angeles during the 1970s and 1980s.

In 1971, a Beverly Hills reader (O.G.) wrote to the Editor of "TV

Times." Reader: "Recently I saw a tall, skinny actor in a television drama who looked very much like the tall kid who was getting slapped around by Leo Gorcey in the *Bowery Boys* films. Is he the same actor?" Editor: "Since Huntz Hall is active in TV these days and did play the stupid kid who was always getting punched around by Gorcey, Hall is probably the guy."[74]

An odd reference to Hall appeared in a newspaper by a reader writing about a college football team to a sports columnist. Tom Stitt: "Dick Sullivan (Jan. 5) is naming Notre Dame as the No. 1 team because it beat Texas, is using the kind of logic that was once attributed to Huntz Hall."[75]

Hall's return to Hollywood received press in "Huntz Hall–Still a Dead End Kid." The author, Cecil Smith, described how Hall has not changed at all: "...the rasping voice mangling the language, spitting out words in jerks and jabs like an alley fighter, the same smashed nose across his face, the same pop-eyed look of bewildered belligerence... after 36 years!"[76]

Smith: "Toward the end Huntz Hall and Leo Gorcey owned part of the action–'we were the first actors in Hollywood to get a percentage,' Huntz declared. And made lots of money? 'Blew lots of money,' he said. Too often, all of them, particularly Huntz, took the image of the tough brat home: there were scrapes, arrests, charges of 'never growing up.' 'They didn't let us grow up,' Huntz says. 'But when I was out on the street again, I did a lot of growing in a short time. That's why I think it would be good for every Hollywood actor.'"

Hall at the time of Smith's interview had been engaged to do four episodes of the TV series *Chicago Teddy Bears* playing a character named Dutch. Hall told Smith: "This show is like my childhood all over again. Even this lot–our old studio. I expect to see Bogie come walking out of the alley. Listen, I had a great childhood. I remember when we made *Angels with Dirty Faces* here, I was 16, I had $150 in my pocket, I owned the earth.

"I'm glad Hy [Averback] asked me to come back and do this. I said to him: 'What's the part?' He said 'Play Huntz Hall.'" Smith concluded: "What else?"

In addition, in 1971, Hall would work as the dialogue coach on the telefilm *Lost Island*, though nothing else is known about that. Further, he would appear as a character named Gilbert in the TV movie *Escape*.

The following year, his life-long buddy and frequent co-star Gabriel Dell worked together with him on an episode of Dell's short-lived TV series *The Corner Bar*. Hall played an old shipmate of the bar's owner. Dell remarked to Carol Kramer: "I have a total blackout of my past." Kramer: "It's obvious from talking to him that 'Dead End' was a dead end, in his opinion. 'Thank God I don't have to live back there,' he says. 'I have no anecdotes. Huntz can give you pages and pages.'"[77]

In 1972, Hall reflected on his career as a Dead End Kid. Hall: "But those pictures really weren't made for American kids. They were made for American adults. They were some of the first social dramas. The public was seeing the dirty laundry, the slums, the garbage. It hurt."

Herbie Rides Again, the 1974 juvenile audience motion picture with 40 supporting players, offered Hall the chance to play a judge.

As reported on July 7, 1974 in the *Los Angeles Times*, Hall played fussy Felix Unger in the familiar play *The Odd Couple*, at the Oaks Playhouse in Ojai, California.[78] Hall played opposite Shelley Berman, but there are reports that at one point he acted with Gabe Dell in one of the revivals of *The Odd Couple*.

Hall got even busier in the next two years. In 1975, he played a character named Gronk in two episodes of the TV series *The Ghost Busters*.

The *Los Angeles Times* reported on January 19, 1975 that Hall was a hitchhiker in a two-part episode of *Walt Disney's Wonderful World of*

Color, called "The Sky's the Limit." The newspaper said that Hall, along with the supporting cast (including Richard Arlen, Ben Blue, Alan Hale, Jr., Jeanette Nolan), was "glimpsed briefly."

In that same year, the theatrical release of *Manchu Eagle Murder Caper Mystery* offered him the role of Deputy Roy to the Sheriff (Jackie Coogan). The still-active actress Joyce Van Patten said she remembered working in scenes with Gabe Dell, but could not recall any with Hall.

In 1976, he played Willy in one episode of the TV series *Matt Helm,* and he appeared as Barney in the TV series *Good Heavens.*

Hall had a walk-on part of a moving man in yet another theatrical release made for the family market, *Won Ton Ton: The Dog Who Saved Hollywood.* An article, "Won Ton Ton Can't Save Bad Script" observed that the film "sounds like a good idea–a slapstick comedy about a mutt in the silent picture era who revives a faltering studio with a string of action pictures. What's up on the screen, however, is a scattershot comedy that can't make up its mind whether to be 'wholesome family entertainment' or a smutty film industry in-joke. It goes both ways."[79]

Gabe Dell recalled his Bowery Boys days at Monogram in an article, "The Charmer in the Dell." Dell: "I liked some of the early ones, such as *Dead End, Crime School, They Made Me a Criminal* and *Angels with Dirty Faces,* but most of them weren't too hot. I'm always surprised to run into people who really enjoyed those things we turned out. I was always a fan of Huntz and Leo though. They were funny actors and should have been every bit as big as Martin & Lewis. There was a terrible caste system in this town, though. And once we ended up at Monogram it was like death. There was such a stigma attached to working at Monogram that if you walked into Schwab's, even the unemployed actor didn't want to be caught talking to you." [80]

In 1977, a cast-and-friends party at The Beverly Hills Playhouse celebrated the two opening performances of the Arthur Ross comedy *The Quadrangle*. The story revolves around "three people in a psychiatrist's office in a 24-hour period." The cast featured Hall as Mr. Thanatopsis, along with Darryl Hickman, Terry Kise, and Barrie Youngfellow. Sally Burton produced, and Gabe Dell directed.

A reviewer acknowledged: "There's the aptly named Mr. Thanatopsis, a Mafia bigwig who seeks to confirm the rightness of his wrongdoing… Hall, true to the character's name, is a dead-on stalker of annihilation."[81]

Finally, in 1977 Hall would escape the limited roles he seemed plagued with. In fact, he got perhaps his most viable role ever (at least Hall was sure it was), outside of being in the *Bowery Boys* series. He got the opportunity to play Jesse Lasky, one of the preeminent filmmakers from the early days of motion picture history. The *Los Angeles Times* simply declared that "Huntz Hall is a ruthless Jesse Lasky."

The theatrical film named *Valentino* had Ken Russell (1927–2011) directing, and it starred dancer Rudolf Nureyev (1938–1993) playing silent superstar Rudolph Valentino, Michelle Phillips as Natasha Rambova, and Leslie Caron as Alla Nazimova.

Gary told Leonard Getz: "Director Ken Russell called him one day and wanted him to play the part of Jesse Lasky. He put on a tie. Russell told him he was the only person who dressed up to see him."

Hall: "I happen to think Russell is a genius. I idolize him. And I think the only reason people put him down is because they're afraid of the truth that he manages to put on the screen. I also happen to be very grateful to him because he's finally given me the chance to prove myself as an actor, and not as a Bowery Boy."[82]

Gary said that his father "really loved getting to know Rudolf Nureyev and Michelle Phillips during *Valentino*."

Phillips leveled complaints against Nureyev for unpleasant behavior.

After working with him for six months, Hall offered a defense. Hall: "I never saw Nureyev act temperamental once. And it was a tough assignment. Director Ken Russell is a perfectionist, and after 25 takes of one scene, it would have been understandable if a performer had *cracked*."

By mixing fact and fiction, *Valentino* came under criticism. However, Russell asserted his belief that he did nothing wrong. Russell: "I only want to be accurate up to a point. I can be as inaccurate as I want–it makes no difference to me. I'm writing a novel. My films are novels, based on a person's life, and a novel has a point of view."

Perhaps the most disappointing aspect to the movie's reception is when a member of Lasky's family challenged Hall's portrayal. Greg Kilday reported: "Jesse Lasky, Jr., son of the late producer, has sent letters to the London newspapers defending his father's honor against Huntz Hall's portrait of his father in the film." Lasky, Jr. noted: "Even the Brooklyn accent was wrong. My father was born in California, son of a Californian, and grandson of a covered wagon pioneer. I recently wrote a book called, *Whatever Happened to Hollywood?* Perhaps the answer is Ken Russell."[83]

Although the film did well in Britain, it failed critically and commercially in America. Russell later considered the film his worst mistake, and that it contributed to his downfall. Nevertheless, Hall never had any luck again to get such a quality part. In 1978, he was back again playing another insignificant part–this time as the armored car driver in an episode of the TV series *CHIPs*.

From April 24th thru the week of May 25, 1979, Hall would appear with Marvin Kaplan in an Orange County production of *The Sunshine Boys* at the Harlequin Dinner Playhouse in Santa Ana, California.

In July of 1979, it was reported that Gabe Dell and Carole Goldman joined Hall in the Murray Schisgal comedy *Luv* at the *Queen Mary* Dinner Playhouse in Long Beach, California. Hall played Milt Manville in the show that ran through August 5th. Dell had several years' experience with the play as he was in the Broadway production.

Hall would be seen on the big screen as the character named Uncle Joe in the 1979 theatrical release *Gas Pump Girls.*

On June 9, 1982, "An Evening with the Bowery Boys" featured Hall and William Benedict, who played Whitey in the Bowery Boys series. They appeared in person at the Vista Theatre where three of their movies were screened; *Ghost Chasers, Dead End,* and *Bowery Champs.*[84]

Hall continued to keep busy with dinner theater work. From September 28th thru October 17, 1982, Hall played in a North County production of *The Sunshine Boys,* directed by Gary Davis, at the Lawrence Welk Village Theater in Escondido, California.[85] The ad read: "Tom Pedi and Huntz Hall bring the same sparkle to the stage as Walter Matthau and George Burns did in the film."[86] Hall played Willie Clark. The theater offered tickets priced between $10.50 and $14.50 for the performance only; and $19.50 to $24.50 for the performance with buffet lunch or dinner.

In that same year, Hall played a character named Turnkey in theatrical film *The Escape Artist.* He also played the Happy Wanderer in an episode of the TV comedy *Diff'rent Strokes* ("Big Brother"). Hall still lived in Hollywood, but now at 7560 Hollywood Boulevard.

Hall, at 62 years old, finally got sober, after a drunk driving arrest not reported by the press. Gary: "The judge sent him to AA. It stuck." Hall permanently and successfully sobered up thanks to Alcoholics Anonymous. Hall would go on to generously assist in the cause to help others with Princess Grace of Monaco's Council for Drug Abuse, a program of the Catholic Office of Drug Education.

On September 23, 1983, a group of friends of the deceased actor John Garfield honored him at the Riviera Country Club in Pacific Palisades, California in order to launch the John Garfield Foundation. His brother Michael set up the Foundation. The guests at the event included Hall, Ida Lupino, Burgess Meredith, Dane Clark, Stella Adler, and others.

Hall had appeared as a Dead End Kid alongside Garfield in *They Made Me a Criminal*. He explained his friendship to Nancy Graham. Hall: "I was 18 and Julie (John) was close to 25. I remember we used to call him 'the poet' and 'the philosopher.' Being New Yorkers, John understood us more. He talked to us about politics and government. We knew about Hitler before the war. John told us to look out for him, that he was a dangerous man."[87]

According to Hall, Garfield was not a communist. Hall: "Julie came from a background of poverty. He didn't like to see the little guy pushed around. The Committee was a terrible thing. John was persecuted. I don't think John's family ever recovered from it. I know this, John loved the American people like I do. He didn't like discrimination. He was brought up with black actors. There is no color on the stage.

"Julie was a guy I loved. We were all younger than he was but when we were working with him, he would sit down with us and talk on an artist-to-artist level. He would say, 'Listen, do you think the scene works better this way?' "

Regarding the John Garfield Foundation, Hall noted: "I'm glad we're doing this. I want to see him remembered. I'd like to see them bring back his acting. They can learn from his pictures. He's been too long in the background."

This interview gave Hall a chance to show his intelligence as well as his respect for a fellow actor. Gary: "My father had some unique social theories, but he was usually proved right. I know he thought of the Dead End Kids as the Beatles of his day."

In 1984, the cable television movie *The Ratings Game* featured Hall as the character named Benny Bentson. Three years later, Hall played Long John in the theatrical film *Cyclone*.

On October 5, 1987, a city proclamation was issued for a Huntz Hall Day in Los Angeles.

The following year he played the priest Father O'Malley in an episode ("Bless Me Father.") of the television series *Night Heat*. A dark point in Hall's life happened then in 1988 as his life-long buddy Gabe Dell died. A spokesperson for Hall said he "was not taking any calls. He is in mourning."[88] Hall and Bernard Punsley were then the only remaining Dead End Kids still alive.

Hall told Broeske: "The trouble with this business is that everyone thinks that everything happens in this town…Darling this is *not* the world. People think if you're not on TV, you're not working. I tell you, it's a big country. There are a lot of dinner-theaters out there." Hall spoke of how he has been keeping busy over the years in "at least a play a year."

In 1992, Hall played a farmer in a film called *Auntie Lee's Meat Pies*. Hall: "It's a cameo. You can do a cameo and be the best thing in the picture."[89]

Hall played his last part in 1993 at seventy-three years old. It was for an episode of the TV series *Daddy Dearest*, in which he played the Pretzel Man.

His credits after the *Bowery Boys*, with the exception of *Valentino*, and some occasionally good character parts, leaves fans with much to be desired. Gary explained the problem with Hall's post *Bowery Boys* career. He told Leonard Getz that his father: "kept holding out for bigger deals, more money, top billed. He didn't play it right. He did commercials for Dash and Toyota."

In a way it's understandable that Hall held out for productions that offered top billing, as he ended his career at Allied Artists with the last seven *Bowery Boys* movies giving him star credit.

Besides his appearances in television and film productions, Hall spent his later years busy speaking at colleges, and signing his autograph for fans at paper shows. Hall said in 1990: "It's lucrative–and I also have a good time. At the last show, I signed 900 autographs in four hours."

He attributed these engagements to people's continued interest in the Kids. In addition, Hall believed that the movies held up quite well.

Broeske asked him why his motion pictures were so appealing as they continued to be shown in syndication. Hall: "Their appeal? That's easy. They're Americana. Then there's the fact that we were the good guys. They were also pretty entertaining. After seeing our pictures, you got rid of your problems. In today's movies, the problems are on the screen."

When reviewing some of his personal appearances, in which he had the opportunity to look back over his career, and the quite varied response from attendees, it is apparent that his behavior reportedly seemed erratic and unpredictable. Opinions of him ran the gamut from quite friendly and engaging to seemingly hostile and abrasive. His son agreed with my assessment of those reports and explained further. Gary: "He was always erratic and unpredictable. He was both sweet and angry. But this was a lifelong issue."

What is difficult in researching Hall's life is finding individuals to critique Hall on the record. I was told stories of how strange and odd he could be at times. One fan told of how he met with Hall and Dell, including visiting Dell's house. Hall had with him about ten 11x14 stills, to which the fan requested to just look at them. Hall adamantly refused to show him the stills. In contrast, Dell provided that same fan with seventeen stills, and even autographing them.

His wife Lee seemed to run everything for Hall. Gary: "Lee wanted to monetize everything–she was his manager as well as his wife–and she had some strange ideas."

Whatever the reason for Hall's odd and standoffish behavior, including his reliance on Lee to handle everything, this did not stop fans from continuing to have much respect for him. The endearing friendship that he kept with some fans has prevented them from ever signing their names to stories of his quirkiness. It seems that no one wants to badmouth him. People simply had so much affection for the man that gave them so much laughter.

The same fan that was given stills by Dell had nevertheless corresponded for years with Hall, receiving many letters in return. That fan would not provide them because he believed it would not be right to print something for the world to see what Hall intended only for his eyes. Again, it is interesting to see the respect that Hall generates years after his death.

Perhaps other fans expected much more from him as they confused the real person, Huntz Hall, a quite intelligent but temperamental man, with the seemingly dumb but friendly and loveable "Sach," the character who Hall played so convincingly.

Comedian Jackie Curtiss used to have coffee with Hall on Sundays at Schwabs. Curtiss made many appearances on TV and elsewhere, and he was known for pairing up with straight man Bill Tracy. Curtiss is quoted as having said: ". . . when I was sitting with him and a couple of other comics, people would never recognize any of us, but they would yell, 'Huntz Hall, We love you!' Everybody.

"A lot of people would not know this, but he was *not* a dummy. His character with the Bowery Boys and the Dead End Kids and everything had nothing to do with his real self. He was intelligent. He was a bright guy, but he never talked in a bright *way*. A couple times when we were alone he would say something and I would go, 'Jesus, that's bright thinking!' He'd say, 'Well, I'm not a dummy. I just *act* a dummy.'"

Gary revealed some of his father's traits, interests, and things that made him the individual he was. Gary: "My father was very funny in person and in groups—he was always 'on' at parties, and he was a wonderful storyteller. As a kid, I knew he was famous, and I went to the set dozens of times when the movies were being made. When I saw the movies as a teenager, though, the Sach persona seemed very different than the person I knew. My father was funny in [a] more New York/comic way than the Sach character. He did do the cheek thing [motorlips], and while I can't my son Oliver can, so it must be a genetic trait.

"He was full of great stories from his studio days that I don't recall that well. When I was at Yale, I talked to Ronald Reagan (visiting the campus), and he told me how he and my father set a director's chair on fire. Whenever you asked him a question about a star, he would have some tidbit of information." Reagan appeared with Hall in *Hell's Kitchen* and *The Angels Wash Their Faces*.

Gary: "Because he had grown up in radio and the theater and had been in the studio system, he was very sophisticated and quite charming. He was incredibly smart, though not a reader. He could add figures in his head and tell you what cards had yet to be played in Blackjack.

"He was a big jazz fan and every time I meet a jazz musician from that era they knew my father. [This is] partly because he and Gabe toured with Charlie Barnett's orchestra, partly because my father spent a lot of time in jazz clubs.

"He loved the ballet too. He was a huge sports fan, especially hockey (the Rangers) and baseball (the New York Giants). He was in the Polo Grounds the day Bobby Thompson hit the game winning home run.

One thing that has not been told is that he loved Abstract Expressionist art, besides being a drinking buddy of that art movement's founder, Willem de Kooning. In addition, it is easy to agree with Hall in that he thought Cary Grant was the greatest screen comedian.

As far as Hall's politics, he was a left-wing Democrat throughout his life. As an activist member of the Screen Actors Guild, he especially supported workers' rights issues. Gary noted: "My father always had very strong, left-wing political ideas. Unlike many 1930s radicals, he never lost his progressive leanings. He was questioned by the FBI in the early 1950s over his support for the republican side of the Spanish Civil War. He wasn't one (like me) to go to marches and demonstrations, but he had a lot of black friends and felt really at home in the black community."

As regards his opinion of the LGBT community, Gary explained: "He had gay friends, but he was possessed of the homophobic attitudes of his generation. He used to say he was OK with the gays as long as they don't flaunt it. I think today he'd be in a better place on that issue."

Hall served as an altar boy in the Catholic Church. However, he left after a priest slapped him when he confessed that he took the Lord's name in vain once too often. Gary would note in his eulogy to his father: "That his only son became a priest seemed to him a combined gift of God and a cosmic joke."

He attended church when his son Gary served as Vicar of St. Aidan's in Malibu, California. His buddy Gabe would go to St. Charles Church in North Hollywood. Gary noted: "I think my father's religious feelings were pretty internal."

He did not like to eat vegetables. He was allergic to sulfa drugs. Hedda Hopper reported it this way: "Huntz Hall, one of the toughest Dead End Kids–pardon me Bowery Boys–balked at taking penicillin tablets. Doc had to give him the medicine concealed in ice cream."[90]

Gary: "He could be unbelievably hilarious. Once he came to watch me give a lecture on Ralph Ellison's *Invisible Man* at UCLA when I was teaching English there. The kid in front of him turned to another student and said, 'I don't understand what Professor Hall is saying.' My father leaned in between them and said, 'Hey, kid: read the fucking book!' That's pretty typical of how he was."

In 1990, eight years after joining AA, Hall told Broeske: "[I'm] going 15 years without a drink." Supposedly, Hall had been in recovery from alcoholism. Technically, it was not accurate, since that would mean he started recovery in 1975, rather than 1982. It is unknown whether Hall was misquoted or that it was just so long back that he did not recall when he quit.[91]

Gary: "Especially after he got sober in 1982, my father was pretty realistic about alcohol. [As you know] both Bobby Jordan and Leo Gorcey died essentially of alcohol issues.

As regards his habits, Gary recalled: "he was a lifelong smoker of Camels–from age nine. He never got over tobacco, even when he was on oxygen. Being Irish, he was predisposed to alcoholism, and I would say his getting sober at age 62 was a real achievement. I think his marijuana use was pretty benign, and in this way he was way ahead of his time. Today that habit seems less onerous than it did in the 1950s.

"I wish my father had had a really good education. Part of his problem, I think, was not having had the discipline of a formation in mental, physical, and behavioral habits. At age 17, he was taken over by the studio system at Warner Bros., and though they taught him how to ride a horse, tap dance, and fence, they didn't help him organize his mental furniture."

Despite his personal habits Hall did not really have self-destructive tendencies, commonplace among the famous. Although he suffered from alcoholism (and later was proud to be a recovering alcoholic), smoked cigarettes and marijuana, and had a bad temper, his life's choices did not derive from the need to indulge out of a lack of self-restraint. Gary said it simply: "He didn't really live a dissolute life, especially in relation to the way many people in music and films do."

Should we regret that actor/comedian Hall never hooked up with a major studio like Paramount or MGM? I think not. Although those studios would have given him much more publicity, a larger pool of really good writers and even better technical talent, it would not guarantee that his motion pictures would be celebrated and remembered any more today than they are.

At the very least, it would have meant that the movies would have lost their casual and improvisational quality that came out of Monogram, the "Poverty Row" quickie factory. Perhaps the conditions that made Hall's movies so endearing may not have existed at the major studios due to the complexity of having more hands and money controlling the outcome. Most certainly, the sheer longevity of the *Bowery Boys* series, at least at a major studio, would have been called into question.

Chapter 6:
A Sad Farewell

"When people would ask me what he looked like these days, I would say, 'Just picture Howard Hughes without the money.'"
Gary Hall, "Thoughts on My Father," Eulogy, Feb. 2, 1999

Sadly, Huntz Hall's last five years were spent without his dear wife Lee, as she passed away in 1993. He had been with her for more than 25 years. Their last years were spent together in homes in North Hollywood and New York.

Gary: "After that he went into reclusive decline–he turned down work and stayed pretty much at home. We would see him regularly for holidays and the like, but he stayed more and more to himself. At the same time, his health problems (heart failure and emphysema) began to increase, and so there were a constant round of hospitalizations."

"I think Lee's death really hit him hard and he stopped wanting to live. They had a complex relationship, but he deeply loved her. By around 1996 or so I was the only person he saw regularly. I would do his marketing, take him to the doctor, and then call the paramedics when he went into heart failure.

A published source noted that Gary said that when people asked him what his father was like at the time, he answered that he was very much like Howard Hughes without the money. One might infer that this statement suggested that Hall suffered from serious mental complexes or psychological issues.

Gary clarified his earlier statement: "What I meant was that he was reclusive. After Lee died, he essentially withdrew into himself, grew his hair long, and didn't see anybody except Kathy [my wife], Oliver [my son], me, and his doctors. He wasn't crazy; he was lonely and depressed. He really loved Lee.

"In December of 1998 he had a massive heart failure episode and went into St. Joseph's in Burbank. He was in the ICU for a while, then they did the heart catheterization on him and determined that his heart problems (valves, blockages) were inoperable and sent him home. He died a week later at home."

Oliver, Hall's grandson, whom Huntz loved very much, was home from college. Gary, along with Oliver, had visited him on January 29, 1999, the day before he died. Gary: "He seemed both happy and exhausted. Kathy and I found his body later that night when we got an alarmed call from an actor friend, Bobby Ball, who said he couldn't get him on the phone.

"His last years were pretty sad. He was more dependent emotionally on Lee than we knew and never got over her loss."

Hall's final home in North Hollywood had been at 12512 Chandler Boulevard, apartment #307. Gary told Leonard Getz: "When the paramedics came and checked his driver's license, they looked at him and said, 'Hey, that's Sach!'" It was on January 30, 1999 that Huntz Hall died.

No different from most people, Hall's personal life was tumultuous at times. One wonders what Hall thought of his life as he neared the end. Gary: "My father was not one given to reflection, at least with me. He never voiced misgivings about personal or professional mistakes. He seemed to take professional ups and downs with equanimity.

"My father and (his wife) Lee talked on and off about writing a book, and he may have been working with a writer at the time, but I wasn't involved and didn't find anything in his things when he died."

Hall died intestate. He never wrote a Last Will and Testament. Gary noted that he tried repeatedly to get him to write one, but he could not overcome his father's reluctance.

Hall's son, in his position as the Rev. Gary at All Saints Episcopal Church in Pasadena, California, delivered the eulogy on February 2, 1999. His ashes are interred at the church's columbarium at that location.

Gary acknowledged: "Although he was widely known in this country and around the world, my father probably didn't have the colossal stardom he should have. For sixty years of his life he loved to make people laugh and he did it brilliantly and simply as anyone on stage and film has ever done it."

Gary aptly concluded his eulogy to his Dad. He noted: "The *Bowery Boys* are not as well-known these days as they should be, but like those of Buster Keaton and Stan Laurel and The Three Stooges before him, the films of Huntz Hall will one day be rediscovered and applauded for the generous and spontaneous way they celebrate community, simplicity, and the pure goofiness of being human. And when you think about it, what is a better life's work than that?"

Bidding Huntz Hall a fond farewell is not easy, especially if one got the chance to really know him. Gary: "He was generous in all kinds of ways. He helped a lot of people up the career ladder. He gave work to actors who needed to qualify for health insurance. He gave a lot of money away when people were in a jam. He almost always picked up a check in a bar or restaurant. He was always giving to people. He really didn't care about money and seemed to be in a hurry to give it away."

We can be happy that even in his death, Huntz Hall did not leave us empty-handed. What he did share with us in motion pictures is his spirit of loving to make us laugh. As you will see in the next three chapters of this book, you can enjoy his character of "Sach" forever. His movies exude his brand of solid and lasting humor that is never dated. Hall's "Sach" remains as lively and funny today as he once was to audiences over fifty years ago.

Huntz Hall, our "American Chaplin," finally deserves the long-overdue appreciation for his contribution to film history. Is it possible for this first biography to revive critical interest and further study into his comedy genius? I think Hall's Sach would be surprised by this idea, saying: "Ohp! Ohp! Ohp!"

Not only did Huntz Hall love to make people laugh, but we love to laugh at his comedy as well. Indeed, he deserves our affection and appreciation for honing his ability to make us laugh in his flawed, though nevertheless quite entertaining movies. My hope is that Huntz Hall's comedy will endure, and may it never be lost or forgotten! Long live Sach!

Alan Lowell, Gary Hall and Huntz Hall. Courtesy Gary Hall.

Barry Bregman (son of musical arranger/record producer/composer Buddy Bregman), Huntz Hall and Gary Hall. Courtesy Gary Hall.

Ben Melzer (Huntz Hall's manager), Gary Hall and Huntz Hall.
Courtesy Gary Hall.

Gary Hall and Huntz Hall Take. Courtesy Gary Hall.

Gary Hall and Huntz Hall on the Allied Artists Pictures set for the 1955 release *Dig That Uranium*. This is my personal favorite of these never-before-published photographs. Courtesy Gary Hall.

Gary Hall Today. Courtesy Gary Hall.

Gary Hall, The Steve Allen Show Marquee. Courtesy Gary Hall.

Huntz Hall, (2nd wife) Leslie Hall, and Baby Gary Hall.
Courtesy Gary Hall.

(2nd wife) Leslie Hall, Gary Hall, and Huntz Hall.
Courtesy Gary Hall.

Part Two:
The Bowery Boys Films

Chapter 7:
Sach's Comedy

1946-1949
Spook Busters (1946) - 3.0/4.0
Hold That Baby! (1949) - 3.0/4.0
Master Minds (1949) - 4.0/4.0

Where is Hall's comedic brilliance as Sach? First, there is his superb delivery of dialogue, offering the right intonation and pauses; in short, excellent timing to deliver laughs every time. In addition, Hall offers some well-chosen, intense and perfect facial mannerisms; a whole array of peculiarities, including bulging his eyes, tilting his head sideways and sometimes upward, pursed lips, and so on. Hall's Sach has to be seen to be truly and fully appreciated.

In short, the reader would be best served to accept these comments provided in these chapters as a rather rough guide to just some of Hall's comedy moments as Sach. By no means can these descriptions replace the actual comedy moments.

As regards his personality, Sach has an uncontrollable habit that makes him oftentimes put his foot in his mouth. Usually Slip hits him on his head, with Sach reacting in pain ("Ohp! Ohp! Ohp!") Whatever

Sach says or does, he always seems to try Slip's patience. In essence, it seems that Sach cannot stop aggravating Slip, which means he gets himself clobbered often.

What never changes in any of the *Bowery Boys* movies is that you can rely on Sach to say or do something silly. As far as Sach's presence is concerned, the *Bowery Boys* movies of least interest are the ones in which the story has very little comic business for him to do. However, the best productions in the series as regards comedy are those in which the story revolves around Sach.

Nevertheless, the comedy of Hall's Sach would not be complete without Gorcey's Slip. The laughs from Sach generally depend on playing off of Slip. In short, Gorcey acted as the one of the best straight men of the era. Though both mug to the camera, they play brilliantly off each other. The proof comes when we compare Gorcey/Hall movies with the disappointing productions made when Gorcey's replacement, Stanley Clements, teamed with Hall.

The final scene, or finale, is described for each film. Some of the best closings to comedy movies are found in these productions. A good closing must be an adequate wrap-up, and it is essential that it leave the viewer with a positive memory of the film, to generate loyalty to the viewer to see the next film of the series. Most of the finales are generally funny or satisfactory to achieve that loyalty.

To conclude each film description, I offer "Sach's Comedy Meter," a rating of how much comedy Sach offers in each film. The comedy is appraised with a scale between a lowest of 1.0 and the highest of 4.0. It is meant to rate the relative amount of comedy that Sach offers in each film.

A rating of 2.5 means an average amount of comedy moments from Sach. Below 2.5 (2.0, 1.5, 1.0) is below average. Above 2.5 is above average. The motion pictures with 3.0, 3.5, and 4.0 are highly recommended, with the latter ratings of 3.5 as very funny and 4.0 as extremely funny.

Please note that some of the release dates here are premiere dates. These will be earlier than the general release dates found in the Credits section.

1. Live Wires
Released January 12, 1946

In the premiere entry in the *Bowery Boys* series, the credits read "Monogram Pictures Corporation Presents Leo Gorcey and The Bowery Boys with Huntz Hall." The manner in which Hall would be credited would change for the early movies until it was decided how it should remain; sometimes the credits would read "with Huntz Hall," sometimes they would read "featuring Huntz Hall," and so forth.

Sach looks better than Slip as he has been working as a process server for an auto finance company for more than a year, and he owns a new suit.

Hall plays Sach as if he is not quite confident about the correct characterization; sometimes he is smart, sometimes tough, and sometimes stupid. The contrast between this film and later ones is significant. As the series progresses, Sach would become more self-assured, eccentric and eventually seemingly dwell in a world all his own. In addition, the other Boys have more to do in the early *Bowery Boys* movies. They would eventually become non-entities as Sach's persona comes to dominate most scenes.

There is still a similarity to the East Side Kids in having familial references. For instance, the character of Mary appears as Leo's sister. She is important to the plot since she is concerned that Slip is always being fired because he gets into fights at work.

Nevertheless, the Bowery Boys would rarely have parents or authority figures. The only exception is with Louie, the owner of the Sweet Shop where they hang out. In this entry, it is called "Louie's Ice Cream Parlor," and Bernard Gorcey does not play the owner yet. He plays a gambler named Jack.

One characteristic of Sach is his misunderstanding of words. The first time here is when Slip observes: "looks more like somebody's trying to incite a riot." Sach answers, "what do you mean inside, the guys outside."

Sach's predilection to making a wisecrack is also evident here. A street seller offers Pierce's Peerless Stain Remover. Sach wants to buy a bottle, but he changes his mind. Then Sach plays Devil's Advocate. Slip wants to buy a bottle, and Sach retorts: "I don't think it's any good." This time Sach makes a smart remark–and as you will see, it is one of the few times in the series that a wisecrack does not result in Slip smacking him.

When Slip buys the product setup, so he could be a salesperson, Sach senses that Slip's venture will put them in jail. Slip remarks: "A few days of selling this and our families will see us as we really are." Sach responds: "Certainly–on visitor's days."

Slip does a demonstration and promises a new suit to a spectator if the ink stain remover does not work. Slip loses. However, Sach bets against Slip and wins a wad of money. When Slip realizes that Sach bet against him, we see the first time that Slip smacks Sach, complaining: "You bet on the other guy–no confidence in me."

Sach brings Slip to his job in the hope of helping Slip find work. Slip gets assigned to go to the High Hat Club to summons and collect from a female singer behind on her car payments. Sach does not believe his eyes when Slip is all dressed up to go to the club to wine and dine. Sach puts a hat on Slip, but Slip slaps Sach in the face. Slip gets into a fight, this time the trouble makes the newspaper. Again, Slip's sister is upset.

The laughs are plentiful as a gangster bullies and scares Slip and Sach. This highlight of *Live Wires* is at the gangster's apartment where they try to subpoena him for the District Attorney seeking the leaders of an auto theft ring.

As in most movies of this series, what is interesting is that Sach does not partake in fighting the bad guys, but he's absorbed in watching and directing everyone else that's fighting.

It is obligatory in the series that the Boys are on the side of the law, and they always somehow manage to help capture the crook(s). Here Sach gets to serve a subpoena to the biggest crook in town.

Finale: Slip's sister punches out a woman who calls Slip, "you Guttersnipe." Sach asks Slip, "Isn't [it] you who say that fighting was vulgar and common?" Slip responds asking, "Don't you see she was at a social disadvantage?" Slip uses that same excuse throughout the film to defend his own actions ("I was at a social disadvantage"). Sach shakes his head and murmurs a doubtful negative response, until Slip quickly smacks him across his face with his hat three times. Sach changes his tune and optimistically answers: "Ah huh."

Sach's role in *Live Wires* is limited and lackluster for his character is not fleshed out or developed much. Uncharacteristically, he is depicted as well dressed wearing a suit. He did not adopt his characteristic cap yet. He seems sullen, and there is not much goofiness either. Sach's typical mannerisms that he becomes known for are non-existent here. In addition, his interaction with Slip shows minimum chemistry. *Live Wires* is one of weakest if not *the weakest* of the entire Bowery Boys series as regards Sach's input. Sach Comedy Meter: 1.0 out of 4.0.

2. In Fast Company

Released June 22, 1946

The credits differ from the first film with the substitution of "with" for "and," as well as the removal of "with" after "Boys." Here it reads "Monogram Pictures Corporation Presents Leo Gorcey with The Bowery Boys Huntz Hall."

The Red Circle Cab Company (RCC) is trying to muscle in on the Cassidy Cab Company (CCC) to sell their company to them. CCC's refusal makes RCC jealous of the competition to the extent they are cracking up CCC's cabs. Early on, the Boys are depicted as petty thieves tasting bananas for ripeness from a street pushcart and not paying for them. Sach joins in: "This ain't ripe." When the pushcart owner incites a fruit fight, and the police officer arrives, the owner says, "I want to prefer the charges." Sach shoots back, "I prefer the celery," as he shoves the celery in the dealer's mouth. The scene ends with Sach barking: "Last time I buy anything from you!"

Sach is showing that he acts as a support to Slip with little asides. He observes things that Slip is doing, for instance when he sees Slip making out with the waitress at Louie's Ice Cream Parlor, Sach remarks: "That boy's a genius–what a liar." Louie is now seen behind the Parlor's counter.

Sach's first impersonation is found here. *In Fast Company* he plays a cowboy in order to create a diversion.

Throughout this film, Sach has various one-liners and word plays. For instance, Slip confirms with Sach that they got everything: "Check, check, check…" Sach takes it wrong. Sach: "No check, simply cash." When Slip is driving a cab with Sach in the front seat, the rival cab manager rides their cab and asks: "What's the idea of two drivers." Sach responds: "Didn't you ever hear of co-pilots? Double service for your money."

While trying to grab a wristwatch in a jaws gaming machine, Sach is interrupted (he claims 8 times already). Sach: "I get to this watch or else." Bobby questions: "Or else what?" Sach answers: "Or else I'll get nothing."

Of special note is the scene of the Boys, the waitress, and Louie getting crammed into the parlor's phone booth. It serves as a tribute to a Marx Brothers' sight gag reminiscent of *A Night at the Opera* (1935).

When Sach fell asleep in the cab he is supposed to watch, the wheels were stolen. This gives Slip justification to hit him in the head with Sach's cab cap.

We see Sach with his characteristic upturned black cap for the first time here. There are alternate scenes whereby Sach is wearing a cab cap. At one point, he wears it with the chinstrap wrapped around him so that Slip cannot take it off to hit him. So then, Slip steps on Sach's foot instead. Sometimes Slip will not slap Sach right away, but instead with a delayed reaction. Nevertheless, the hitting is always because Sach wisecracks with an unwelcome comment.

Briefly, for the first time, there is a moment when Sach is alone. He wanders into a room in the rival cab owner's mansion. He bumps into a tiger rug ("Hello, how are you? How's the family. That's nice"). Then Sach backs away and bumps into another tiger rug ("Hi ya kid, just spoke to your father"). He bows goodbye to it. He looks on the wall and likewise remarks when he sees hanging a rhino and a kangaroo head. The scene is a foretaste of the later movies, in which some of funniest moments are when Sach is alone exploring and commenting on the objects in his surroundings.

The owner of RCC confronts one of his underlings about the destruction being done to CCC by his men. Characteristically, Sach does not get involved in the fight scene that ensues. Instead, he speaks into a car pipe as if he is fight commentator as he describes the punches.

Finale: Sach drives and crashes the cab when he turns around to see Slip and his girl fighting in the backseat. Sach is in the totaled cab offering the film's last line: "Taxi, Mister?"

As with *Live Wires*, Slip dominates *In Fast Company*. However, Sach has more one-liners here, and he frequently raises Slip's ire with his stupid responses. Unfortunately, Sach does not run as far with the lines, as he will in later productions. However, Slip usually responds to Sach's remarks by hitting him in the head with his cap or hat. Sach Comedy Meter: 1.5 out of 4.0.

3. Bowery Bombshell
Released July 20, 1946

The credits go back to the format of the first film. They read "Monogram Pictures Corporation Presents Leo Gorcey and The Bowery Boys with Huntz Hall."

Here Sach wears a white cap with an upturned black bill. Some of the exchanges between Slip and Sach seem to go a little further than in the two previous movies.

When Slip asks Sach to turn the lights on in a photography darkroom, Sach hits the burglar alarm instead. Sach explains: "It looked like a ordinary light switch. How do I know about it? What do you think I am another Edison or something?" Slip responds: "You haven't got the brains of a moron." Sach answers: "Oh yes I have!" Slip: "Stop bragging about it!"

Sach gets his picture on the front page of the newspaper, mistaken as the bank robber. Slip: "Stupid Sach probably bragging all over the East Side, bragging about getting his picture in the paper." Sach goes into hiding, and there is a $1,000 reward for his capture. This plot device is reminiscent of Abbott & Costello's *Hit the Ice*. The parallel includes the presence of Sheldon Leonard as a gangster.

Besides giving him a $1,000 bill, a man stuffs money in his clothing to frame Sach. Sach tells Slip: "You better be nice to me, it's ain't every man that's worth $1,000." In one scene, Sach wears his cap backwards. When Slip says he is going to take good care of Sach, an embarrassed Sach offers for the first time a distinctive (and slightly effeminate) hand wave.

In order to evade a police detective, Sach disguises himself as a knitting granny with laryngitis. Slip calls him "Mother Whistler." In addition, what acts as a fine tribute to Warner Bros. gangster movies, Slip and the Boys disguise themselves as gangsters.

The highlight of this film is the sequence showing Hall's fine dramatic ability as a paranoid Sach. Alone in hiding, he gets up with a pillow on his head, and then he hears voices saying he is going to jail. He is scared, even asking Louie to hide him. He thinks the cops are closing in on him.

A henchman beats up on Sach and Slip. Then they believe the crook will explode because he drank an explosive formula invented by a Professor. Slip kicks Sach in the ass for starting all the trouble because he wanted his picture taken. When Sach kicks the crook in his ass, they realize it turns out that just the crook's spit is explosive.

Finale: A spare tire with "Dead End" written on it falls over the heads of Slip, Sach and the Professor. As regards inventing the formula, the Professor asks: "Aren't you gonna congratulate me?" Slip and Sach hit the Professor over his head.

The story in *Bowery Bombshell* seems to give just a little more attention to Sach than *Live Wires* and *In Fast Company*. Sach Comedy Meter: 2.0 out of 4.0.

4. Spook Busters

Released August 20, 1946

The credits first title card reads: "Monogram Pictures Corporation Presents Leo Gorcey and The Bowery Boys." The second card reads: "in Spook Busters." The third card reads: "with Huntz Hall Douglass Dumbrille."

This film opens with Sach sitting separately away from the gang at graduation ceremonies (College of Insect Exterminators) wearing a pointed cone over his head with the word "Dunce" written on it. We see him sad, even ready to cry, and embarrassed. He does a distinctive hand wave implying "get out of here" when Slip narrates: "There was a hunk of IQ."

When Sach comes in chasing a moth, he causes a ruckus. Slip makes a sullen Sach release it since he does not have a license and he did not graduate exterminating school.

The Boys take on the job of searching for Louie's mouse. Sach is eager to be a part of Extermination Company by banging walls. Slip is banging and searching, but he is hearing Sach. He continues and backs into Sach, as Sach's eagerness to help turns into interfering.

Slip is clearly shown here as the type of character that tends to takeover situations. Louie, speaking to Gabe, describes Sach: "A nice boy, but a crazy moron."

When the Boys go to do an exterminating job at a deserted (and spooky) mansion owned by a magician, a scared Sach is found hiding under their jalopy. Although Sach gets easily confused, here he manages to get inside the entrance gates before everyone else.

Sach has plenty of amusing one-liners here. Slip: "This house has been in the state of un-occupancy." Sach: "I thought it was in New York." Sach: "Every time I try to use my brain I get in trouble."

They walk into a room full of magic tricks. Slip thinks Sach is imagining that he is seeing things–but they are there.

When Sach sees Gabe's French girlfriend, he reacts: "Hubba, Hubba, Hubba, Hubba." Sach is clearly not as funny here as he will become. In later movies, he gyrates his lips upon seeing a pretty woman (referred to as Sach's motorlips).

Slip: "When are you going to stop trying to be an imbecile?" Sach: "Well, if I fail I'll start at the bottom again." Slip: "You'll never get off the bottom."

As Sach plays the organ, he disappears through a revolving wall. This leads to a "Sach alone" scene as he wanders into a laboratory. He speaks to himself saying: "This is a funny place for a drug store." There are gas masks, and what he thinks is a radio–but it is a television. He turns it on to see a graveyard, and says: "I don't want to listen to no mystery." The TV monitor reveals the Boys are searching for Sach as they look for a trapdoor. He opens a door to leave and sees a caged gorilla.

After being chased by a henchman, Sach locates the Boys. Sach proves helpful at times, as when he tells Slip that if you move the gravestone, it will lead to the basement thru a trapdoor.

The scientist wants to use Sach as a guinea pig, specifically he wants to do an experiment to remove Sach's brain and transplant it in the gorilla. Sach: "Oh! Oh! Oh! Oh! Oh! No you don't, no you don't." Doc: "I only want a little piece." Slip: "How much do you think he's got?" Sach: "He's right Doc, I have none to spare…Hey Doctor, how about doing this operation on a Wednesday, Wednesday 1982?"

Sach offers his frightened and dopey stare. There are more one-liners about Sach's brain. Sach: "Well you gotta get my Mommy's permission, I'm a minor." Sach: "If he takes my little brain, I won't be able to think." Slip: "Is that bad?"

Sach (with Slip's help) tries to postpone the operation and escape by using the ruse of asking for a glass of water and then splashing it on one of the henchmen. This film's highlight occurs when Sach hilariously delays surgery by fooling the henchmen (played by Charles Middleton and Richard Alexander–Ming the Merciless and Prince Barin from the *Flash Gordon Space Soldiers* serial). Sach reminds them of a deceased patient that the doctor has operated on. Sach convincingly fakes it and begs the unseen Charlie not to hurt him. He feigns that Charlie is attacking him, even having Charlie seem to be throwing things out of a room. Sach turns the tables by scaring the frightened henchmen. Sach: "Run for your life, Charlie's got an ax!"

With Slip effectively narrating, he impersonates the surgeon who fumblingly tries to stop the operation on Sach. He splashes ether on the henchmen, and the scene changes into slow motion fighting. Fast motion action follows when Sach finally realizes that he freed the gorilla and runs away.

Finale: Louie calls to tell Slip his mouse just had puppies. The final line goes to Sach: "His mouse just had puppies? Here we go again!"

Spook Busters offers some very good humor from Sach. The story has even more emphasis on him than the first three. Of particular note is Sach's convincing portrayal of being scared. Sach Comedy Meter: 3.0 out of 4.0.

5. Mr. Hex

Released December 7, 1946.

The credits first title card reads: "Monogram Pictures Corporation Presents Leo Gorcey and The Bowery Boys." The second card reads: "in Mr. Hex." The third card reads: "with Huntz Hall" followed by six other players. This format continues for most of the series.

The scene opens at "Louie's Sweet Shop." Before this film, it was named "Louie's Ice Cream Parlor."

We observe Slip stacking playing cards into a monument. Sach energetically comes in and knocks them over. Slip uses his hat to hit Sach's head. Sach is seen in the background wiping his eyes.

A love song that a young woman is singing in the jukebox saddens the Boys, including Sach. Slip gives Sach his handkerchief so he can clear his nose and wipe his eyes. The singer's mom is sick, and in need of money to care for her, as well as to finance her singing career.

Slip sees an advertisement offering a $2,500 Boxing Tournament Prize. Slip pushes "Sach the Simpleton" to enter. A scared Sach displays his cowardice. With the help of a celebrated hypnotist, they tap into Sach's super-human strength so he could win the fight.

One of the film's highlights is when Sach is being hypnotized. The hypnotist transfers control to Slip via a coin–what Slip calls the genie. There is a montage sequence of fighter Sach Sullivan being put under hypnotic influence. In short, Sach's strange powers come from making him believe he is a great fighter.

When Sach is boxing with his own shadow, his shadow turns on him and knocks him out. The nightclub owner tries to take advantage of his new female hire. Slip and Sach come to her rescue, but the owner knocks them both out. Once Slip shows Sach the genie, Sach knocks out the owner and his cohorts.

The crooks find out the secret to Sach's strength is the genie. A counter-hexer, "Evil-Eye" Fagin, is hired. When Sach sees Fagin in the boxing stands, he loses his nerve and strength. Trouble for Sach ensues when the genie is stolen. As soon as Sach learns that Slip used the wrong coin, he loses his confidence, as well as the round.

Finale: When Slip sees a paper ad concerning $5,000 prize for champion wrestler, Sach (with bandage across his nose) insistently refuses and runs away.

Although the story centers on him, Sach is not given much to say or do in *Mr. Hex*. Nor does it seem as funny as the previous *Spook Busters*. Sach simply becomes the pawn of Slip to win fights. The limited comedy that arises is due to seeing his cowardly resistance and hypnotic compliance to the scheme. Sach Comedy Meter: 2.5 out of 4.0.

6. Hard Boiled Mahoney

Released April 26, 1947

The credits first title card reads: "Monogram Pictures Corporation Presents Leo Gorcey and The Bowery Boys." The second card reads: "in Hard Boiled Mahoney." The third card reads: "with Huntz Hall" followed by other players.

Here Sach enters talking about being fired from the Elite Detective Agency. He is wearing a deerstalker, acting like he's smoking a pipe, and exhibiting the stereotypical mannerisms of Sherlock Holmes. There are good exchanges as he walks around looking silly in his detective getup.

Slip and Sach are mistaken for detectives when Sach pursues getting his last week's salary, and they get involved in a case of a missing sister, reminiscent of *The Maltese Falcon*. They are advanced fifty dollars, and Sach thoroughly misunderstands the women's story as indicated by his incorrect comments. The woman describes her sister: "She's very attractive… she's 5 feet 6, she has blue eyes and red hair and she weighs about 115. I think that's all." Sach makes faces and declares: "Sister, that's enough!"

As will be Sach's normal interaction, he wisecracks and continues to make faces as Slip insults him. In one example, Sach makes a joke by a word play. In his wisecrack, Sach makes "hasn't" sound like "Hasson" Sach: "I have a friend named Hasson once, but he hasn't been around lately." Of course, Slip slaps Sach's head for this wisecrack.

Sach believes in his own exceptional mental ability, declaring: "Brains, brains, my head's crawling with them." Nevertheless, Sach shows fear as he jumps across a roof to the adjacent building.

The chase scene is interrupted when the Boys are mistakenly caught up in a live show, *Prof. Quizzard and his Brain Trust*. This spoof of radio quiz shows is the movie's highlight. Sach is introduced to the studio audience by host Dr. Quizzard as a famous psychologist, Dr. Millstone. The Boys change into collegiate robes they remove from the real professors, and then sit on the stage as panelists.

Sach first starts calling Slip "Chief" in this film. Sach reveals that he is named after his Aunt Sachela.

Prof. Quizzard tells a testimonial of someone who used the sponsor's product, Fickle's Cough Syrup. Prof. Quizzard notes that after the syrup, he does not cough anymore. The Professor asks the audience: "Why?" Sach answers: "He's dead." Everyone laughs. Then the Boys joke around.

The Professor asks: "How many hairs are there on the human head?" Sach answers: "One. . . .Uncle Herman has an average head and he has just one hair on it." The audience claps to encourage the host to award Sach the "oodles and oodles of goodie-goodie prizes" (radio, wristwatch, and insanely an electric toaster that works underwater, as well as a year's supply of Fickle's Cough Syrup).

None of the Boys could correctly answer: "For what General was the Washington Monument erected?" Nevertheless, the audience enjoys the crazy answers they offer. Sach tells an old joke: "I was in the last war. I saved 500 men. I shot the cook." Everyone laughs wildly.

After the show is over, Sach briefly disguises himself as he stands in front of a cardboard cutout wearing a police officer's cap. Sach: "Hey look at me fellows, I'm a cop. You are all under arrest. Come along quietly. . ."

Finale: The earnings of $50 are wiped out by the expenditures, not considering the damage to the car, Louie's store, and the penthouse.

They all hit Slip over his head. Slip's girlfriend responds by punching each one of Boys out. Slip tells her: "Ain't going to no dream island." Girlfriend: "Oh yes you are!" Then after he's punched Slip changes his opinion. Slip: "I guess maybe I am."

Hard Boiled Mahoney is not directly about Sach, although his Sherlock Holmes appearance offers some ongoing humorous moments. This is more of a group effort with Slip taking charge. The Sach highlight is his goofy quiz show appearance. Sach Comedy Meter: 2.5 out of 4.0.

7. News Hounds

Released August 13, 1947

The credits first title card reads: "Monogram Pictures Corporation Presents Leo Gorcey and The Bowery Boys." The second card reads: "in News Hounds." The third card reads: "with Huntz Hall" followed by other players.

Here in this film, Sach first offers one of his characteristic repetitive responses (different from *Spook Busters*). He says: "Oh! Oh! Oh!" Later in the series, he will sometimes add the "p" sound to make it "Ohp! Ohp! Ohp!"

Slip and Sach are seen working at *The Chronicle* newspaper. Slip is a copy boy. Sach, wearing a solid black cap, is first seen hiding with his camera in a desk which is labeled "DARK ROOM KEEP OUT." He is a photographer in this movie, and at times, he grimaces like Stan Laurel.

Sach is positioned on top of four stacked tables in Louie's Sweet Shop to get a shot of the Boys. He loses his balance when the tables sway, and he comes crashing down.

To cover a story, Slip makes a press card from a tailor's signs. Sach takes the tailor's big sidewalk billboard sign that says "Press," and he wears it to enter a building, but a police officer stops him.

A kid puts a jam sandwich on Sach's eyes, which makes him blinded and clumsy. The explanation Sach gives to Slip shows Sach's hysterical reaction as he exaggerates how the child knocked him down. He describes him as a tough monster that came along to choke him, and so on. Slip hits Sach over the head a couple of times, and he tells the Boys: "Sach is what might be classed as a very demonstrable boy–also slightly psychiatrical."

They visit one gangster as Slip playing "Pete the Blaster," and Sach as his lieutenant, "Herman the Crow." Pete and Herman are supposed agents/friends of another gangster. When smacked by Slip, Sach yelps. Sach takes a photograph of Slip with the gangster talking to a fighter about a fix. The photo evidence proves the linkage of crooks, and indicates the top fixer, "Mr. Big."

When Sach hurts his hand, he moans: "Ooh! Ooh! Ooh!" Slip and Sach's impersonation, is exposed, and Sach humorously reveals his cowardice. His camera with the film evidence is lost after it is thrown out the window as the Boys make their escape from the crooks. The kid finds the camera, and he kicks Sach in his ass down a flight of stairs, but Sach retrieves his camera and the photographs.

Sach offers us a laugh whenever he could. He comes into the courtroom, he goes to sit on the wrong side next to the gangsters. He quickly switches when he realizes his mistake. Sach's delivery makes the scene on the witness stand funny as he points out each of the guilty, saying: "It was him."

Finale: Sach tries to get some good photographs by sitting on top of the four stacked and swerving tables at a "Welcome Star Reporter" celebration for Slip. When Slip asks him to take a bow, he leans over and falls down with the toppling tables. Slip winds up with the cake around his head.

Sach takes a photograph and tastes the cake. Sach: "Hold it, hold it for an exclusive. Got it! Got It! Oh! I got it, Oh! My favorite kind. Oh I love this type." He goes to bite more into the cake around Slip's head. Then Slip uses his hat to hit Sach repeatedly over his head.

Although *News Hounds* has been faulted, the scenes with Sach save this film and make it an average entry. Sach Comedy Meter: 2.5 out of 4.0.

8. Bowery Buckaroos
Released November 22, 1947

The credits first title card reads: "Monogram Pictures Corporation Presents Leo Gorcey and The Bowery Boys." The second card reads: "in Bowery Buckaroos." The third card reads: "Featuring Huntz Hall" followed by other players.

The opening scene of this movie has Sach looking at magazines on a rack at Louie's Sweet Shop. He finds a comic book called "Hair Trigger Western Yarns" while Louie is singing "Louie the Lout." Sach yawns, and he supposedly goes into a dream. However, the transition is seamless, and so it is not convincing that what we see after that moment is not really happening.

Sach views a picture of a naked baby, and misunderstands what it means. Sach: "Poor–don't even have any clothes on." The treasure map drawn on Louie's back is copied onto Sach's back. Sach sings "Oh, Susanna" as they head out west. His upturned baseball cap is suddenly replaced with a skunk hat, parodying the raccoon hat of Davey Crockett.

Sach spills the beans by showing the map and telling an American Indian why they came out west; that is, to find the gold, find a bald-headed baby girl and to find "Blackjack" who framed Louie and murdered a man. Later he complains that an American Indian hand poked him inside his camp tent. Slip calls it his imagination. When that hand offers beads, Sach concludes: "Beads is for a girl's imagination."

When a gang confronts Sach whether there is another map, since his map has been removed, he is defiant: "I'm no blabbermouth."

Sach fits in well here as the not-too-bright sidekick of a Western hero and Slip succeeds as the tough gunslinger. However, Slip still slaps Sach, but it seems Slip dominates the film, with Sach's input minimal. When the baby girl, now a luscious singer, is located in the saloon, she says after performing that she is going to change her clothes. Girl-crazy Sach quickly offers: "I'll go with you." Slip and Gabe stop him.

By the conclusion, Sach is calmly singing "Oh Susanna," and he comes riding back with Blackjack's henchmen. Slip asks, "How did you do it, Daniel Boone?" Sach: "I surrounded them." Slip doubts him: "*He* surrounded them." Slip responds by hitting Sach as we see him awaken from what was really a dream.

Finale: Sach complains: "I have beautiful dreams, don't I?" Slip slaps him, and Sach asks: "What are you hitting me for?" Slip: "For waking up. Go back to sleep." Slip and the Boys hit him repeatedly, as Sach laments: "Oh fellows, it was only a dream!"

In *Bowery Buckaroos*, as elsewhere in the series, Sach pays the price for his funny remarks and wisecracks by being smacked around. Overall, Sach humor is limited in this OK take-off of Westerns and the Old West. Sach Comedy Meter: 2.0 out of 4.0.

9. Angels' Alley

Released March 7, 1948

The credits first title card reads: "Monogram Pictures Corporation Presents Leo Gorcey and The Bowery Boys." The second card reads: in "Angels' Alley." The third card reads: "Featuring Huntz Hall" followed by other players.

This movie opens with Sach chauffeuring Slip to a date. A young fan of Slip named Boomer wears a pinned back hat just like Slip.

Some funny moments include when Sach takes the whole roast at the dinner table, he says: "My, what a beautiful pork chop." In addition, he plays pool by sucking in air to get the ball into the hole, otherwise he cannot get shots.

A prankster gangster running a car theft ring hires Slip's ex-con cousin to commit a burglary. When the Boys arrive at a deserted warehouse to stop Slip's cousin, Slip tells Sach: "You're afraid of your own shadow." Sach: "No, I'm afraid of yours."

Slip takes the blame for his cousin's break-in and suspicion of burglary. He refuses to talk, which leads to being sentenced to 18 months in a workhouse, but the sentence is suspended.

Whitey, referring to Slip being arrested: "He might get ten years." Sach: "Yeah and they'll put his picture in the papers and Slip will be famous."

When Boomer is in the hospital after being hit by a car, Slip is down in the dumps. The film's highlight is when Sach, also saddened by the accident, manages to cheer up Slip via mimicry. Sach invites Slip: "Play some pool? How about some snooker? Wanna see my new trick? Wanna hit me with your hat?" None of those suggestions interests Slip, so Sach offers what he calls "some new imitations."

Sach's does an impression of what sounds like Ronald Colman who tells of someone who idiotically cut off his own leg without surgical equipment. He also does impressions of Jimmy Durante and James Cagney. Then he sings a silly jingle of "Figaro," ending with "I can't figure this guy out." Finally, that makes Slip laugh, and he responds, "You're O.K. Sach."

Often Sach shows his ability to do something to help bring a positive result. For instance, here he drives their jalopy to the crooks' hideout so Slip can spy and catch his cousin meeting his gangster boss. Sach gets Whitey and Chuck to create a diversion so he can get to be with Slip and the gangster. Sach manages to make even the gangster laugh. Gangster: "Is that your face?" Sach: "I ain't practicing witchcraft." Gangster: "You oughta with that one." Sach takes the insult as a compliment. Sach: "Thanks a lot!"

The gangster does not get upset with Sach since he likes Sach's self-deprecating humor. Sach is unfazed and even laughs, when the gangster squirts him with water. When Sach squirts the water back at him, there is a moment of tension as we wonder whether the gangster will get upset. Then Sach smartly squirts himself, and says: "Now we're even." That works, and the gangster laughs again.

Sach often punctuates tense moments with a repeated phrase. For instance, Slip is on the telephone calling the District Attorney. Sach is next to him also on another telephone dialing the mayor. When the mayor answers, Sach nervously responds: "Ooh! Ooh! Ooh! Ooh! Ooh! " He gives the telephone to Slip and squeezes out from under the wire as if he was playing a game with the wire. The phone rings and Sach again says: "Ooh! Ooh! Ooh! "

The "Sach alone" scene here is one of his masterpieces. Sach is walking down the street, speaking to himself, when he spots a car to use. Sach: "Slip told me to get a car. Oh! Oohhh a black and white one... " He sees a large speaker on the fender. Sach: "With a phonograph, and a red light. I like this one!" Actually, this is a police patrol car. He drives off and hears a police transmission call on the radio, instructing the police: "See the landlord." Sach says: "Silly police calls, I don't want to see the landlord, I have a place to live."

Then Sach hears another police transmission: "Calling all cars, calling all cars, a stolen police car, a stolen police car." Sach is oblivious and nonchalant, saying: "Cops shouldn't steal cars. Well can't trust anybody these days." The radio continues: "Stolen police car 102 last reported going east on Pell Street." Sach: "I'm on Pell Street. If I see that young fellow I'll teach him that crime doesn't pay." The transmission continues: "Suspect is wearing dirty, cream colored jacket, a baseball cap." Sach: "Looks like he stole mine (touches his head). Nope."

When he finally realizes the police are pursuing him, Sach drives into the crook's hideout, and he begs Slip to save him.

Finale: The police arrive, and as usual, Slip takes all the credit. Slip: "I guess I cleared that case up, pretty good, huh?" Sach asks incredulously: "You cleared it up? (He whines and cries). How do you like that? I bring the cops, I save his life, and he clears it up. This is the last picture I do with you." Sach sticks his tongue out at Slip.

Unfortunately, Hall is not given as much business in *Angels' Alley* as one would like, and the story does not involve him adequately. Anyhow, it does imbue Sach with humorous edges. The ending redeems this film as Sach makes the welcome mistake of taking a police car to Slip and the gangster's chop shop. The police follow the police car that Sach took, and so Sach carelessly, though inadvertently, manages to save the day. Sach Comedy Meter: 2.5 out of 4.0.

10. Jinx Money
Released June 27, 1948

A mysterious umbrella stabber kills a gambler who won $50,000 in a card game. The first time we see Slip and Sach, they are being ejected from Louie's Sweet Shop. Slip tells Sach that it is time they "segregate"(he means separate) —South to Brooklyn for Sach, North to the Bronx for Slip.

However, they find a folded newspaper that is full of money. Then the Boys wash and dry the money. They have Louie's Shop boarded up with signs saying, "Keep Out," "Building Condemned Ord. No. 71,001,"

"Quarantine Measles," "Fire Gate No Parking At Any Time," "Beware of Dog," "High Tension Wires," etc.

In rare close-up shots, we see the startled reactions of the Boys when Louie arrives and questions whether the bills are real. The last close-up is the longest and it is of Sach crying, as they take the money to the bank in a bucket to check its authenticity.

Sach keeps seeing that umbrella stabber. When a thief comes to the back of Louie's to hold them up for the money, Sach asks him: "Say, you mind if I call a cop?" When Slip asks Sach to conduct a search of the dead thief, Slip calls Sach: "Maniac coward." Sach takes it as a compliment: "Truest words you ever said."

A Police Lieutenant tells the Boys that they must report the money they found or have a fine imposed of $100 and a thirty-day jail sentence. This is a no-brainer for Sach: "Oh that's a cinch, Here's the $100, Whitey will do the 30 days."

Again, Sach sees the shadow of a man with a hand with an umbrella. The Lieutenant screams at Sach and Sach responds: "If you lost your voice you'll find it in my ear." Sach grimaces like Stan Laurel.

Sach passes a shop called Tommy's Umbrellas. He goes into a dream when he falls back down a flight of stairs. He dreams of a man with an umbrella who knocked him down. He finds himself being afraid of umbrellas, especially when Whitey approaches him with one.

A gangster holds Slip at gunpoint to obtain the money. Sach arrives with a wrapped up package–supposedly the money. When the gangster leaves, the umbrella man stabs him and takes the package.

Sach expresses terror as a corpse falls out of a closet when Sach opens it (Sach: "Timber!").

It turns out that Sach outwitted the umbrella man since he kept all the money on him. The umbrella man got laundry wrapped in the newspaper. The money goes back to the Boys since no claims surfaced.

Slip gives out $20,000 of the money he promised to the charities, some other people, and taxes. With nothing left, Sach observes: "At least you got the rubber band the money came in. Boy am I gonna have fun. I'm gonna make a bean shooter."

Finale: When Louie realizes that the Boys are now broke, and that he will not get the money due him, he throws things at them as he chases them out of his shop. Outside Sach asks: "I wonder what made Louie go all to pieces?" Slip: "Money is the roost of all evil." They see money in the gutter. Slip tells them to resist temptation. Then they all run for it. Louie goes outside his store, and he takes the $5.00 they found. Sach: "I wonder what Gravel Girty's doing?" Slip: "Drop dead." Then Sach plays dead by falling back.

Comic fans will know that Gravel Girty is an ugly female character from the "Dick Tracy" comic strip. She lived in a gravel pit, and had associated with the crooks.

There are some acceptable comedy elements in *Jinx Money*, but the humor from Sach is limited. Sach Comedy Meter: 2.0 out of 4.0.

11. Smugglers' Cove
Released October 10, 1948

As an office cleaner, Terrence "Slip" Mahoney mistakes a letter addressed to another Terrence Mahoney, and he thinks that he inherited a Long Island manor.

Sach's habit of confusing the wrong usage of a word is evident in this film, as it is throughout the series. Slip: "Hey, I got a Manor." Sach misunderstands the word, and he responds: "I ain't got no manner."

Upon exploring the house, Slip learns that there is a diamond smuggling racket operating there. When Sach strays into a cave tunnel, he sees water flowing and asks: "Where's the ferry?" He goes a little further and says: "Ooh a subway, I'll take the express."

The crooks hold the Boys in captivity, Slip says: "Locked up in the cellar of my own home. This is a fine howdy you do?" Again, Sach responds incorrectly: "Howdy you do?" Slip takes his hat and slaps Sach over the head several times. Sach yelps in pain.

While locked up, Sach offers his method to escape. He tells Whitey to go home and bake a cake inscribed "Happy Birthday Sach" with a hacksaw inside it. Eventually, Sach goes crazy being locked up: He bangs the doors, moaning and hollering, "I gotta get out, let me out..."

Slip proves to be no brighter than Sach. Eventually he realizes that it is not his house. The real heir with the same name arrives at the manor. Slip informs him that smuggling is going on.

Slip referring to diamonds says: "Must be 1000 carats." Sach responds: "Carrots, what's vegetables got to do with diamonds, silly?" The real Terrence Mahoney heir leaves the manor saying he just wants "Peace and rest." Sach retorts: "And may you rest in peace."

Finale: The Boys abandon Slip, now proud owner of his Spanish adobe. Slip: "Just goes to prove that bread cast upon the waters sometimes comes back as burnt toast." Sach appears in a secret panel of a painting and attempts to spook Slip. But then he confesses, "Master, I couldn't leave you." As expected, Sach gives Slip his cap so Slip slaps Sach.

Smugglers' Cove is not a strong entry for Sach fans since so much of the film focuses on the smuggling ringleader and his activities. At times, the Boys seem to be subservient to the plot. Sach Comedy Meter: 2.0 out of 4.0.

12. Trouble Makers

Released December 10, 1948

This film opens with the Boys offering a chance to see the stars through a telescope positioned on the sidewalk for a nickel. Of course, Sach manages to use the telescope to follow a passing woman. When Slip asks him what he sees and to describe it, Sach answers: "a heavenly body…beautiful."

Sach sees a murder on the twentieth floor of a nearby hotel via the telescope. As Bowery detectives, the Boys get the beat cop (Gabe Dell) in trouble with his captain. As a private eye, Sach shows his incompetence by knocking over everything to the annoyance of the hotel manager. Sach almost strangles the manager to death in his eagerness to re-enact what he saw.

Sach referring to Gabe says: "I know, I let him lock me up. That oughta get him a promotion." Slip: "That'll get him a strait jacket." The morgue attendant asks Slip and Sach if they came to see "the strangulation victim?" Sach responds: "No, this guy was choked."

An ex-con confuses Sach with an ex-con that got a facelift. One of the highlights of this movie is when Sach plays along with the mistaken identity as he gets tough with Slip. It shows, albeit ever so briefly, Hall's ability to do much more than just act as a goofball.

While looking for clues in the room, Sach finds a foreign coin. "Money, I'm rich." He tries to use it at Louie's Sweet Shop to treat the Boys to no avail.

Finale: Slip is hawking peeks through his telescope to see the man in the moon. Sach fools Slip when he impersonates an old-time cop wearing a mustache, copper helmet, carrying a bobby, and speaking with a British accent. He asks Slip for his license. Slip turns around and sees Sach. Sach: "Fooled you, it's me, Sach." Then Slip takes the copper helmet and slaps Sach. The Boys join in by hitting Sach with cardboard signs.

Trouble Makers offer an average amount of Sach laughs. Sach Comedy Meter: 2.5 out of 4.0.

13. Fighting Fools

Released March 17, 1949

This movie revolves around a family connection as a fighter is killed in the ring, and his brother follows in his footsteps. We see the brother's comeback as a fighter with the help of the Boys.

As boxing ring workers, Slip offers the programs, Chuck peddles the soda, and Whitey hawks ice cream. Sach is most hilarious as he sells the hot dogs with a string attached to pull the dog from the roll just before the customer goes to bite into it.

Again, Sach's tendency to misunderstand words is manifested. Slip referring to the brother: "Gotta handle him with kid gloves." Sach: "Kid gloves? He ain't a kid no more."

At one point, Hall shows his ability to play a real tough guy as he did in *Little Tough Guy,* and he acts serious insulting the fighter's girlfriend.

When the Boys hang signs for a benefit bout, Slip quotes from Shakespeare's *Hamlet*. Sach: "What weight did he fight at?" Slip responds simply by throwing soda at him. Sach takes it, happily tasting it. Sach: "Cream soda, like it."

The upstairs of Louie's Sweet Shop is turned into a training ring. Sach shows off to the kid brother by hitting the punching bag. When Sach punches the bag, he knocks himself out. While sparring Sach tries to trick the fighter by saying his shoelace is untied, but the fighter responds: "No it isn't, it's yours." Sach looks at his own shoes and he is knocked out.

Sach will even volunteer himself to be slapped when a despondent Slip has his managing license revoked. Sach asks: "Hey Chief, why don't you slap me around a little? Maybe it'll cheer you up!"

Crooked gamblers try to force Slip and the fighter to throw a bout when they kidnap the kid brother. Sach cleverly uses the trick hot dog to find out where the kid brother is being held by kidnappers, and then again to get the kidnapper to leave the kid brother unguarded.

In short, Sach manages to save the day when he rescues the kid brother from captivity. In addition, Sach discovers a chunk of metal shaped like a hot dog is being used in the glove of the fighter's challenger. He switches it with his trick hot dog. When Sach shows Slip the metal, he receives a hug of appreciation. Slip: "Sach, I love you."

Finale: At a victory celebration, Sach, wearing a chef's hat, gives Slip one of his trick hot dogs. Apparently, Sach substituted the piece of metal shaped like a hot dog. Sach: "Compliments of the house, Chief." Slip takes a bite and spits out some teeth. Sach looks into the camera and asks: "Is there a dentist in the house?" Slip takes his hat off and he repeatedly hits Sach's head.

Fighting Fools is a slightly above average entry in regard to the comic moments with Sach. The most memorable scenes are those with Sach's running gag of feeding people his trick hot dogs. Also, there are his many sassy quips that ensure a quick slap in return from Slip. Sach Comedy Meter: 2.8 out of 4.0.

14. Hold That Baby!
Released June 26.1949

Sach's first scene here has him with a laundry bag trying to make a date speaking somewhat like Cary Grant. What's funny is that he is trying to woo "Cynthia," a mannequin in a store window.

Slip and Sach lose their jobs when they crash their laundry truck. The clothes explode out all over the street. With the help of Louie and his shop's back room, the Boys run their own Laundromat.

Sach's Comedy

To pacify a baby, Sach does some rumba dancing with rattles. He also daydreams of "Cynthia" while he holds a child in his arms. To hide a baby from the beat cop, Sach even dresses up as a mother wheeling her baby carriage. He says to the cop: "Good morning, flat foot." Sach manages to mix up his baby with another one by switching carriages.

At a Sanitarium, Slip refers to Sach: "Dead from the neck up." Sach observes: "I like this place–friendly people." Sach fits in perfectly with two patients playing imaginary poker. Sach to nurse: "I'm gonna like it here. You got a game room?" Sach speaks to a statue: "Like to play some gin? See a card trick?"

One of the best scenes is when Sach wanders alone into a room marked "Surgery." This seemingly ad-libbed scene has him coming upon various items, and he offers a comment about each one. He picks up some things, such as surgical tools, etc., taking them with him. He accumulates in his arms a pile of items to take with him: "Mmhh, a toy shop, beautiful….Indian nuts…I'll give Whitey a manicure, hasn't had one in ten years or has he?" He picks up a skull imitating its voice, "I knew him well, 1000 times he bore me on his back. I was heavy too….I'll take you." He puts on the doctor's lighted headpiece, "Play pirates now with Whitey…a basin, put all this in a basin…a flashlight, I'll get that for Louie so he can see people in the dark." Sach sees a sterilizer and calls it "a pressure cooker: give that to my mother…." Talks German looking through an ophthalmoscope…

All of this reminds us is that Sach has a fertile, infantile imagination. Sach sits down in the examination chair and thinks he is going to get a shave and a haircut when two doctors walk in. One doctor thinks he's a schizophrenic; the other doctor says he shows strong symptoms of kleptomania. A doctor examines inside his ear and says, "[I] can't seem to locate the brain." Sach tells him: "Look harder, it's there." Doctor: "Eureka,

I located it, it's no bigger than a pen point." Sach: "I told you it was there." The doctors conclude that they will do immediate surgery on Sach.

As Sach hugs a nurse, he says: "This I like, could I take her with me?"

Sach is depicted at times as unpredictable. For instance, he plays the tough guy, even pulling a gun out. Of course, we too are fooled until the word "B A N G" pops out of what is revealed to be a toy pistol. Sach laughs.

The obligatory fight in the *Bowery Boys* film series takes place here with the Boys fighting the crooks in their Laundromat. Sach nervously moves around, waving his arms, avoiding involvement in the brawl. When the cops arrive, Sach sprays a crook (and mistakenly a cop) with a bug-exterminating gun.

Finale: Sach speaks to Cynthia in window. Sach: "One weapon, my everlasting love for you." Slip: "Are you still wasting the company's time talking to this dummy?" Cynthia walks out of the store showcase, proceeds to punch Slip, and asks: "Who's a dummy?" Sach: "That'll teach you to call my girl names, come sweetie." Slip: "Sometimes I doubt my own vervacity, whatever that means."

Sach shines here, with overall good humor pervading *Hold That Baby!* This entry offers the first substantial "Sach alone" scene in the surgery room. Sach Comedy Meter: 3.0 out of 4.0.

15. Angels In Disguise

Released September 9, 1949

Though this film seems to be a serious film noir crime film with a voice-over narration by Slip, it is actually played for laughs as well. Sach's cheek/lip flutter, referred to as motorlips, makes its first appearance in this film. This time Slip and Sach work at a newspaper as copy boys bent on investigating the shooting of Detective Marino (Gabe Dell).

The Boys visit the wounded detective at the hospital. Sach stares at a girl passing by in the hospital. Slip observes: "I can see what was running through Sach's mind." We first see nurses giving Marino a back massage. Then we see Sach moaning in the adjoining next bed so that he can get the nurses to give him attention.

Nurse to Sach: "How does that feel?" Sach: "I'll let you know in a couple of hours." Nurse: "He needs medical aid." Slip to nurse: "I think suffering a mania for feminine pulchitrude." Slip hits Sach over his head. Sach: "I feel much better. Punch killer."

Sach makes Slip lose while playing pool, but then he wets the opponent's cue stick, so Slip could get another shot and win.

Throughout the series, Sach's bonehead responses drive Slip to respond by slapping him, usually on the top of his head, but also across his face. Some examples here: When detectives want to take Slip and Sach in, Sach: "I'll stay with Gabe." Slip hits him over his head. When Sach repeats Slip's statement, Slip again hits him over the head. Sach tells Slip his ideas ("Hey Chief…."). Slip responds: "You're spaghetti, get back to work." Sach: "I don't feel like working." Slip goes to hit Sach, but Sach changes his tune. Sach: "I feel it, I feel it."

The exchanges between Slip and Sach are nonsensical at times. For instance, when Slip sees Sach using the ink to work on the newspaper artwork, Slip interrupts him: "Hey Rembrandt, hello pastel nose." Slip: "…there are times when Sach is as yellow as a ripe banana." Sach responds: "I am not!" Sach to Slip at morgue: "I'll race you to the door." Sach remarks: "I've been to the Bronx Zoo." Slip responds: "Why did they ever let you out?"

A bookworm crook says to Sach: "I'm reading Spinoza." Sach asks: "Who's he? A Spanish dancer?" Crook: "Horace Debussy Jones, interesting name, very euphonious." Sach takes it as a compliment. Sach: "Thanks. I think you're a phony too. Glad to meet you."

After Sach takes a drink, we are treated to the first time he does his distinctive motion of his cheeks and lips, Sach's motorlips. This will be a regular feature of the later movies, frequently offered whenever Sach sees a pretty girl.

Slip narrates: "...Integrity should be rewarded." Slip offers to Sach: "Come on, I'll buy you a lollipop." When Sach asks, "Hey Chief, hey chief, what about my lollipop?" Slip: "I'll hit you right in the head with a lollipop."

While waiting for Louie to arrive at the gangsters' office, Slip narrates: "I hated the whole idea." Sach responds: "Gee you're in a hateful mood."

Finale: With the gang smashed, Slip and Sach are in the hospital after being beat up. Sach's nose was almost broken, and both have bandages on their faces with their legs in traction. After ringing the buzzer for the nurse, a male nurse goes to Sach's side. Sach is dismayed and starts to cry as Slip gets a pretty nurse to help him. Slip is delighted: "Well Sach, murder. Guess he who laughs last laughs the most. Ooh! I'm gonna break a leg every day from here on."

Angels in Disguise is Slip's film throughout. Nevertheless, Sach helps bring a few laughs to lighten the film's serious tone. Sach Comedy Meter: 2.0 out of 4.0.

16. Master Minds

Released November 20, 1949

The film opens with Sach's bulging eyes reading "Famous Predictions of Nostradamus." Louie comes in and tells Sach: "I ask you to mind my store. And the minute my back is turned, you not only mind it, you empty it! Who's gonna pay for all this ice cream and candy that you're shoving down your throats, I'm asking you who?"

Slip arrives and tells Sach to take off his hat, pulls his head back by his hair. Slip demands: "Did you eat that box of candy?" Sach: "No, there's a few pieces left." Slip: "That's different, for a minute there I thought you were becoming a glutton. All morning long I pound the pavements looking for a job for you, and you sit here running up a bill. I got plenty of bills, I can't pay them now." Slip takes his hat and slaps Sach, which triggers Sach to grab his jaws aching with toothache pain.

We learn that Sach exhibits the ability to predict whenever he gets a toothache after he eats candy. When Sach starts staring, Slip thinks he is on a fortune-telling mission because of the book, and he wants to take the book back to the library. Slip: "They got some nerve giving compounded literature like this to a mental incompetent like you, liable to give you a nightmare."

Yet Slip devises a moneymaking scheme when he creates a sideshow at a carnival for Sach. The sign reads:

ALI BEN SACHMO

THE BOWERY PROPHET

HE PREDICTS STARTLING EVENTS

OF THE FUTURE

Slip gives Sach candy and tells him: "Now Sach old boy you just stay here and build yourself up a nice little toothache." Sach: "I don't want no toothache." Slip: "You don't want one?" Sach: "No." Slip slaps him and says, "Maybe that'll give you one."

There's a "Sach alone" scene. This time Sach talks to himself about his candy: "Boy what a life, nothing to do but sit around and eat candy, and more candy, and sugar and ice cream. Boy when I get wealthy I gonna buy a candy store. Wonder what a vegetable tastes like? You get toothaches. I don't mind toothaches too much–but they hurt." Then he's affected by the candy when his tooth suddenly aches with the pain. . . "Oooh! Oooh! Ahhh!"

This film parallels the previous year's Universal release *Abbott & Costello Meet Frankenstein* as regards the idea of brain transfers. Here a mad scientist kidnaps Sach in order to transfer his brain electrically to Atlas–a werewolf-like creature. He supposedly has the body of Hercules, and the brain of Aristotle.

When the Doctor tells Atlas to say hello to Ali Ben Sachmo, Atlas offers a growl, and Sach remarks: "Uh, College boy!" Sach fights his fear and throws a kiss to the giant Atlas. Sach: "Atlas, I bet you make a good square dancer." After Sach is bound to a stretcher, he asks: "Doctor may I have one last wish? Could I call the police?"

With Sach missing from the circus backstage, an enraged Slip says to Gabe: "If that mutton chop gets parted with that magic tooth, I'll tear his head off." Louie refers to Sach as "That little schlemiel." Slip: "Could have made so much money–that imbecile has to disappear."

Sach is given a brain transfer treatment. His brain (with voice and mannerisms) goes into Atlas' oversized body. He escapes and arrives at Louie's Sweet Shop to frighten Louie and the Boys.

The treatment wears off, and kidnapped Sach-acting-like-Atlas reverts to being just plain old Sach again. He calls Slip and the Boys to tell them of the mansion where he is being held.

While locked away, Sach eats candy again and acquires the gift of prophecy. Atlas-acting-like-Sach is seen leading the Boys into the mansion, but he reverts to the growling Atlas. The mad Doctor orders another treatment for Atlas and Sach.

The Boys arrive at the mansion to free Sach-acting-like-Atlas from the locked cell. Sach takes Slip's hat and hits him repeatedly over his head and Slip frantically runs away. Of course, before Sach reverts back to his real self, Sach-acting-like-Atlas and Atlas-acting-like-Sach battle each other.

Finale: Slip is called to the carnival backstage since Sach is holding up the show. Sach is being fed candy, and Slip complains to Sach: "Gabe tells me you won't get a toothache, you ungrateful dog, after me spending all your money buying you candy. The show's ready to start. What are you trying to do drive us into bankruptcy?"

Apparently, Sach is unable to predict anymore since he says he swallowed the tooth with the cavity. Sach turns into the growling Atlas as soon as Slip starts criticizing him, such as calling him "you double-crossing rat…you idiot."

After frightening Slip, Sach jumps up and down in jubilation and laughter, hugging Slip: "I fooled you. Boy can I act!" Slip: "Yeah! You fooled me. Just for that I gonna give you a little reward." Sach: "Sugar?" Slip: "Lumps." Slip takes his own hat and repeatedly hits Sach over his head.

Although Sach was hypnotized to be a super-fighter in *Mr. Hex*, this film is the first one with Sach having special abilities. In addition, the story of *Master Minds* revolves around Sach throughout. First Slip exploits Sach, and then the scientist exploits Sach. This weird story of electrical transference and reversion of brains is not explained at all, but the notion makes for a very entertaining film nonetheless, thanks to some good work by Hall and company. Sach Comedy Meter: 4.0 out of 4.0.

Chapter 8:
Sach's Comedy

1950-1953

Best Films (Highest Score):
Lucky Losers (1950)–3.5/4.0
Blues Busters (1950)–3.5/4.0
Let's Go Navy! (1951)–3.0/4.0
Jalopy (1952)–3.0/4.0
Loose in London (1953)- 3.0/4.0
Clipped Wings (1953)–3.0/4.0
Private Eyes (1953)–3.8/4.0

17. Blonde Dynamite
Released February 12, 1950

This movie is one of the entries where Sach is slapped many times.

Slip and Sach are standing in front of D'Amour Escort Bureau, where they are going to find work as male escorts. Slip: "Sach, when we get in here I want you to put on your best save your fair." Slip means *savoir-faire*. Sach: "You knew how to save yours we wouldn't have been here." Slip slaps Sach. Slip: "Don't be funny, save your fair is a French proposition, and it means keep your trap shut-t." Slip emphasizes the 't' in shut. Sach reiterates emphasizing the 't' three times: "Shut-t-t-t!" Both are ejected out the door of the escort service seconds after they enter.

Slip decides they will open their own escort bureau. Sach asks: "What are we gonna use for manpower?" Slip mentions the Boys' names. Sach asks again: "As I said what are we gonna use for manpower?" Slip slaps Sach. Slip: "Maybe even you." Sach: "Ooh that's better, that's better." Slip: "Let's go." Sach: "Where we going?" Slip: "We're going to the bank to float a loan to finance this deal. Since our friend Gabe Marino has been working at the bank he's must pack a lot of weight." Sach: "You've been packing a little yourself lately." Slip slaps Sach.

Louie is stressed out, and the Boys give him a sendoff to a vacation to Coney Island. When Gabe laughs at the idea that the Boys will mind Louie's shop, Sach laughs too. Slip slaps Sach with his hat.

As escorts to the opera for wealthy women, Sach eats cracker jacks, and Whitey eats a candy apple. Sach's client got a prize of a mousetrap. Then the Boys decide they are quitting the escort business. Sach tells the Boys, saying he's gonna tell Slip to stop pushing him around. Sach admits: "I got no talent. I'll just loaf."

When they see the girls sent by the crooks, Sach and the Boys put on their tuxedos. This scene is comically speeded up. With four girls and five Boys, one Boy is left behind. Of course, Sach gets beat: "Now I know how Cinderella felt. Oh well, that's life, chin up." Sach plays with his toy top. The girls attempt to give Mickey Finns to the Boys to keep them from going back to the Shop. The Boys outwit them, and the girls are drugged instead.

The crooks plan to drill into the bank, starting from under Louie's Sweet Shop. They force bank employee Gabe to provide them the safe's combination. The crooks call Sach "the stupid one," and they fool him into believing that they are government men digging for uranium under

Sach's Comedy

the Shop. One of the henchmen observes: "This joker's not only stupid, he's a moron besides." As usual, Sach responds: "I heard that, thanks for the compliment."

Sach asks: "How do I know you're government men, you got credentials?" He's shown a Division of Parole card and he responds: "Just wanted to make sure, thought I was stupid, heh?" Sach is allowed to help and he pledges loyalty to keep their secret. Sach: "Just like the Boy Scouts–maybe they'll give me a merit badge."

Sach has a ball digging a tunnel under the Shop. They give Sach a rock, which they say is uranium–he is so gullible he believes it.

With the drinks being switched, the girls are dead drunk. Slip and the Boys return to the shop to find Sach digging along with the crooks. One crook pulls a gun on Slip to get him digging. Sach tells Slip: "Don't fool around with us government men."

Louie returns and goes berserk upon seeing his Shop sign read "Park Avenue Escort Bureau." Louie: "Those little gremlins. . .those good-for-nothing hoodlums, what did they do to my Sweet Shop, Oy Vey. . .they massacred my darling Sweet Shop, holes, what are they building a subway in my store. . . . At my age I should be a groundhog. . . . Those scoundrels. I'll kill them. I'll murder them and there ain't a jury in the country that'll convict me."

Slip makes a joke: "Hey Louie, why don't you drill for a while, you used to be at the National Guard." When Louie struggles to hold the drill steady, Sach volunteers: "Give me that, I'll drill, I used to work for a dentist. Drill, a National Guard." Sach finally gets the play on words (referring to drill sergeants) and laughs. Slip slaps Sach.

The crooks drill themselves into police custody. Sach gives Louie the rock and tells him: "Louie, here's your uranium, it belongs all to you." Louie asks the policeman: "Officer, what's the penalty for murder." Policeman: "The electric chair." Louie: "Then start warming it up for me!"

Finale: It turns out that the rock is uranium and the Shop is built over a vein, and Louie will be rich. Slip credits Sach, and Sach this time slaps a surprised Slip for not believing him. At a party of celebration, Louie makes a toast to his wife. However, the happiness quickly ends when he is told that according to his property deed, the mineral and oil rights found on the property belong to the descendants of a previous owner. Slip grabs Sach as Sach looks at him. Sach starts to get up and leave. Louie faints. Slip slaps Sach repeatedly.

Overall, there is an average amount of comic material with Sach in *Blonde Dynamite*. The highlight is in the movie's last section when Sach is duped into digging for uranium. Sach Comedy Meter: 2.5 out of 4.0.

18. Lucky Losers
Released May 14, 1950

Slip and Sach work on Wall Street. Sach is seen in a garbage can of ticker tape. Their boss apparently committed suicide, and Slip goes on a mission to find out what really happened. The pursuit leads to a nightclub, which is just a blind. Actually, it is mostly a secret gambling establishment owned by a crooked nightclub owner.

Slip: "Holy mackerel, supposed to take this letter to the post office and register it. Why didn't you remind me?" Sach: "That's simple, 'cause you didn't remind me to remind you." Slip: "Why didn't you remind me to remind you to remind me?" Slip slaps Sach.

When Slip asks Whitey to turn on the television set in Louie's Sweet Shop, Sach insists he knows how to do it since he is smart as he works on Wall Street. As Sach is nearly electrocuted and Whitey tries to help him, Slip calls them: "Nice pair of idiots, wonder if they were born at the same time?"

The Boys learn from a card sharp everything he knows about card and dice gambling in a lengthy montage sequence.

Slip and Sach arrive at the nightclub. Sach: "Boy this place is swank with a capital 'c.'" Slip: "The letter is 's,' you only use 'c' when it's plural." Sach: "I thought you used 'c' when you spoke Spanish."

When Sach dances with Slip, Slip kicks Sach in the leg to stop him. Slip tells Sach that in order to get into the club's back room gambling section they will "need some way of identification, like a button or a card or something." Sach: "I got plenty of cards, pick a card." Slip slaps Sach.

The bartender throws a cloth at Sach when he asks for a napkin. Then Slip slaps Sach, and Sach complains: "I'd rather get hit with a napkin." Later, Sach throws the napkin at the bartender and laughs.

When Slip enters the backroom: "So much money in here I can almost smell it." Sach: "What a beautiful odor." Slip: "Everybody's smoking. Maybe we should take that last quarter we got and buy a pack of cigarettes." Sach: "But I don't smoke."

Then he does his motorlips when he sees a passing cigarette girl (announcing "Cigars, cigarettes"). Sach starts to follow her: "Never too late to learn." Slip: "Cigarette girls are too rich for our blood. Put that quarter in a cigarette machine." Sach: "Yeah! But maybe she'll give me one puff for a quarter, hah Chief?" Slip: "I don't think so. Cigarette machine." Sach: "Sorry honey, romance killer."

Sach mistakenly puts quarter in a slot machine above the cigarette machine. He pulls the handle and out pours the money. Sach loses one of the quarters he won, and he searches everywhere. He then finds it, puts it down on the gambling table, and wins a stack of chips.

It is funny indeed when a pouting Sach complains: "I don't want those chips. I want my quarters! Who wants those buttons? I don't like buttons." Sach: "Gee Chief, am I sorry I didn't get your cigarettes. I put the quarter in the cigarette machine. And out came quarters. Am I stupid?" Slip: "If you get smart I'll never talk to you again."

The crooked club owner meets with them. Slip and Sach disguise themselves as Slippery Mahoney and Sacramento Sach (Sach starts to say Seattle). Sach is introduced to a Countess, and he quickly becomes amorous: "How about tonight at 11?" Sach does his motorlips.

Sach sees a twenty-dollar bill and throws it away from the table. He sees the game as "playing for buttons" (referring to the chips). When they work at the club, the boss tells them to take a break from the gaming tables. Sach: "What did we quit for?" Slip: "We didn't quit, we're just on relief." Sach confuses that phrase (meaning home relief): "We're not on relief, we got jobs."

Sach: "All work and no play makes a fellow very stupid. You don't want me to be stupid?" Slip: "That's something I'm afraid even I couldn't prevent."

When the club owner socks a playboy to death, Sach's eyes dramatically widen as he looks on in terror.

Sach goes to shake the hand of someone from the District Attorney's office, and he mistakenly shakes Slip's hand and Slip smacks his hand.

Sach sees a gun. He starts to run away, and he falls to the floor under a table, saying: "Firearms, the Fourth of July." Slip announces one of their routines. Everything, including the chips, is thrown from the tables to hit the crooks. Louie is still gambling alone amidst all of the chaos. Instead of helping to fight the crooks, Sach is choking Whitey, saying: "I got one of them."

Finale: Television host Gabe dedicates his show to Sach and Slip for smashing the local gambling syndicate. Sach on TV: "Oop, television, are we on? Ladies and Gentlemen, it's really a pleasure to be here. I guess you'd like to know a little more about my life. Well, when I was born, I cried like a baby (laughs). I was so amazed I couldn't talk for a year and a half. At six months old, I ran away from home. Six months later I came back, my father took one look at me, and he ran away from home. (Laughs) He ran to the mountains. Went to one cabin, didn't pay his rent. Went to another cabin, didn't pay his rent. Went to another cabin, didn't pay his rent. Soon he became known as Rent-free of the Mountains. (Sach howls.)

While watching TV at Louie's Shop, Whitey remarks: "Gee that Sach is clever, he sends me." Louie: "When you go, take him with you." Sach howls again. Gabe: "Thank you Sach, thank you." Sach: "Yeah but I'm just getting started." Gabe: "Yes but I only got 15 minutes." Sach: "I'll kill you. I'll kill you." Sach does his Stan Laurel grimaces.

Slip goes on television, gets tongue-tied, loses his voice, and falls down. Sach: "How do you like that? The man of courage–fights gangsters with firearms, afraid of a little mike? This is a mike? Kill it! Kill it!" Sach hits the microphone with a box, screams in fear, and falls down too. Gabe: "Why I guess that's all folks."

Lucky Losers has been denigrated by some, and it has been compared to *News Hounds* for losing focus. However, I find the many funny moments with Sach make it a much better than the average entry in the series. Sach Comedy Meter: 3.5 out of 4.0.

19. Triple Trouble

Released August 13, 1950

The film opens with the Boys wearing masks as they stop a warehouse robbery. However, the police arrive and blame them.

Sach gets upset when he hears the gravelly-voiced convict Bat Armstrong talk about prison conditions. Slip slaps Sach. Whitey's ham radio leads Sach to say that he loves ham, especially with schmaltz.

Sach is reading *My Thirty Years Behind Prison Walls*. Slip pulls it off him: "What are you reading that propaganda for?" Sach: "Because I'm conditioning myself for a prison career." Slip: "Maybe this will help condition you." Slip goes to hit him with his hat, Sach bends his head over and covers it with his hands. Sach: "Maybe what will help condition me?" Slip slaps Sach in the face with his hand. Sach: "Well shut my mouth." Slip: "That's what I was trying to do." Sach sticks his tongue out at Slip.

Slip: "There are 6 and 7/8 robberies every hour on the hour." Sach: "6 and 7/8, same size as my head." Sach: "Hey Whitey, how long is a short wave?" Slip: "It's slightly longer than your brain." Sach is impressed: "College."

Sach is whistling while he is dreaming. Slip: "Wait till I turn off the peanut roaster." Slip slaps Sach with his hat. Sach whistles down and stops.

Slip pleads guilty so he can try solving a crime while in prison. He is sentenced to three years. The judge gives him probation, but Slip waives it. Another old joke follows. The judge says: "Order." Sach: "I'll have a ham on rye." Sach gets angry and shouts back to the judge. Sach: "You're out of order, don't you talk that way to our counselor!" The judge insists: "Order, order, order." Sach: "I'll have a ham on rye with mustard."

After the trial, the lawyer (Gabe Dell) asks: "Slip, you just set my career back ten years, what are you trying to prove?" Sach answers: "Insanity." Slip to Gabe: "We'll be doing the community a great public service." Sach: "Sure, we'll be in jail for the rest of our lives." Gabe: "Slip I hope you knowing what you're doing." Slip: "I know what I'm doing." Sach: "I don't." Slip slaps Sach. Sach sassily says, "You're getting very sneaky lately."

Now they impersonate two convicts: Pretty Boy Gleason (Slip) and Benny the Blood (Sach). Sach asks the warden: "Can I have the Sunday funnies delivered to me?" Slip: "Who's gonna read them to you?" Sach: "You will Chief." Sach: "I want an outfit with a belt in the back." Slip:

Sach's Comedy

"I'll give you a belt in the head." Sach: "Watch out, the warden's a friend of mine, ain't you warden?"

Sach humorously displays cliched effeminate mannerisms.

Upon entering the prison cell, Sach says: "I want a room with a view. This room is crowded." A man is knitting in a cell. Sach: "What are you doing?" Prisoner: "I'm knitting a sweater. What does it look like I'm doing?" Sach: "Knitting a sweater? Are you serious? (laughs like Ed Wynn). I bet you play with dolls on the side." Prisoner gets up menacingly: "What did you say?" Sach: "I forgot."

Sach passes the time by playing with jacks. "Oh Slip, I made my foursies." Slip says to Bat: "He's always clowning, he's got a sense of humor." Sach avoids being smacked by blocking. Sach grabs his hand, but Slip slaps him with his other hand. Sach: "What a sneak."

The other Bowery Boys visit. Butch asks: "How's things on the inside?" Sach answers: "We got everything we need on the inside, except one thing." Chuck: "What's that?" Sach: "To be on the outside." Sach does his Ed Wynn laugh again. Later Sach is playing hopscotch in the prison yard.

In front of another convict, the Boys act tough for Louie. Slip imitates Edward G. Robinson and Sach imitates James Cagney.

When talking about money, Sach says Louie has 50 or 75. Bat thinks he means 50 or 75 thousand dollars, and communicates with his ham radio to have Louie robbed. Sach childishly asks Slip: "What idiots, what imbeciles. How can they rob Louie's safe from behind prison walls? Stupid." Slip: "You're through now?" Slip grabs Sach by the collar. Sach: "Just about." Siren rings. Sach: "Saved by the bell." Slip slaps Sach with his cap. Sach: "You fouled me." Slip: "The only time you were in a foul is when you were born." Sach: "I'm going home with Whitey." Slip pushes him.

The Boys are given solitary confinement. Sach: "It's dark in there.

But I'm afraid of the boogeyman. Nice place to grow mushrooms."

When Sach is released from solitary confinement, he hugs the guard thinking it is Slip. Slip corrects Sach: "Hey broccoli head, I'm over here."

Bat is upset that the Sweet Shop robbery yielded just $75 and some worthless jewelry. Slip suggests to Bat that he is being doublecrossed– but not by him, but by the gang and his mother.

Sach is put in a cell with another convict who pulls out a knife and says that he likes to see blood running. Sach is scared, and he falls down backwards. In short, Sach takes every joke or exaggeration seriously.

Slip punches Sach to get to see the warden, but it does not work. Bat realizes it was an excuse to get to talk to the warden. Bat believes Slip and Sach are simply stool pigeons. Therefore, he uses them as cover when he breaks out of the prison.

Whitey saves the day since he deciphered another criminal message. After breaking out, Sach asks Whitey: "Did you take care of my baseball cap?"

Finale: Sach goes on the ham radio and imitates Bat scaring Louie and the Boys. He says that he was sending crooks over to the Sweet Shop to get even. Sach: "Hey Chief, what are you doing?" Slip: "Bat Armstrong is coming to see us. He got loose." Sach: "Bat Armstrong, are you serious? That was me. Wasn't that a cute joke?" Slip slaps Sach repeatedly. Sach reacting in pain: "Ooh! Ooh! Ooh! Ooh! . . ." Slip: "Give me that microphone. Over and out." Slip continues to slap Sach.

Triple Trouble offers an average amount of Sach humor. Sach Comedy Meter: 2.5 out of 4.0.

20. Blues Busters
Released October 29, 1950

The film opens at a hospital maternity ward. Louie is complaining to the Boys that Sach's hospital stay has made him "so much in hock that I had to make a loan on my loans." We surmise that Sach has had a serious operation.

A nurse is reading "Red Riding Hood" to him. Sach: "What should that nasty wolf do to that little girl? You can't trust wolves." Two nurses are rubbing him down. Sach: "It's a miracle I pulled through... send in the next shift... it was horrible...they took out my liver, my kidney, and my heart, I feel like an eggshell...." As Sach is offering us the dramatics, Slip looks at the chart that says:

Horace Debussy Jones Room 302 Dr. Bollin
SIMPLE TONSILLECTOMY
Pulse: Normal
Temperature: Normal
Respiration: Normal
Remarks: Everything normal (except patient)

When Louie gets the bill and realizes he spent all this money on tonsils being removed, he calls the Boys "junior confidence men." Louie wants all his money back. Louie elaborates: private room $6 a day, flowers $5 a day, $200 surgical fees, twelve nurses at $9 a piece, ether $10. Sach: "Louie they were cheaper by the dozen." Louie: "Poison gas they should have given you...."

Sach: "Gee Chief, my throat hurts." Slip: "Maybe if I cut your throat it would stop hurting." Sach: "That would be manslaughter." Slip: "Since when are you a man? This whole predicament is your fault. You hypermaniac." Sach: "Stop picking on me, I'm sick." Slip: "I'm sick too, sick of you. Now get out of here." Sach: "But Chief." Slip: (mockingly) "But Chief. Go hide your head in the corner."

We hear singing. Slip thinks it's the radio, and tells Whitey to turn off the radio. It turns out that Sach is singing. Slip observes that the operation developed the "greatest voice since Caruso. He sounds like

Crosby, Jolson, Jessel, and the Andrews Sisters all on the same record."

Slip slaps Sach when Sach starts to dance with him. Slip is convinced that Louie's Sweet Shop should be turned into a club for Sach to sing. The shop is renovated to become Louie's Bowery Palace. It is packed with customers to see and hear Sach, now dubbed "The Bowery Thrush." Note: Louie's Sweet Shop turned into the Palace is an amazing transformation. However, it is not at all believable given the huge size of the Palace.

Another club owner from across the street visits with his female singer. He admits that he will have to close his club if Sach keeps singing to packed houses. He sends a crew to disrupt Louie's club, and the place is left in a shambles. However, the next night the Palace is miraculously back in business.

Walking down the street, Sach is distracted by a toy store window. Sach: "Boy, look at that beautiful erector set and that pair of skates, I wish the Chief would increase my allowance so I can enjoy the luxury of life." Sach does his motorlips when the female singer drives up and lures him, saying "Hey handsome, come here." She asks for his autograph on her lampshade. A mass of adoring female fans causes him to go in the car with the female singer to her apartment. At her apartment, Sach talks about the movie that they saw. Sach: "Sure glad the sheriff caught the rustlers in the end."

When Sach is left alone, he drinks from a bottle, calling it "strong coffee." He spots the nuts and proceeds to fill his suit jacket's pockets with them. Sach: "Ooh nuts, boy I hope she don't catch me."

Oftentimes, Sach seems to know the difference between the real and the fake, but prefers the fake. He sits crunching away at her plastic grapes. Sach: "Grapes, I love grapes, nice grapes, these taste better than the real ones."

Sach's Comedy

After finishing off a whole full cluster, he notes: "Gee that was a nourishing meal, I wish she had some more grapes." The female singer comes out in evening robe: "How do I look?" Sach: "You sure got tasty grapes." The female singer takes it as a compliment on her appearance: "Oh Horace, darling you're divine."

Sach autographs the lampshade and almost everything else, including the walls. After having signed most of the apartment, wringing his tired hand saying, "I'll come back tomorrow night and do the ceiling." However, she makes him sign one more thing before leaving–a contract making him the singer for the other club.

He returns home after 4 a.m., having missed doing his show. Sach: "How do you like that silly girl, she couldn't even tell time." Sach explains he was trying to create good will. Slip: "For that you can go in the corner and sing 'How to be a Moron' 500 times." Sach: "'How to be a Moron,' very cute title, it would never be a hit, not commercial enough." Slip slaps Sach over his head.

When Slip learns that Sach is now exclusively singing for another club, he does not believe this is true, telling the other club owner: "I'm beginning to think that you're suffering from hallukinations, which are probably induced by the excessive use of a cigarette that ain't exactly legal." With that, Slip offers his humorous way of referring to marijuana.

Slip calls Sach "hatchet nose." Slip tells Sach: "Get out, I never want to see your ugly face again." Sach is surprised: "I'm ugly?"

The show goes on without Sach at the Palace. An off-key Slip sings "Dixie." The Boys do a ridiculous slapdash dance routine. Because of a poor response, the Palace closes.

One of the most touching scenes in any of the *Bowery Boys* movies happens here when Sach meets up with Slip on the street and gives him a wad of money. The following exchange ends with a bittersweet smile made by Slip that makes you believe the connection between Sach and him. Yes, this is proof they truly cared about each other:

Sach: "Chief, Oh Chief."

Slip: "Hi ya Sach."

Sach: "How are you Chief?"

Slip: "Good, I feel fine, real fine."

Sach: "I wish I felt that good, I feel rotten."

Slip: "How can you feel rotten? It's the first time in your life you're living. You're on top of the world."

Sach: "Yes, but it's lonesome up there. I want to come back, Chief. Please take me back."

Slip: "I couldn't do that. You're in the big time now. Wearing expensive clothes. Meeting important people. You reached the pineapple of your career."

Sach: "Yeah! But I wish things were like they used to be. Conning Louie out of banana splits. Going out looking for jobs and trying not to get them."

Slip: "Yeah those were the good old days. But it seems so long ago."

Sach: "Why did I have to go and get my tonsils out?"

Slip: "I don't know I guess it was just a jerk of fate."

Sach: "How's Whitey? Is he still taking his vitamins?"

Slip: "I told you Whitey's great, we're all in great shape."

Sach: "Here's eight hundred dollars, maybe you can use it."

Slip: "Eight hundred dollars. That's a lot of money."

Sach: "It is, well take it anyway maybe you can help pay some of Louie's debts with it."

Slip: "I couldn't take that Sach, it would leave you broke."

Sach: "Broke, me broke, I'm loaded I got a pocketful of nickels."

Slip: "You're holding out, huh? I was only kidding. This would help pay some of Louie's bills though."

Sach: "Gee, thanks for taking it Chief, you're a pal."

Slip: "Gives me his life savings, and then he thanks me. Good old Sach."

Sach: "Well, I gotta go Chief, so long, see ya later."

Slip: "So long Sach."

Sach: "Chief?"

Slip: "Yes."

(Sach takes his hat and gives it to Slip.)

Sach: "Just one for old times sake, please."

(Slip takes his hat and weakly slaps Sach over his head.)

Sach: "Thanks a lot Chief. But you didn't have your heart in it."

The tables are turned on the other club owner when the female singer spills the beans about what they did to get Sach's signature on the contract. Sach returns with a hoarse voice, and he is unable to perform at the new re-opening of the Palace.

The finale has Sach asking: "What are you getting excited about fellows? All's I did was go to my family doctor, and he looked at the tickle in my throat." Slip: "He didn't per chance remove that tickle, did he?" Sach: "Per chance he did. And he said it was a perfect specimen." Slip: "Stand back everybody. He said you were a perfect specimen, huh? You wanna bet? This is going to hurt." Sach offering a self-reflexive moment: "Is there a doctor in the audience? Oh!"

Slip: "Do–re–me–fa–so–la–ti–do, Do–re–me–fa–so–la–ti–do." Slip hits him over the head with his hat back and forth to the notes.

Though *Blues Busters'* story may be simplistic, particularly lacking any real conflict or tension, the real problem is that the film offers little humor. It lacks many one-liners and the slapstick is rare. Even the rescue of Sach results from a simple play on the female singer's jealousy. There are some long and sometimes dull stretches of Sach singing, though the lip-synching by Hall is excellent.

On the positive side is Slip's exploitation of Sach's newfound singing ability, which allows Sach to still dominate the entire film. The movie seems more polished overall. The idea of Sach turning into a professional singer is still very funny, and it makes you appreciate Hall's ability to make it all so believable. The emotional effect of the scene of Slip and Sach meeting is unforgettable. Most importantly, Gary said that this was among his father's favorite movies. Sach Comedy Meter: 3.5 out of 4.0.

21. Bowery Battalion

Released January 24. 1951

Without Gabe Dell taking part in the series any longer, it seems that the comedy level is gradually upped.

The opening scene has Sach running outside to see airplanes flying overhead. He thinks it is an air raid, actually it is a mock one. He takes a kid's pistol to fight them. The kid calls him a dope and an idiot.

Sach gets the Boys, with the exception of Slip, to join the Army. Slip says: "I gotta stop them. They'll set the Army back a thousand years." Slip inadvertently signs up when he goes to visit the Boys.

Sach: "I'm hungry, when do we eat?" Slip: "We're on our way to mess right now." Sach: "Mess, I don't want mess, I want food." Slip: "Sach, for some inexplicable reason in the army mess means food." Sach: "I bet you the food is a mess."

Confusion ensues when they enter the officer's hall. They are thrown in the guardhouse several times, first for wearing the officers' clothes. The sergeant is frustrated in training the Boys.

Because Sach gives away the password ("scrambled eggs"), Louie (now a Major with a secret formula) is kidnapped. While he is being rescued, Sach is put in charge to guard the spies. Sach shows himself unreliable as he turns his back to untie Louie, and he gives the gun to one of the spies. However, the day is saved when Sach is given a push in the face, which causes the vases above the spies' heads to fall and be knocked onto them.

Finale: The boys are presented medals, and then the Sergeant leads them to the guardhouse. Sergeant: "As far as I'm concerned, this is the greatest finish of any picture I've ever seen!" The Sergeant gives us a hearty laugh.

At times, the comedy in *Bowery Battalion* seems somewhat labored and forced. It centers so much on the Sergeant's reaction to the Boys as Privates. In addition, the plot and comedy moments connect so much to Louie, and the sparse humor with Sach is confined to brief moments. Sach Comedy Meter: 2.0 out of 4.0.

22. Ghost Chasers

Released April 29, 1951

Sach and Slip are at Louie's Sweet Shop. Whitey is conducting his own séance. However, Whitey helps Sach (using Whitey's card membership) to get into Margo the Medium's séance. Sach feels around the seat. Whitey: "What are you doing?" Sach: "I don't want to sit in a seat that might be occupied by a ghost."

We meet Edgar the Ghost who says he is a Pilgrim opposing and exposing witchcraft who comments on events throughout the film. Edgar on Sach: "He has a nose like Cyrano."

Sach and Whitey sit on garbage cans. Sach (referring to Slip): "That guy is not only narrow-minded, he's very stupid. Stupid, one of the most stupid guys I ever met in my life!" Just then, Slip comes by. Sach: "Oh how are ya Chief, I was just telling Whitey how stupid you are." Sach recoils off the pail in expectation that Slip is going to hit him, although this time he does not.

Sach bangs the pail and startles Slip as he goes off in preacher mode with the following as he is thinking that Slip is now a believer in Whitey and clairvoyance. Sach: "Hallelujah! Hallelujah! Chief, you are now one of them. You have been given the gift of clairvoyance. Hallelujah! You'll be able to see beyond the walls of Jericho. You are a master. Oh dearest, dears. Oh mystic of mystic, whom your slave kisses your hand. Hallelujah!" Slip hits him over the head. Sach the over zealous preacher is quieted. Sach: "Oop! Hal-le-lu-jah!"

Sometimes Slip hits Sach after a delayed reaction. Slip: "I'm just a poor old man trying to make a living." Sach: "You can say that again." Slip slaps Sach in the face with money: "That's for the crack you just made."

Edgar the Ghost befriends Sach. Only Sach can see him. Sach: "I like you. You're a good ghost." Edgar moves from the bottom to the top of the stairs. Sach: "Gee I love that trick. Is it hard to do?" Edgar: "You must die first." Sach: "Die? I'll stick to my card tricks."

Louie goes to a fortune-teller. Sach is fascinated and awestruck with Edgar as he does amazing things such as go through a door by drawing one with chalk on a wall. Sach slides down the banister to escape. Sach helps prove the Medium is a fake when he shows Slip a room with the phonograph and masks, skulls, etc. Now the Boys have enough evidence. Louie runs away not knowing it is Sach who is wearing a wolf-like mask.

Sach to Louie: "Who's gonna drive the car? You know I can't drive a car. They wouldn't give me a driver's license on account of my ridiculous I.Q."

Sach to Edgar: "You got any slugs?" Edgar: "Slugs?" Sach: "Yeah nickels. Jitney." Edgar: "Oh you mean coins?" Sach: "Yeah!" Edgar: "I think I have Shillings." Sach: "Shillings? I don't want to call London, I want to call the Bowery."

Professor: "The only person that you cannot hypnotize is the idiot or a moron." Sach: "A moron. I'm being paged!" The Professor's claim that Sach being a moron cannot be hypnotized contradicts the earlier *Mr. Hex* where Sach was effectively hypnotized several times, and as you will see later he is hypnotized in *Spy Chasers* and *Hold That Hypnotist*.

Here Sach acts like he is hypnotized. When one of the professor's assistants moves his stiff body, Sach takes advantage and sneakily smacks him in the head and then kicks him in the ass. Sach slaps the hypnotized Slip, and the latter wakes up to punch Sach back in retaliation.

Finale: The Medium is proved part of a fake spirit racket. Slip and the Boys grab Sach while he is speaking to Edgar in the Sweet Shop. Slip tells Louie to get an ambulance, put a pencil in his mouth, and so forth, to stop him from ranting. Edgar: "Obvious my friends do not believe in ghosts." Edgar looks at the camera and asks the audience: "Does thou?" He winks and smiles.

Although the idea is interesting that only Sach can see and communicate with Edgar the Ghost, the comedy of *Ghost Chasers* (as with *Bowery Battalion*) centers on Louie. This seems to make the slapstick with Sach limited, and definitely less than satisfying. Sach Comedy Meter: 2.0 out of 4.0.

23. Let's Go Navy!
Released July 29, 1951

This is producer Jan Grippo's last film. Ben Schwalb would take over producing, and he would bring in Edward Bernds to direct. The slapstick elements to the movies will increase consequently.

The film opens on the following sign:
DANSANT AND CHOWDER PARTY
ENTIRE PROCEEDS GO TO THE
NEEDY FAMILIES OF THE
GREATER BOWERY
Slip Mahoney
CHAIRMAN OF THE UN-PERMANENT
CHARITIES COMMITTEE

Sach and Slip add up the money raised, but Sach's addition is completely faulty. Two sailors, one with a tattoo of the name of "Marie," rob the Boys. The Boys go down to the police station, and when Sach gets tough and forceful the Boys are threatened with arrest. Slip decides they should check with the Navy recruiting office to report the robbery. Instead, they manage to join the Navy.

A recruiting officer confuses the Boys with enlistees that left the office. Sach: "Hobbernocker. What a silly name." Later when Slip is not able to read the name, he gives that one to Sach. Slip: "You be this guy." Sach: 'I don't want this name. I want my own name. It was a gift from my mother and father. This is Hobbernocker, nocker, nocker nocker–whatever it is, I don't want that!"

Sach is questioned as to how long he was in the Navy, how he wears his tie wrong, and how he ever got into the Navy. Then he drops his sack full of comic books onto the deck in front of the Commander. The latter asks him: "Now what have you got to say?" Sach: "Someone stole one of my comic books." This unexpected response makes you laugh.

In fact, everything Sach does is funny here. For example, he washes the deck, vacuums the deck, and then uses the waxer to polish the deck. The result of this is that Longnecker slides off the deck. The running gag throughout this movie is that Longnecker is always getting wet.

Commander: "You seem to make an effort to get into trouble." Sach: "Oh! it's no effort at all." Commander: "I cannot reconcile your actions with your background. I see here where you are credited with an M.A. from a State University." Sach: "Yes sir, I also get a P.S. from Louie." When asked why he joined the Navy, Sach says: "To see the world and have a girl in every port."

When he thinks a drill is a real fire, Sach turns the water from a hose on, and he floods the deck. When Slip attempts to wake up a dreaming Sach, the latter hugs Slip thinking he is Cynthia. Slip slaps him and he wakes up. When Sach is almost caught searching the sleeping sailors to find the one with the tattoo, he runs in the shower room and feigns a shower with his clothes on. Longnecker tells Sach he is showering without any water, Sach says: "Water, I knew I forgot something. Thanks." Again, he soaks Longnecker.

The Boys go to an island to contact the native Chief, a tattoo expert. Sach talks some foreign language to him. Slip tells the Boys: "I didn't know Sach could talk French." Slip to Sach: "Sach, Sach, that's great. What did he say?" Sach: "I don't even know what I said." Slip pushes him away.

Sach sees a pretty girl, and he gives us his motorlips. Sach befriends the Chief's parrot named Davy Jones, who bites Sach and Sach bites him back. Sach brings the parrot onto the ship.

While the ship is running a test firing drill, Sach is in the barrel of the guns. The Boys get him out just before it is fired.

The old gag of the table shell game is revisited. This is the game of guessing where the ball is hidden after scrambling the three cups. Slip loses, but Sach plays with his last five dollars. The parrot helps by telling him which cup does not have the ball ("Ah! Ah!"). Sach wins wads of money totaling $2,000, which he wears all over himself. This allows the Boys to replace the $1,600 that was stolen.

Sach: "Wait a minute, what about me?" Slip: "I'll split the four hundred dollars with you." Sach: "Oh no you don't wise guy, none of that. I want my original five dollars." Slip: "Well here take it." Sach: "That's not it. Oop! There it is, lucky five. (He kisses it)."

As fate would have it, the same sailors rob the Boys again. However, Longnecker comes down the street upon them. The parrot repeats that it is a stickup, etc., which brings Longnecker to start punching the sailors. As usual, Sach is on the sidelines giving directions during the fight. He thinks he gave a punch, but it is really given by Longnecker's girlfriend.

Sach to the girlfriend: "Where did he go? Ooh my magic punch, I'm in good shape. Want to go a few rounds?" Of course, Longnecker gets wet again by a street sweeper passing by. We learn that Louie had shown the two sailors the telegram that Slip sent, so they knew the Boys had money on them.

Finale: *Let's Go Navy!* has the Boys going back to the Navy office to receive letters of commendation. The same mix-up that occurred with the group of enlistees happens again as at the start of the movie. The Boys are signed up for the Navy once more. Slip: "Well fellows, here we go again." Parrot: "Here we go again. Anchors away. Batten down the hatches. . . ." Sach has the final line: "Old sailors don't die, they just sail away."

The story of *Let's Go Navy!* tampers too much with believability. Besides the unlikely event of being robbed by the same sailors twice, there is also the mistake of being enlisted at the beginning and at the end in the same way. Nevertheless, there are so many funny gags throughout this film, from the minor sight gag of their exploding jeep to Sach winning the shell game. This time, Sach saves the day; though not through some special power, but via the assistance of Davy the parrot. Sach Comedy Meter: 3.0 out of 4.0.

24. Crazy Over Horses

Released November 18, 1951

This film marks the first time we see the comical caricatures of Slip and Sach in the credits.

The film opens as the Mahoney Collection Service offers to help collect money owed to Louie. Instead of collecting money, they bring back a horse named "My Girl."

In the first minutes, Hall displays his fine acting ability and range as he quickly moves from comical idiot to vicious and dead-serious loan shark, and then finally to the needy and crying beggar.

At first Sach jokingly thinks the debtor is dispossessed because he sees old furniture outside the building, but Slip corrects him and explains that the guy "sells that junk." A smiling Sach says: "Well, I ain't buying none." Slip tells Sach that they are going to collect by acting tough. Sach tests out his tough act on Slip. He then hands Slip's hat to him and Slip summarily slaps him over his head.

Then mean-looking, tight-lipped Sach growls with toughness, viciously shaking the debtor and demanding "Will you stop with that hearts and flowers, we want that money, you're gonna give me that money, I'm gonna tear you apart, let me [have] that money!" Finally, we get Sach's sympathetic pouty face ready to buy the debtor's sob story, which Sach plays as comical melodrama sighing to Slip, "please give us a little more time...."

When the debtor offers 'My Girl' as payment instead, they all look out the window. As Sach sees the debtor's daughter with their horse, it is an automatic "Ahhh!" He does his motorlips several times, as he gets uncontrollably excited. Sach and Slip think the debtor is giving away his daughter, not the horse. Debtor: "You'll be doing me a big favor if you take her off my hands, it cost so much to feed her."

Slip starts to explain that there are laws against such, but Sach interrupts: "Don't worry about the law. We'll do it black market." Sach tells Slip: "If he's crazy enough to sell her, let's be crazy enough to buy her, she'll be nice to have around the store." However, Slip quickly realizes their misunderstanding.

Slip explains to the debtor and his daughter: "Oh! I used to be an exercise boy." Sach: "You could do with a little exercise now." Slip slaps Sach with his backhand. The debtor and his daughter share smiles as we do too to see Slip respond to Sach's wisecrack.

Sach rides the horse down the street, and acting like a deep-voiced cowboy, he sings: "Home on the Range." Slip turns down an offer of $1,000 for the horse because he believes it is a racehorse and the buyers have something sneaky in mind.

This story revolves around the switching of horses, 'My Girl' and 'Tarzana.' Louie's difficulty handling the horse leads Sach to offer a hand. Sach: "My Girl, this is your honey Sach." Sach is tumbled out after the switched horse kicks him. Slip offers his insult: "I think before you were born, someone scared your mother." Sach realizes it is not "My Girl" after he asks her questions. He also thinks that Louie slaughtered the horse to use as hamburger meat. Sach barks at Louie while eating his hamburger: "You, I'm going back to the Hamburger Association!"

As usual, one of Slip's insults is taken by Sach to be a compliment. Slip: "Sach, everyday you're mind is degenerating more and more." Sach: "Gee, thanks Chief!"

Slip pulls Sach away by the nose for being overly friendly with a security guard.

Sach goes to ask someone at the stable where "My Girl" is. Slip stops him: "What are you an interrogator?" Sach: "You know I don't drink." Slip: "Whitey, switch the horses, and do it with dispatch." Sach:

"I thought we were going to do it with 'Tarzana.'" Slip: "I thought I told you to keep your mouth shut!"

Sach is blamed for messing up the switching, and Slip throws Sach out of the gang. Slip: "I don't want to see you again until eternity ends." Sach: "Chief, what are you gonna do without me?" Slip: "Everything right. Now get going!" Sach responds: "Alright for you Slip. After I gave you the best years of my life, you throw me out of the gang. I'm leaving, but when you get in trouble, don't call on me for more."

The Boys switch the horses again. Sach tells the horse: "You're the cause of all my troubles, you made me an outcast." Sach gets an idea to switch the horses back when he is left alone to his own devices.

A dated and especially inappropriate scene of humor comes when Sach disguises himself in blackface, since he wanted to look like a stable helper. The problem is he overdoes it so that he looks like a minstrel man with burnt cork, whitened lips and hands, and a deep voice à la *Amos 'n Andy*. Indeed he looks silly, but this unnecessary lapse into pre-World War II humor is offensive by the exaggeration. Even his light hair sticking out of his cap makes it look phony.

Sach greets the black stable worker: "Say hello to your sister Shiskebob." Of course, this effort actually messed up the situation for he inadvertently returned "My Girl" to the stable, and brings home "Tarzana."

Sach tells Slip what he did. Slip grabs him by his throat. Sach insists he brought back "My Girl." He is kicked out by the horse and declares: "wrong horse." Slip regarding Sach: "After this job we'll have to send him to a sanitarium."

Next, the Boys let the crooks do the switching back this time, although the Boys could have easily done it again themselves. Apparently, the crooks switch the horses thinking that the Boys are getting "Tarzana" and that they have the real racehorse "My Girl."

The swindle that the crooks were working required that they have "My Girl," and they run her as "Tarzana," increasing their profits on the latter long shot horse winning the race (when really "My Girl" is winning). However, the crooks bungled the set-up by actually getting "Tarzana" and losing their bets.

There is an unrealistic aspect to this somewhat confusing story. It is when a tall Sach is used as a jockey. Sach is on his horse sticking his tongue out before the race. Slip's frustration in getting Sach to move his horse up in position in the race is the funniest moment in this movie.

Slip speaks to Sach on what Slip calls "that electrical equipment," what we today say is a very large, oversized walkie-talkie radio. Slip: "Hey bird brain. . . All right Sach now let her out. Let her out. (More angrily) Hey cement head let her out! Catch up with the other horses. I don't care how, go over them, go between them, go under them–but catch up!"

Finale: At a party celebration, Sach the jockey starts to offer a speech of thanks. Sach: "You know something, I could have gotten killed. Why you! (He smashes the cream pie in Slip's face). Oh you. Ooh! Whipped cream (Sach tastes some from Slip's face)." Slip: "Now that's what I call besmirched gratitude." Sach offers his Ed Wynn laugh. Slip goes to slap some cream in Sach's face.

Crazy Over Horses offers a somewhat limited story about a swindle concerning switching horses, but the plethora of gags with Sach keeps it somewhat entertaining. Note that this movie does not have the typical fight at the end to catch the crooks. Sach Comedy Meter: 2.5 out of 4.0.

25. Hold That Line
Released March 23, 1952

This film opens with Sach the scientist mixing chemicals at Louie's Sweet Shop. Slip calls him 'Test-tube Head."

Sach greets some college professors who have an idea to improve their situation. Sach: "How do you do do da, do do da?" Inadvertently, the Boys are shuffled off to college. Sach arrives at the college with a raccoon coat and ukulele. The Boys are now at a location in which they seem totally out of place.

Slip uses smart gibberish and astounds the professor when answering a question in class. Sach is busy in the chemistry lab: "Some of this... Put some of this...." The German professor asks him what he's making. Sach: "Medicine to end all medicines...." Professor: "Smells like it will end everything." Sach: "Well, I put some C2O4, and some SE2HO2, and for a topper I put KH2O2." Professor: "Stupid, stupid, you are boiling a high explosive." Sach made TNT, causing an explosion.

There is also a "Sach alone" scene in the lab mixing chemicals. This is a partial excerpt of his monologue: "Nobody here. Oh Boy, all alone now. I can invent till the cows come home.... I put a little bit of that... take some of this right there, that's enough, Oh boy some of that, let me see, nope, green's not my color... don't like green. Let's see I'll take some of this, and some of that and for the last one... (He mixes it back and forth pouring from one metal malt glass). Oh boy, for a scientist Horace Debussy Jones." Sach drinks what supposedly is a vitamin formula, which gives him strength to bend the metal cups.

Again, Sach has acquired special powers. Sach stands out in pole throwing, and then playing in the football games.

Sach sings "Men of Ivy." Slip hurts himself when he smacks Sach's steel-like face. Now Sach has muscles of iron, and he reveals to Slip the secret that it comes from his own vitamins he made in the lab. Sach is nicknamed "Hurricane Jones of Ivy."

Sach: "Boys, I want to be in the girls fraternity, rush me you fools." All the Boys dress up as women for a hazing initiation in their own neighborhood. Sach drops his bag on the policeman's foot. Policeman: "What do you got in the bag?" Sach: "My lipstick." Policeman: "Heavy lipstick." Sach: "Yeah I got a heavy date." Sach powders the policeman's face with a pie-sized puff.

Louie laughs at the Boys dressed as girls, so they make Louie dress up too. Hall has the most convincing mannerisms playing a girl as when he laughs, he shrugs his shoulders, and holds his hand against his cheek and cocks his head.

"Strong boy" Sach is driven to a woman's apartment. Of course, Sach's response to a potential amorous situation is, as usual, his motor-lips. He dances and kisses her. Sach is clobbered by a pistol's backside, and he is kept from playing in the football game, similar to missing his performance in *Blues Busters*. The crooks plotted this to have taken Sach out of a game since they want the school to lose.

Nevertheless, the school is winning, and Sach is rescued. Slip makes a batch of vitamins and brings Sach into the game by trying to revive him. Unfortunately, the vitamins made by Slip are tested on the Dean, and they surprisingly shrink the latter in size.

Finale: Sach is back in the lab inventing. Sach: "There it is, my new invention, 'Flying Z.' One drink of this and I fly." Slip: "Oh he's really flipping this time." Sach goes to the window. Sach: "Ohps! I feel a flight coming on." Slip: "Sach, don't go out that window! Get back in the room Sach, you can't fly! You can't fly!" Sach jumps off the window ledge. Slip: "What happened to him? Nobody gonna ever believe this."

Hold That Line is a below-average outing as far as humor originating from Sach. Sach Comedy Meter: 2.0 out of 4.0.

26. Here Comes The Marines
Released June 29, 1952

Slip is drafted. Sach joins too, but he does not like the uniform.

Sach wants to buy toothpaste at the commissary, but he cannot get it to come out. The clerk asks him: "Why don't you take the top off?" When he does, he inadvertently squirts it all over the clerk's face. Sach: "You know something, you're right."

Sach boasts that he can be the Marine staff doctor, and then he is mistaken to be one. He does eye testing, etc. Colonel Brown: "Insubordination, impersonating an officer and doctor. You know what you can get for that?" Sach: "$10.00 a visit."

Sach enthusiastically mixes a large amount of spicy ingredients to make a pot of soup. When asked by the Captain what he is making, Sach calls it: "Horace DeBussy Jones's Special Bouillon." It burns a huge hole thru the ladle. Sach: "A little strong. I get it, my culinary days are over." This self-realization by Sach that he is incompetent at cooking reminds one of *Modern Times* (1936), in which Chaplin leaves quickly from a shipyard job as soon as he realizes he screwed things up.

Colonel Brown believes that he knew Sach's father. This begins a series of promotions for Sach; first as Sergeant.

Slip's charm induces fear whenever he takes charge and demands others give him respect, even if he has to fake it. However, Slip is no longer in charge, and so he talks back to Sach here as he is trying to fight back this new arrangement.

Sgt. Sach takes pleasure in lording it over the Boys. However, the power goes to Sach's head as he annoyingly blows his whistle for everything, even when he says "Good Night," or when he sleeps and snores. While he is sleeping in the barracks, Slip gets even by putting a dud in

Sach's arms to scare him. It turns out that the missile is not a dud, and by saving his men from an explosion, Sach is promoted to Staff Sergeant.

In a seemingly unrelated sub-plot, Sach is made to win at a crooked gambling operation connected to the murder of a whistleblower. The crooks are aware that they were being watched because Slip brought along intelligence officers.

For camouflaging foxholes so well, Sach is promoted to Technical Sergeant by the Colonel. While dancing, Sach humorously cuts in on another couple. He tells a woman who is working with the crooks about his barracks. Later that night, she shows up, hiding in his bed, in an attempt to make trouble.

Sach shows his inability at problem solving, and so he relies on Slip to help. Sach: "Save me, Chief save me, I'll never pull my rank again."

The Colonel investigates an accusation by the Corporal that there was a woman hiding in Sach's barracks. When the Colonel finds a mink, he asks: "What is this?" Sach: "That's my jacket, it's a cold war."

Sach's arrest for harboring a woman in the barracks warrants a court martial. Slip is now in charge of Sach. With the Colonel reassigned, Sach is no longer the big cheese. When Slip gives his name to the new Colonel, the latter remembers Wildcat Terry Mahoney, the toughest Sergeant. When the Colonel asks Slip if there is any relation, Slip smiles.

Finale: Slip is the new Sergeant. He blows the whistle to Sach's annoyance. Sach: "Say sir, you never told me your father was in the service?" Slip: "He wasn't." Sach: "He wasn't? Then who's Wildcat Terry Mahoney?" Slip: "I never heard of him." Sach: "You never. . .Oooh!" Slip: "Get going! March!" Slip smirks. Sach covers up his face as Slip continues blowing the whistle.

Sach stops being funny in *Here Comes the Marines* since he's no longer being slapped around. Initially it is funny to see him here boss-ing around Slip and everyone else. However, the reversal of roles is not even mildly amusing for long. This is not a favorite film for Sach lovers since the running gag of Sach being in charge tends to be overused and quickly gets to be tiring halfway through the movie, and especially annoying is Sach's constant blowing of his whistle.

This experiment in changing Sach's character from being Slip's foil proves unsatisfying. Sach Comedy Meter: 2.0 out of 4.0.

27. Feudin' Fools

Released September 21, 1952

The film opens in Louie's Sweet Shop, where Sach seems bored and depressed. Slip: "You guys like a banana split?" Sach: "I don't wanna banana split." Slip: "You don't want a banana... what's the matter, what are you sick?" Sach: "No, I'll have a steak."

Sach makes an observation: "Everyone's a private eye. What happened to public eyes?"

Sach inherits a Kentucky farm. He dons a skunk coon hat and the Boys are caught up in Smiths vs. Jones feud à la the famed Hatfields and McCoys conflict.

The Boys take to the hills. Sach offers us various humorous moments. He eats peas by cutting them in half, and then eats them one-by-one. Sach milks a cow. Sach: "What do you need, a college education to milk a cow?" He squirts the milk directly in the bottle. He obtains chocolate milk from a brown cow. Sach: "What do you expect to come out of brown cow? Green milk?" Sach feeds chickens and eats the feed. Sach even crows like a rooster.

Some bank robbers need a bullet removed from one of their gang, so the Boys disguise Louie as a doctor. An attractive country girl walks into the shack where the bank robbers are holding the Boys. Sach goes under the table with the girl when a fight ensues between the bank robbers, the Smiths, and the Boys. When a routine is called by Slip, Sach explains to the girl: "Oh a, they fight, and you and I stay here." Sach does his motorlips.

The Sheriff arrives to say that robbing is "agin' the law." Sach: "Robbing a bank is agin' the law?" Sheriff: "Yeah!" Sach: "That's a good law!"

Finale: The bank offers a loan of $5,000 to develop the estate, and Sach is happy to sign. Slip gets ready to head back to New York, but Sach wants to stay to be a farmer. Slip grabs the pen from Sach: "What's the matter with you? You flipping your melon? When it comes to the business end of this organization, I am Mr. Jones."

The Smiths: "Jones? You hear that man?" The bullets start flying. Slip runs out the cabin into the hills. Slip's controlling need to always take over backfires this time. Sach: "Give me that gun, got him, right in ..." Sach fires the gun. "The End" title comes on the screen, and Sach grimaces and nods his head yes, and blinks to indicate he shot him in the ass!

Feudin' Fools takes the Boys on an expedition to hillbilly country, and it valiantly looks for laughs where few can be found. Sach Comedy Meter: 2.0 out of 4.0.

28. No Holds Barred

Released November 23, 1952

The film opens now in Louie's Ice Cream Parlor (more often it is called Louie's Sweet Shop), that is held up at gunpoint as the Boys arrive. A tough-nosed Sach stands up to the thief, and he tells Louie put your money away. The spurned thief runs out after twice hitting Sach over his head with a gun to no avail.

Of course, a doctor examines Sach's head to find it as hard as a rock. Sach does not feel anything. He has an extremely strong skull from calcification, which is temporary. Slip calls him "Calcium Head." Sach: "I got an idea. I'll rent it out as a sledgehammer." Slip sees a wrestling poster advertising if you stay in the ring for ten minutes you win $1,000.

Louie complains that the Boys used his two passes to see the wrestling match, and he had to pay to get in. Sach accidentally stands up when they ask one audience member to be the challenger to the champion.

Everyone laughs and boos when they hear the name of "Horace 'DeBussy' Jones." Sach's attempts to avoid fighting are funny. Then the champion bangs his head against Sach, and he is quickly knocked out. Sach wins and collapses.

Slip says he will get him ready for the next match. Louie: "Why don't you shoot him now, and save time?" Slip is offered $5,000 by a crook who tells Slip you will need the money for training and he can supply the connections. He turns it down. Slip starts his own training camp in the back of Louie's, but the noise is bad for business. Louie tells Slip and Sach: "This is Louie's Sweet Shop, not Sweat Shop." However, wait, this statement by Louie contradicts the sign shown at the movie's opening shot.

When Sach's power migrates to another part of his body, his title changes. "Hammer-Head Jones" is transformed into "Steel-Fingers Jones." When the finger power is gone, it travels to the elbow, hence "Iron-Elbow Jones."

Sach's power disappears before each bout. Slip insults Sach for this ridiculous situation. Sach carries on crying: "My elbows ain't iron anymore, they rusted away." Then with his power in his toes, "Terrible-Toes Jones" wins the Heavyweight Champion Title.

An attractive woman named Rhonda Nelson has a flat tire outside of Louie's. Sach reacts with his motorlips. He jokes with her: "I knew your brother Half Nelson and your father Full." Slip wins her favor as they go outside.

Slip sits in the car with Rhonda, and he expects Sach to do the repair. Slip calls Sach 'Moose Nose.' Slip's mistreatment annoys Sach. We see what might be considered a passive-aggressive side to Sach. Sach says to himself: "I'll get even with him." Sach jacks the car carelessly to disturb the lovebirds.

As Sach has shown his vulnerability to being charmed, even Slip is no better off sometimes. Slip goes to a party that Rhonda invites him to. She is really part of a crew trying to find out where Sach's strength is. Slip: "I'll be there with bells on." Sach wisecracks: "I'll be there to ring them."

A silly female fan of "Terrible Toes" asks Sach: "Would you like to give me a little kiss?" Sach: "What and ruin my reputation?" Fan: "Oh how can one little kiss ruin your reputation?" Sach: "It's been my reputation that I never been kissed." Sach explains: "But honey you're not my type." He asks her if she likes martinis, and hands her an oversized martini-shaped punch bowl.

Sach cuts in when he sees an attractive woman dancing. The man taps Sach's shoulder. Sach takes that as an invite to dance: "Oh anytime." He dances with the man, and then pushes him away: "You know something, you're a pretty bad dancer."

Sach hilariously and cleverly pretends to be a waiter with a Jerry Colonna/Jimmy Finlayson-type mustache. Slip initially calls him Cornelius, then realizes it really is Sach. He runs through several vocalizations sounding like British, Cockney, Dracula-Hungarian and Swedish-German. Then Slip keeps Rhonda's head turned so Sach could mime to him that she is connected to the gangsters trying to get information.

When she looks at him, he quickly goes into a friendly and happy waiter. He talks French. She asks: "I thought you were an English butler?" He spills the tray of drinks to get her away from Slip.

When the fan sees Sach the waiter, she insists he's "Terrible Toes

Jones." After escaping, Sach is next seen stamping his autograph for a dollar. Slip explains that he bought Sach the stamper since Sach would have worn himself out trying to spell his name.

Slip and Sach are both fooled now when they are asked to pose for a photo getting into a car. They are immediately taken to the crooks' hideout where they are forced to tell where Sach's power is.

Sach refuses to go in the ring again. However, Slip uses a sob story to get Sach to fight again. He tells him that the bout is for the Orphan's Milk Fund. Slip's teary pleas and suggestions, replete with background melodramatic violin music playing, finally convinces him. Sach: "I'll do it, I'll do it for the orphan kids." Regal music plays for the 132-pound "Terrible Toes" as he fights the 325-pound champion he beat at the beginning of the movie.

Sach is pushed into the ring. This time his power is in his derrière. Sach fumbles not knowing where his power is. As Sach leans over the ring's ropes to talk to Slip, the champion eventually plows into Sach's backside, and is knocked into confusion. It causes the champion to wrestle his manager instead.

Finale: Sach: "I did it, I did it without power!" Slip: "That's what you think." Sach: "Well where is it?" Sach: "Ohhhh, what are you gonna call me now?" Slip: "Well, we'll call you..." Sach interrupts with his nervous whine: "Ahh-hah! Ahh-hah! Ahh-hah! Ahh-hah!" Slip: "How about it?" Sach: "Ahh-hah! You say it and we're out of pictures."

No Holds Barred offers an uncanny illogic in which Sach's powers keep changing locations. There is no logical explanation of how his powers relocate, and the few gags limit the movie's laugh power. Overall, this movie may seem to offer less slapstick satisfaction than the other Sach "special powers" entries. Noticeably, Slip never slaps Sach even once. Although it is not as humorous as it might have been, this is one of Hall's three favorites of his own movies according to Gary. This raises it to an above average rating. Sach Comedy Meter: 3.0 out of 4.0.

29. Jalopy

Released February 15, 1953

Jalopy revisits the story of Sach the inventor as in *Hold That Line*. Sach mixes up a high explosive formula at the rear of Louie's Sweet Shop once again. Slip calls him "Horace DeBussy, Test-Tube Head."

The test-tube formula explodes into what Sach calls "a beautiful blonde out of my bottle." Sach does his motorlips. A blonde-haired woman appears coincidentally and introduces herself as "Bobbie Lane." Sach greets her by raising his cap by the bill, and he calls her Robert.

Sach wants to drive Slip's car, "Mahoney's Meteor," in the race. In referring to the engine, Sach declares: "I can put her together and take her apart blindfolded." Slip asks: "But can you do it without a blindfold?" Sach: "Certainly, but that's asking a lot of me."

Slip drives it, and the car boils over. It crashes into the track wall. Sach walks on the track to help Slip. Sach chases after his lucky cap. When he gets it, he says: "I just bought it the other day." The track announcer calls him "that idiot." Sach causes a pileup on the track, so he runs away. Slip follows, with angry drivers pursuing them. Sach's panic and fear is hilarious as he backs off from the menacing drivers. Sach: "Fellows, relax, relax, relax, relax, you left your motor running, fellows, fellows, don't get excited, don't get excited…don't get excited!"

Sach: "If you hadda let me drive the car, I would've won the race." Slip: "I'm gonna let you drive," pointing to the floor waxer. Sach: "This? Not me, that's below my dignity, I'm a genius." Slip: "Well genius serve up some elbow grease and get to work." Sach then alone questions: "I wonder if there's a union for geniuses?"

Sach's Comedy

When Sach waxes Louie's floor, he fiendishly sneaks into the machine what he calls his "magic syrup....never knows unless one tries." The syrup causes the waxer to fly off in the air with him holding on. Sach: "Hey fellows look at my invention." It then explodes and falls out Louie's window and goes up in the air outside, crashing in front of the store. Before it crashes, Sach is being pulled around by it. Sach: "Oh! Oh! Oh! Oh!...."

Slip thinks to put Sach's syrup into his jalopy, saying "Sach, you're a genius." Slip tests the formula out and finds his car spinning around at tremendous speed of one second per lap. Sach supplies his tongue-tied fearful response when he sees three guys approaching them: "Ahh-Ahh-Ahh-hah!"

Sach almost reveals his secret formula to the crooks by hinting positively when they get warmer in guessing how the jalopy runs so fast.

Slip calls Sach "Eagle-Faced Nose," demanding that he make more formula. Sach: "Now wait a minute, fatso...certainly I remember it, I'm a genius." Sach tastes it, and burps: "There it is Professor, old boy, the stuff that makes cars go faster and beautiful women appear."

When the formula beaker is thrown on the floor, a cloud of smoke reveals beautiful Bobbie again. Bobbie tells Slip there will be girls at a shindig. Sach: "Girls, who needs girls? I have all the girls I want in this bottle and besides that, it makes cars go faster." Slip yells at Sach: "SHUT UP!"

At a party, Slip dances with Bobbie. Sach arrives with the Professor, both wearing top hats. Sach says to the Professor regarding Slip: "What's he doing dancing with my invention?" Sach cuts between Slip and Bobbie, and starts to dance with Slip. Slip: "Boys are supposed to dance with girls." Sach to Professor: "Right now, we're gonna dance with girls." Sach does his motorlips, and he dances with Bobbie. (The big martini punch bowl from the previous film is seen on the table.)

Sach is told: "You look like the brains in this outfit." Sach is flattered and joins the gangsters. He acts tough with Slip and demands the bottle. Sach throws it on the floor creating an explosion, and they escape.

Back at the lab, Sach explains: "My formula takes five ingredients to make a high explosive. . . ." Slip: "This will take all night." Sach: "Don't worry I made it simple. I'm a simpleton you know."

While Sach makes it, Slip sees a hand from outside the window taking the beakers. Slip places another beaker there–one that is hot–and you hear a painful holler. A fight ensues, as the gangsters demand the formula. Sach and the Professor watch as a fight goes on, agreeing: "Highly exciting!" Sach throws scoops of ice cream at the crooks as the boys are fighting. Sach hits Louie: "Ahh, Oh! Oh! Oh! Well, well, well, it was Louie's favorite anyway."

Sach drops the bottle–and nothing happens. Slip: "You put us through all this trouble for nothing?" Sach forgot an important ingredient; namely, the seltzer.

Slip enters the race. Sach did not come with the formula when the race starts. When he arrives with it, he runs alongside Slip's car. Suddenly, Slip along with Sach standing on the car's sideboard is going backwards at top speed. Slip: "I think you mixed the stuff wrong." Sach: "What makes you think so? I know, the seltzer was flat." Slip: "I think your head is flat." Slip manages to catch up in lost laps, and he wins the race.

Finale: There's a party celebrating Slip's win. The cake has a car in the center. Sach runs out with another bottle of explosive, and he drops some, which reveals a sexy blonde-haired woman who Slip walks off with. Sach: "Ahh-hah! Ahh-hah! Hah! Hah! Hah! Now I gotta get one for myself." He splashes more liquid, and a geeky woman appears. Sach: "Oh. No. No. No. That's not for me. Professor." Professor: "For me." The

Professor's excited and exclaims: "With horn-rimmed glasses."

Sach gives Louie the beaker with the formula and walks off. Sach: "For you. Louie, have a ball. Oh Chief, wait for me." He walks out as he does his motorlips. A disappointed Louie tries splashing it: "Nothing works for me." Louie starts to cry.

Jalopy is an enjoyable first production under Ben Schwalb's control. Sach the inventor of beautiful girls fits in perfectly with what we would expect of his wacky persona. This movie is also the first entry with that memorable opening theme music, known as "Hail, Hail, the Gang's All Here." It is a 1917 song whose words were written by D. A. Esrom, with music adapted by Arthur Sullivan from Gilbert and Sullivan's 1879 comic opera *The Pirates of Penzance*. Marlin Skiles offered a superb arrangement, with slight variation in several of the following Bowery Boys entries. This opening background music to the credits differs from the theme used in the earlier *Bowery Boys* movies. Sach Comedy Meter: 3.0 out of 4.0.

30. Loose In London

Released May 24, 1953

The film opens at Louie's Sweet Shop, where Slip is telling Louie his gold, silver and uranium stocks are worthless. When Sach tries to say something, Slip stops him: "Oh shut up!" Sach acts knowledgeable since he had read books about making money.

A paper airplane lands on the table and Slip asks: "What's that?" Sach: "Air mail." He chuckles, and a rare self-reflexive glance at the camera tells us he wants us to know he is joking for our pleasure. Sach learns he is a potential heir and blueblood, and his Lordship uncle wants to meet all of his potential heirs.

Sach learns he has to nest in the trunk because they are short in the number of tickets. Louie is accidentally stowed away onboard. Sach does his "Ahh-hah! Ahh-hah! Ahh-hah!" Then he starts crying.

In London, Sach corrects Slip's description of the famous sights, each time interrupting him and saying: "WRONG AGAIN!" Sach is informed, and knows all the facts about London's sights; House of Commons, Tower of London, Trafalgar Square, and the changing of the Guard at Buckingham Palace. Slip wants to know how Sach is so knowledgeable. Sach: "Because you're smart and I'm stupid. What do you think I was doing in that trunk?" He pulls out *Mitchell's Pocket Guide to London*.

Sach does not know that the relatives are poisoning the uncle to get his fortune. Sach picks up a glass monocle that fell into a tray of Ritz crackers. He puts cheese spread on it, and eats it. Sach: "It's good." Sach takes several sandwiches as the waiter passes.

The slapstick is abundant, including Sach tripping and falling, knocking over a tray of food onto other guests, and he falls on a table and crashes into a wall, etc. Also, there are several good scenes when a terrified Sach is alone as he hears and sees things in the mansion, including Sach getting in bed with a black-hooded man who pulls the blankets off him. In addition, some odd and absurd comical moments include when a supposedly stuffed fox mounted on the wall comes alive and bites Sach's finger, ear and nose.

Slip calls Sach a "schizophreniac." Slip: "I got a dog that's got more brains than you than you have, his nose is not so big but he's got more brains."

As in the other movies in the series, women easily prey upon Sach. When a conniving femme fatale flatters Sach, it causes him to go off in his fantasy mind. She tells him: "We could be all alone." Sach responds with his motorlips.

Sach's Comedy

A solitary Sach is walking around the mansion searching for his uncle. He is startled when he runs into Slip. He unwittingly avoids all sorts of attempts made to hurt him. In his search, he gets his head caught in a hanging noose. He picks up a sword and fences. He sticks his head into a guillotine, and just misses having it chopped off. He sees one of the family members apparently passed out. That person had been knocked out just before he was ready to stab Sach from behind. Sach assumes wrongly, saying, "These people gotta stop drinking that sweet wine."

When a relative points a gun at him, Sach asks: "Sir, could I say one thing? H–E–L–P!" The butler frees the Boys. It turns out the uncle was conking everyone.

Uncharacteristically, Sach gets into the fight. There is a rare moment of sword fighting by both Slip and Sach. Sach is hit over his head. Sach: "Bells. I hear bells. I like bells. Very pretty." Then we get the delayed reaction of him being knocked out cold.

Finale: Sach and the uncle are not related, and Sach is given 1,000 pounds as a token of gratitude. Sach says he wanted to go fox hunting, but Slip tells him there is no fox hunting in the heart of London. Sach dashes off chasing a fox: "Tally-ho, yikes, yikes." His "uncle" runs off after Sach: "Wait for me, yikes, yikes, tally-ho, tally-ho!" Slip looks at the camera and says: "Don't tell <u>me</u> they're not related."

Loose in London is director Edward Bernds' first *Bowery Boys* movie, with the story written by Elwood Ullman and Edward Bernds. Interestingly, as with *No Holds Barred*, there is no slapping in this film, which seems out of place here with Bernds now at the helm. Sach does not wear his characteristic baseball cap once they leave the Sweet Shop. Sach offers an above average amount of comedy moments. Sach Comedy Meter 3.0 out of 4.0.

31. Clipped Wings

Released August 14, 1953

Once again, Louie's Sweet Shop is here called Louie's Ice Cream Parlor. With thunder overhead Sach declares: "Ain't fit weather for man or beast!" Sach puts a slug in the Atomic Jet kiddie ride. He is wearing his flying gear. When the ride takes off wildly, the plug has to be pulled to stop it. We learn that Sach has been taking a ten-lesson correspondence course to learn flying.

When the Boys go to see their Lieutenant friend, held for spying at the Air Force, they mistakenly go to the Recruiting Office. When Sach fools around doing a drill with Slip to make him a Sergeant, he aggravates him. Slip slaps Sach.

They do not realize that they are signing up as rookies until they run through the application and aptitude tests. Sach is friendly with the female Sergeant. Sach filled out the required form; and of course, he misunderstands the questions. Slip asks Sach what he put down for "General Remarks." Sach: "Nothing, I ain't no General."

As regards the aptitude tests, they both fail. Slip is forcing a square peg in a round hole. The staff labels them morons as they have a combined I.Q. of Minus 18. This exaggerated comedic remark hampers this movie's believability.

For some unknown reason, Sach is assigned to the women's barracks, "C" (a W.A.F. Detachment). A staffer asks: "Where did you get the drag?" When Sach admires his muscles and profile in a mirror, the women in the barracks whistle. Sach does his motorlips. The girls flock to him as the female Sergeant, "Sgt. Pruneface" to Sach, goes to find out how this mistake was made, checking with the Lieutenant, the Captain, the Major, and then Commanding Officer.

Sach gets amorous around the bevy of beauties. He throws kisses: "Bye girls." He is confined to the laundry room as temporary quarters. Sach peeks through the door as the Sergeant returns accidentally hitting Sach in the head. During the night, Sach awakens due to a dripping faucet. He is tangled in the clothesline and around the Sergeant. She tells him: "You may not be an idiot, but you'll do until a real one comes along." Sach is ordered to stay up and wash all the clothes he knocked on the floor. He falls asleep while doing the laundry.

A very funny purely visual moment that needs no dialogue is seeing Sach with a shower cap on his head, a towel protectively wrapped around his chest, and carrying a towel held over his arm patiently waiting on the women's shower line.

Sach arrives late to meet Slip. He says it is because he has fifty beautiful girls as buddies, and they just had tea and fudge. Slip keeps himself from slapping Sach, because he says he did not want to bend his hat.

Sach is easily influenced as a commissary woman gives him candy as a reward for promising to let her know if he sees their Lieutenant friend.

Slip expects Sach to climb a ladder to sneak in to see their friend. Sach: "I don't want to go up there, I get dizzy in high places." He quickly changes his mind when Slip suggests: "Just imagine you're flying your own private plane for the first time." There is the gag of Sach removing a ridiculous number of items (crowbar, hammer, rope, coat, shirt and tie, etc.) from a little shoebox to help the Lieutenant escape.

The Air Force jails and then releases the Boys and the Lieutenant for lack of evidence, in order to trap the spies who seek military secrets.

Sach covers Slip's mouth when Slip starts to answer Louie's questions about flying. Sach: "Anything you want to know about flying, ask me. I used to be a graduated flyer." Slip sinks his teeth into Sach's hand.

Sach screams in pain: "Ahhhh! What's the matter with you, didn't you have lunch?" Then Sach makes a wisecrack, Slip slaps Sach with a backhand swipe while he is standing behind him.

Slip and Sach go into a remote controlled plane. Sach keeps reading the manual with each chapter titled: "How to Face Death in the Air," Chapters 6, 7, 9. Sach: "Relax Chief, enjoy it. It's nice and peaceful up here." Then bombers fire ("Chapter 10, Now that you are dead"). Slip calls Sach: "Now what have you done you stupid maniac!" Sach pulls the steering wheel up and out, and he hands it to Slip. Sach retorts: "Stupid maniac, hah? You drive."

As they are plunging down to the ground out of control, Sach jubilantly declares: "I like this." Sach shuts the engine off with the result that they land safely. Slip: "Sometimes I don't know what I'd do without you." Sach: "I know, you'd be working in a garage." Slip: "You'd still be my helper."

They land near where their Lieutenant friend is being held and tortured by the spies. A fight ensues, and Sach directs the activity staying in the background. When he hits the crooks over their heads, he then runs to hide.

Finale: When Sach sits on a needle with truth serum, he screams in pain: "Owl-l-l-l! I'm lucky it wasn't a finishing nail." Sach does his motorlips. Sach: "Sir, I must tell you the truth, it was nothing but dumb, stupid luck. And Slippy old boy, I must tell you the truth, you're nothing but an egotistical, ignorant egomaniac. And that's the truth." Sach grabs Slip by his jacket, shakes him, and hits him over the head with his own air force cap. Slip responds with a shocked look.

This movie is above average in terms of Sach's comedy. Along with *Let's Go Navy!* this stands as one of the Boys best service movies. According to Gary, *Clipped Wings* was also one of his father's favorites. Sach Comedy Meter: 3.0 out of 4.0.

32. Private Eyes

Released December 6, 1953

This is the last film in which Leo Gorcey gets top billing. The first title card reads: "Allied Artists Pictures Corporation presents Leo Gorcey and The Bowery Boys," the second card reads "in Private Eyes," and the third card offers "Featuring Huntz Hall with" the rest of the cast.

The film opens at a Bowery Boy's Club meeting for kids located behind Louie's Sweet Shop. Sach shows Herbie some boxing with fancy footwork, but Herbie knocks out Sach. Sach hears the bell ring, and suddenly he has a special power to know what everyone else is thinking, especially when they are lying.

Slip declares: "Now wired for mental telegraphy." As usual, Slip sees an angle to exploit Sach's newfound talent. Slip asks Louie to give them money to buy a detective business where they can use Sach's ability. Sach: "I'm gonna be the big wheel in this outfit and you're gonna take 70%? And give us 30. Uh uh! Uh uh!"

Slip: "Sach my thought was completely inoculated, as a matter of fact to show what a good sport I am, I'll give you 30% and I'll take 70%." Sach: "That's more like it. You can't fool me anymore. I'm getting smart. Right Butchie. Get that thought out of your mind and you too" (he smacks Butch and hits Chuck). Sach starts to go hit Slip. Slip: "You do and I'll tear your arm out of the socket."

Sach gets barbells stuck over his foot. Slip explains: "He just wanted to know how stupid you can get. With him the possibilities are absolutely unlimited." He manages to pick them up only to fall back into a water cooler, and he gets the water flowing over his face.

At their Eagle Eye Detective Agency, Sach is wearing a deerstalker hat backwards, and file drawers hit him as he closes another one. Slip learns that he was misled by his friend and thought the rent was paid up to date. He puts it to Sach that he should have known. Sach: "What do you expect from my little brain–miracles?"

A desperate beautiful girl who is in trouble rushes into their office as Sach predicts. She says she suspects someone is trying to kill her. After locking up a letter from her, Sach is told by Slip to put the safe's combination in a safe place. Sach locks it in the safe. The girl sees a shadow, and she disappears without her stolen mink coat.

When a police officer comes by and sees the mink, he says: "If I didn't know you guys so well, I'd have to take you in. This is dynamite." Sach: "I thought it was fur." Slip slaps Sach backhandedly. Sach: "Ohp!"

An enraged Slip is ready to hit Sach when he learns what he did with the safe's combination. Slip: "You know what I'm gonna do to you?" Sach stops him saying: "You do and they'd hang you. Ohp! Ohp! Ohp! You might hurt my power."

While Sach is alone in the office, he talks to himself. His elbow is stuck to a dish and he complains about always being picked on. Sach: "If only had a rock or hammer, there must be something around here." He searches the office, finds a gun, and goes to shoot the safe. Sach: "I'll blast you, goodbye safe." It does not work. Sach: "Not making these guns like they used to." He makes a 'Sach bomb' by putting gunpowder in a bottle. He ignites it, and he places it under the safe.

The telephone that was left on top of the safe rings. Sach: "Hello. Hello. What do you want? Oh yes. I'm very busy. I'm very busy. I'm working on an experiment. The what? The Sperry radio survey? What do you want? Yes, I own a radio. My favorite program? Well, a, I have a few of them. I have a *Tony and His Educated Lion*, and a *Orry and his Sister Flo*. Very funny also. *Pete and his Piano*. No. I don't like him, it doesn't do anything for me. *Lou and Luise*. Well now you're talking. Oh they're very comical. They give me a terrific bang." Then the bomb explodes.

The safe was blown open and destroyed. However, Slip laments that the "the explosion flabbergasted his receiving apparatus." In other words, Sach lost his power to read minds. When Sach gets excited that he found the paper with the safe's combination, Slip puts a netted garbage can over his head.

There are times when Sach can be very tough and mean, as here when he smacks Slip and a crook. Sach: "Oh boy, fingerprints." Sach poured a large amount of powder on the arm of a chair. Slip responds by pouring powder in his hand. Sach: "What are you gonna do Chief, take your fingerprints?" Slip: "Yeah! And I'm gonna get a very good depression." Slip blows the powder in Sach's face. Sach: "Ohp! Ohp! Ohp! Ohp! Oh! There goes my private eyes with my dog." Sach washes his face and dries it with the envelope he accidentally finds.

The crooks kidnap Herbie and hold him at a sanitarium. Sach arrives disguised as a stuffy old lady patient, Mrs. Abernathy, and Slip as a heavily accented and bearded Viennese doctor, Dr. Hockenlopper. Slip walks into the walls, and Sach hits a patient over the head. Sach/Mrs. Abernathy complains to the nurse: "I'm a very sick woman." Slip refers to the envelope he gives to Sach. Slip: "If you lose it, I'll break every bone in your head." Sach: "You already done that."

A sanitarium staffer realizes Slip is wearing a fake moustache. In addition, Sach is caught fixing his wig. More importantly, Sach reveals that he is a fake patient, and he foolishly gives the envelope to a supposed insurance agent who is also involved in the fraud.

Sach gets his clairvoyant powers back again after getting hit again. In reference to the agent, Sach reveals: "He's lying." There is a madcap chase for the envelope. Herbie and Sach save the day as they knock out the crooks by clubbing them.

Unlike *Loose in London* and *Clipped Wings*, the heavy reliance on slapstick here, especially at the sanitarium, shows director Edward Bernds finally influencing things. For instance, there is a typical Three Stooges gag here when a wheelchair patient (Emil Sitka) is repeatedly knocked over out of his chair. In addition, Sach frantically runs, saying, "I'll save you Chief!" However, he falls in a mineral bathtub with the crooks.

Finale: The reward money is used for a party held for the Bowery Boys' Club. Slip, referring to the good behavior of the children: "I wonder if this could be permanent?" Sach: "Certainly it's permanent. I tuned them in. No more rough house." Slip: "Well I'm glad to hear that." Immediately a fight erupts among the kids. Slip: "Hey, just a minute, knock it off fellows. It's time for the pie. Just make sure you divide it evenly." Slip and Sach get pies thrown in their faces. Louie laughs. Louie: "They divided it up evenly alright, ha, ha, ha, ha!" Of course, then Louie gets a pie in his face, too!

Private Eyes is a fast-paced film that flows well and has many funny moments. At times, it resembles the madcap and zany comedy of the Stooges. Among the best scenes is the one when Sach is alone making a bomb to blow up the safe. Sach Comedy Meter: 3.8 out of 4.0.

Chapter 9:
Sach's Comedy

1954-1958
Best Films (Highest Score):
Paris Playboys (1954)–4.0/4.0
The Bowery Boys Meet the Monsters (1954)–4.0/4.0
Jungle Gents (1954)–3.0/4.0
Bowery to Bagdad (1955)–4.0/4.0
Spy Chasers (1955)–4.0/4.0
Dig That Uranium (1956)–3.8/4.0
Crashing Las Vegas (1956)–4.0/4.0
Hold That Hypnotist (1957)–3.0/4.0

33. Paris Playboys
Released March 7, 1954

    This is a leap forward for Hall. The credits change here with Leo Gorcey and Huntz Hall now sharing equal billing. The first title card reads: "Allied Artists Pictures Corporation presents Leo Gorcey Huntz Hall and The Bowery Boys," the second card reads "in Paris Playboys," and the third card offers "with" the rest of the cast.

    The story concerns Sach being mistaken for a missing French scientist, Professor Maurice Gaston Le Beau, who invented a secret rocket formula.

Sach plays with a fork and a spoon as he tries to get it in a glass of water. Instead, it goes into Slip's coffee. Slip: "What are you playing golf with Louie's silverware?" Sach puts on a chapeau Louie was wearing and tries to talk French. Just then, several Frenchmen enter to mistake his identity.

Then the old joke, Slip: "Order, order, order." Sach: "I'll have a malted." Slip slaps Sach.

Sach sees his picture in the French newspaper: "Ohp! Ohp! Ohp! Ohp! Ohp! Ohp! That's me, that's me." Louie: "What would Sach be doing in Paris?" Sach: "Are you kidding?" Sach does his motorlips. Slip says Sach does not even know one word of French. Sach: "Are you kidding? I certainly can. I know one word–schlemiel. Ain't that what you always call me in French, Louie?" Louie: "You're a schlemiel in any language."

The Frenchmen agree to pay all expenses for Sach, Slip, and Louie to travel to Paris, besides giving Sach a salary. The rest of the Boys have become literally excess baggage here, so to speak. Besides, they do not really add anything to the movies. They have become extraneous and unnecessary.

The newspaper reports that Sach as Le Beau is believed to be a victim of amnesia, and so Sach flies to Paris to restore his memory. On the plane, Slip reviews with Sach all the people Sach is supposed to know.

Sach-LeBeau is affectionate, kissing all the females. He even kisses a man, and pokes the man's foot with his walking stick.

When Sach makes his tie, he gets his finger stuck: "Oh! Oh! Oh! Oh! Oh!" Slip goes over the names of all the people he supposed to know again. When Slip asks him about Mimi, Sach: "Why that's easy, that's my girl." Sach does his motorlips.

At the dinner table scene, in order to put Sach-LeBeau at ease, the guests agree to follow exactly everything as he does. Therefore, instead of eating the caviar, they crunch the ice cubes that chill the caviar. Sach throws peanuts up in the air and catches them in his mouth, and the guests imitate him.

Sach says they may want him to whip up some rocket juice: "I got it, I'll bluff them, I'll make them think I'm stupid." Slip: "That's the easiest job you ever had in your life." Sach: "Very funny." The conspirators try to find out the formula by hoping to restore Sach's memory. In the lab, Sach creates havoc, sprays foam all over them, and shoots a flame thrower at them.

Sach paints while talking with a French accent. He gets his finger stuck in the palette, and forgets himself screaming and writhing in pain: "Oh! Oh! Oh! Ah! Ah! Ahhh! Ahhh!" Slip helps remove it. Surrounded and followed by a bevy of beautiful women, Louie is also painting, and says to Slip and Sach: "Just call me Tou-Louie Lautrec." As regards the diminutive painter, Slip says to Sach: "I wonder how much it cost to have your legs chopped off? I'll get a price for both of us."

At dinner, the waiter delivers cocktails that percolate with steam. Sach sips some and his hat pops off and he does his motorlips, Slip's bow-tie spins around, and steam comes out of Louie's ears.

Sach reads a murder mystery book in bed. A stranger enters with a butcher's knife and throws it at the headboard, just missing Sach. Slip checks and finds no knife there. The next day Sach is packing. Slip: "I didn't hear you." Sach: "I'm going home." (Sach yells "home," in Slip's ear.) He spells it to Slip: "H.O. U.S.A. Last night was the last time I almost saw Paris, I'm getting out of here." Slip: "That's the way you feel about it, I'll carry your bag for you." Sach does not realize what's coming: "That's my Chief, always thinking of me." Then an angry Slip breaks the bag over Sach's head. Sach takes the bag off unaffected, and says: "Cheap suitcase."

Sach: "I'm gonna sit in Louie's Sweet Shop and have a big fat malted." Slip: "There you go, always thinking of yourself." Just as with Bud Abbott conning Lou Costello, Slip portrays Sach as selfish. Sach: "Well I guess you're right Chief. I'm sorry, I'm nothing but a lowdown, thinking of saving my own life. I'm sorry."

Louie asks where is the real Professor LeBeau. Sach: "I don't know where he is, but if I know him, I know what he's doing." Sach does his motorlips, which always indicates he is thinking amorous thoughts of women. Then we cut to see the real LeBeau on an island with females catering to him. When he finds out his girlfriend is with Sach after noticing the story in a two-month old newspaper, he gets jealous enough to head back to Paris.

A "Sach alone" scene has him in LeBeau's laboratory mixing up some liquid food in a beaker for unseen fleas in a tray; namely, "Napoleon and Josephine." Sach: "Go ahead, go ahead Josephine, Josephine let Napoleon get some, go ahead Napoleon, go ahead, take some of that. Make you the strongest flea in the world." The flea roars, frightening Sach. "Ahhhh! Down Napoleon, down. I didn't know it was that potent."

LeBeau arrives angry and throws Louie out, asking: "What's that crazy foreigner doing in my house?" It is a superb transition for Hall to switch from one persona to the near opposite. LeBeau is upset when he sees the painting, and he goes to fix it. Mimi arrives, LeBeau is affectionate, and Mimi is happy he is well again and they plan to take a honeymoon.

A comedy of confusion ensues as the separate appearances of Sach and LeBeau perplex all. Slip wants to duel. LeBeau smacks Slip over his head repeatedly with Slip's hat demanding: "Get out of my house!" Both Louie and Slip say: "Sach is going nuts." Louie says: "A doctor wouldn't do any good. He's gone completely meshuga." Slip: "Then I'll get a meshuga doctor."

Sach confounds them, and he denies chasing Louie and hitting Slip. They walk away saying they are getting a doctor. Sach: "Get two doctors, one for each of you. (To himself) These guys are idiots. I thought I was an idiot."

Sach is alone looking in a mirror. He picks up an object. Sach exclaims: "Such long nail files." He is referring to swords on both sides of the mirror. Sach and LeBeau confront each other as Sach sees LeBeau in the mirror instead of himself. Sach fixes his tie. LeBeau calls Sach: "An imposter... trying to steal my Mimi!" Slip uses a sword to fight LeBeau. Sach looks on as usual, "Thata boy Chief, Stick him." Slip finally does several double takes when he sees the real Professor LeBeau and Sach together.

The conspirators arrive to force Sach to the lab to write down and mix the formula for them. Sach mixes up chemicals, blows off foam, and then pours it into the rocket. Just then, the real LeBeau is brought into the lab under gunpoint saying he is the real Professor. Sach lights the rocket as the conspirators realize Sach is not LeBeau. The mini rocket flies around the room and crashes into the wall. It causes an explosion that disorients the conspirators. Slip: "Hey, it worked." Sach: "Oop! That sour cream will do it every time."

Finale: Sach receives a medal of commendation. The real LeBeau is upset because Sach ("this imbecile") used sour cream in the formula and it worked. LeBeau apparently had spent 10 years and did not come up with the right ingredient. Sach tells the awards presenter: "And I have something for you." Presenter: "*Qu' est-que ce?* What is it?" Sach: "An electric razor. You plug it in.... Brrrrrrrrrr-ouuuuuu (Sach makes believe he's shaving presenter's beard off) thirty years younger, have a ball." They laugh and Sach hugs both cheeks of the presenter's face.

Paris Playboys is great fun as Hall is in top form as Sach. This is one of his best motion pictures! Sach Comedy Meter: 4.0 out of 4.0.

34. The Bowery Boys Meet the Monsters
Released June 6, 1954

As starting with the last film, the credits show Leo Gorcey and Huntz Hall with equal billing from now on. The first title card reads: "Allied Artists Pictures Corporation presents Leo Gorcey Huntz Hall," the second card reads "The Bowery Boys Meet the Monsters," and the third card offers "with" the rest of the cast.

This film opens with Louie's Sweet Shop window being broken by a kid. Sach, wearing a black shirt, says: "Can't trust those midgets." Sach suggests giving them a playground. Sach: "The lot next to Acme Warehouse." Slip calls the owners after Louie's suggestion to contact them.

Slip talks to Derek Gravesend on the phone. Derek tells his brother Anton: "Anyone who can mangle the English language…no mental giant…just what we're looking for." Derek suggests a human head for Anton's robot named Gorog. In addition, Derek wants his ape to have a human brain with an ideal potential measuring between +5 to +7, and no more.

The remark is made that someone with such a low potential would not even come out of the rain. Then we see Sach outside the mansion getting soaked as he stands away from the awning. Slip yells at him to come up next to the door. Sach manages to get his arm stuck in the doorknocker when the butler opens the door.

Grissom: "In the library, if you please gentlemen." Sach: "Just my luck, I haven't got my library card with me." Slip pushes him. Sach: "Don't get physical."

Amelia Gravesend makes a sweater for her nephew. Sach asks: "Aren't the sleeves a little short?" Amelia: "The sleeves, these are the sleeves, you silly." Sach accepts her explanation with his many 'Oh's': "Oh! Oh! Oh! Oh! Oh! Oh! Oh! Oh!"

Francine, the femme fatale vampire niece, is hungry for men, and so she tries to get friendly with Sach. She caresses and touches his neck and suit. Francine: "A lovely suit, so becoming to you." Sach: "And very expensive. Imported Bowery burlap, it came with two pairs of pants." However, this time Sach does not offer his usual motorlips shtick.

Derek and Anton distract him with food. Then we get Sach's view about pickles. Sach: "Oh I'm crazy about pickles, but ain't they ugly? I got an idea about how to make them prettier. Certainly, you see when you're about to plant the seeds, you turn them inside out. Yeah, instead of having warts they'd have dimples."

Sach thinks the headpiece of a brain potential apparatus is a space helmet. "I feel like a space cadet...." Sach makes a whoosh sound. Sach's brain potential measures +6. This is perfect for the brain transfer, so Derek decides to keep them overnight by telling them he needs to consult his lawyer about giving them the land.

Here even Slip sometimes misunderstands language, just as Sach does. When Grissom tells him, "Take this chair, 1775," Slip thinks he is referring to the price. Slip: "Anyone who paid over three bucks got rooked." Sach also has his usual problem: "Oop, get a load of this crazy corn popper." Grissom: "I'm begging your pardon sir, it's a bed warmer." Sach: "How can a bed fit in this thing?"

Slip has been calling Grissom, "Gruesome." Grissom corrects him. When Sach says: "Goodnight, Grissom." Grissom gets mixed up and corrects Sach saying: "It's Gruesome, sir."

Anton tests a potion on Grissom, and he turns into a longhaired monster, and then quickly turns back to normal. Derek tells Anton to destroy that potion and concentrate on experiments with the robot. Anton puts the bottle on the shelf.

Sach lies in bed reading *Murders in the Rue Morgue*. The old jokes are offered. For instance, Slip: "How can you read in the dark?" Sach: "I went to night school." Sach is left alone, and he picks up a skull on the night table, "I wonder what time it is? Two o'clock." He puts the skull back down, and after a moment he realizes it's not the clock and screams.

He darts across the room and opens the closet door to reveal a skeleton. He finds he is attached to it. When he breaks free, and opens the door, Grissom acknowledges: "Oh! So you found our skeleton in the closet? I'll take it away. Relax Mr. Jones. Relax. Relax. Relax. I leave you with this parting thought: the living of today are the skeletons of tomorrow."

Upon hearing someone at the door, Sach opens it, and in enters the Robot. Sach asks: "Chief, where did you get those crazy pajamas? I always knew you were a square. You look like a walking television set. I think I'll get Kukla, Fran & Ollie." Sach goes to touch the dials, realizes it's not Slip, and starts screaming. The robot drags Sach, but the radio control is used to call the robot back, so Sach is left on the floor. With another knock on the door, Sach opens the door: "Come in monster," Sach hits Slip over his head by mistake.

The next day Slip asks Anton about getting the lot. Slip: "Look fatso." Sach: "Fatso? Look who's talking." Slip backhandedly slaps Sach. Anton: "We just want your heads." Derek enters and reiterates: "We need your heads in the interest of science."

Derek aims a gun. Slip: "If that old thunder-buster will shoot, I'll eat my hat." The gun fires. Sach: "Start chewing, would you like some ketchup?" Slip slaps Sach with his hat.

Slip and Sach are locked in the closet. Sach knocks on the wall and operating tools fall on Slip's head. He does not slap Sach in retaliation, as one would expect.

While Slip is sawing the wall, the ape is grunting but Slip thinks it is Sach making funny noises. Sach offers his hand to help, but Slip smacks it. Sach: "Ooo! Ooo! Ooo! You'll break my piano hand." Sach goes through the hole in the wall, and he comes face to face with the ape. Sach is terrified and he comes back in the room with Slip.

Sach goes back through the hole and the ape holds Sach against the wall. Slip enters the room not noticing the ape. Slip: "What are you standing there for?" Sach: "Say hello to your uncle." Slip: "Where did you get the fur piece?" Slip realizes it is the ape and screams in terror.

Sach is being led to Derek's lab, while Slip is being put on an operating table. Derek reassures: "Don't worry Mr. Jones, I have something particularly interesting arranged for you. Into my laboratory, if you please." Sach: "Is it animal, vegetable or, monster?" Derek insists: "Into my laboratory." Sach realizes: "It's monster." Derek wants to transfer Sach's brain into the ape. However, the ape is armed with a knife, and he frees Slip from being strapped on the operating table. Then Slip, using the radio controls, directs the robot to hit and chase the ape.

Sach is on the operating table under Francine's watchful eyes. She removes his strap, and says she will help him. Sach: "Oh you're so sweet to me. Someday I'm gonna do something nice for you." Francine: "Oh you will–sooner than you think." She rubs his neck and cheek. Sach does his motorlips. Sach is freed. The robot chases after Sach one way, and the ape comes at him the opposite way. Sach sits down in front of the man-eating plant, which grabs him and tries to eat him.

Then Anton and Derek pull at Sach from opposite ends since each want him for their own use. Slip tells Sach to throw him the microphone. Slip calls the robot with the mike, and he gets him to squeeze Anton and Derek's heads together. Sach gets the microphone, and starts directing the robot to kill them. Slip calls Sach: "That maniac with the microphone." Anton stops the robot by breaking up the equipment.

Anton, Derrick, and Grissom grab Sach. The bottle with the bad formula falls off the shelf and splashes on Sach. He drinks some of it, and he turns into the hairy monster. Sach starts hitting Slip as Slip thinks it is a mask. Then, while choking Slip, Sach returns to normal. Sach was wearing Slip's hat, which Slip demands back. After the escapades at the mansion, Slip gets the agreement signed to give the kids the lot.

Finale: Louie's Sweet Shop is in a shambles as the Boys return with the kids. Louie holds balls that damaged his store window. They are home runs hit by the robot Gorog, the big star of the kid's baseball team. With the robot standing behind them, Slip says: "We gotta figure out a way to put this iron numbskull to some better use." Sach: "You're right Chief, we gotta figure out a way how to put this bunch of junk to work. Let's put our heads together." Then the robot bangs their heads together repeatedly.

The Bowery Boys Meet the Monsters is a fast moving movie which offers Sach and Slip many crazy comic moments, especially as they try to constantly get away from the "monsters" in the Gravesend mansion. This is another one of the best of the *Bowery Boys* productions. Sach Comedy Meter: 4.0 out 4.0.

35. Jungle Gents

Released September 5, 1954

With the last film, the pattern has been established that Leo Gorcey and Huntz Hall now share equal billing.

The movie opens with a police car chasing a robber who hides diamonds in the windowsill of Louie's Sweet Shop. Sach can smell diamonds since he has taken powerful new antibiotic pills (50,000 micrograms) for a sinus infection. Slip calls it "a sinus infatuation."

A police officer asks the robber what he did with the diamonds. Sach interrupts: "You're fibbing, I can smell diamonds as plain as anything." Sach finds them and he is taken to the police station for questioning, but he insists that he located them by smelling them.

The owner of the jewels says that they should go to Africa with Sach, saying: "You'll never have to work again." Sach: "What do you mean again?" Slip slaps Sach.

Indeed, they go off to Africa. With Slip narrating, Sach has a bug sprayer and wears a cap with a veil to fight off the mosquitoes. When we hear a large splash, Sach comments: "That was a large one."

Sach is given a map to guard. A chimp walks in wearing Slip's hat and kisses Sach. Sach: "Chief I didn't know you cared....Chief, you look good. Africa did something for you, well." Then a terrified Sach realizes: "You're not the Chief, you're a killer ape."

Slip tells Sach to pitch camp. Sach: "How can you throw a camp around?" Slip: "It does not happen to mean to throw a camp around." Slip struggles to explain. Slip: "Why do you always gotta ask me those silly questions for?" Sach: "So I can hear your silly answers."

Sach is alone, camping out. Sach: "Boy this is the life.... Nothing greater than lighting a fire the hard way rubbing two stones together." When he has difficulty doing that, Sach relents: "Nothing like lighting a fire the easy way with kitchen matches." Sach accidentally burns the map. Sach: "If the Chief finds out... I won't have to worry about the lion, cause the Chief'll kill me."

Sach is asked to read the map by another member of the expedition. He rips the page, 'A Perfect Fittin' Girdle" ad from *Greer's Mail Order Catalog*. He fakes that it is the map. Sach, intentionally misleading that it's about the road topography, says: "Curves, you can say that again, curves, lots of curves...the big bulge around equator, wow, what a bulge, sure is a tight squeeze."

Again, Sach does not pay attention to things that happen. For instance, when a lion comes by and touches him, he thinks it's Slip.

Slip: "You don't know nutin,' (emphasizing) n-u-t-i-n and I should have stopped at n-u-t, because that's you!" Slip finds out that Sach, who he calls "Professional Nose," used an "ad for lady's griddles."

This movie offers us a glimpse of a more serious Sach who knows of his own stupidity. He realizes that he destroyed the map, and he is afraid to say something. The audience is let in on this. Sach says nothing about it, and we know it's gonna come out eventually.

Sach agonizes over it, he tries to do everything to cover-up, substituting the ad, and for first time he is afraid to tell Slip the truth. He truly feels bad about something he has done wrong. He seems different than what you would expect of his character. Sach offers a dramatic sadness, and he is prepared to take a gun and kill himself.

Sach: "Slip, give my brain to science." Slip: "They'll give it right back to you." Sach: "You'll be sorry for that remark."

Slip encourages Sach to use the gun. Louie: "Slip, the gun is loaded." Slip: "I'm glad, relax Louie, he hasn't the nerve to shoot a fly." A shot is fired, and Slip starts crying. Sach returns: "I missed." Slip: "You missed, but I won't."

Self-absorbed Sach, in trying to commit suicide, seems out of character. Sach is so much in his own fantasy world, and he is not usually concerned about what others think about him. The usually upbeat Sach tries to be smart in his own way, and he wants to be part of the world and be remembered.

Sach's suicidal pouting seems unnatural: "I don't care what happens to me." His tune changes as soon as he sees the lion: "I didn't mean it, I didn't mean it, I take it back Mr. Lion. . . . Oh Mr. Lion I was just making conversation. Some of my best friends are lions."

A jungle girl arrives to kill the lion by stabbing him multiple times. Sach: "Honey you were great. If I ever run across another lion, I'll get in touch with you. And you're beautiful too. . . . What's your name?" She tells him "Anatta," and she rubs his face. Sach does his motorlips. Sach: "Oh you wanna kiss. I don't go around kissing girls." Anatta kisses him. Anatta insists: "Kiss, kiss, kiss." Initially Sach is upset that she kisses him.

Sach cooks for Slip, "Clam Chowder à la Sach." A clam bites Sach's nose and he howls in pain, ruining the whole dinner. The natives capture them. The Boys try to destroy Sach's diamond-smelling ability by giving him a cold so he will not be valuable to the natives. A witch doctor tries to heal him. Sach, with a hoarseness that makes him sound like Jimmy Durante, asks the dancing witch doctor: "Where did you take your internship, at the Savoy Ballroom? Hey Witchey, I know a lot of doctors in New York who can't dance a step. It's a wonder they got their diplomas.... Hey Doc, you mind if I lead?" Sach is at his funniest here when he joins in with the witch doctor's dancing, even suggesting some steps.

Then Sach dresses up as a witchdoctor to help escape captivity. The Boys grab him when he enters, and Slip is surprised to see it is Sach. The cold is cured. Sach explains: "He mumbled me out of it.... And then he did the shuffle off to Buffalo and I'm cured." Slip tells him to say the magic words so the natives will bury their heads in the sand. Sach: "... Let me see now, wada wada fu fu, they bend down. Wada wada fi fi, they bend up." Slip: "Just don't fi fi when you supposed to fu fu or I'll give you a witty on your watty."

To Slip's consternation and annoyance, all Anatta wants to do with Sach is "kiss, kiss, kiss." Sach: "She doesn't know any more English. That's as far as we got." Slip: "That's far enough."

In searching in a cave for diamonds, Slip and Sach run into each other hitting Sach's nose. This is not the reason why Sach has trouble smelling for diamonds. Actually, it is because he left the pills that gave him the diamond-smelling power in the witch doctor's robe.

A faceless and masked giant in a cave scares Louie and Sach. Then

Sach accidentally comes across the diamonds when he pulls a lever and they flow from a wall shoot.

Throughout the movie, Slip calls Sach different names, including "Jungle Romeo," "Banana Nose," and "Manic Depressive."

The thieves arrive with guns aimed at the Boys as the giant comes back. They shoot the head off the giant, and a fight ensues. As usual, Sach directs them in how to fight: "Get him. Get him. Be brave Louie. Get him." The giant is unmasked to be Trader Holmes, who saved the Boys by scaring off the diamond hunters.

Sach to Slip: "Take care of my diamonds, I got an appointment." Slip: "Where are you going?" Sach: "Kiss, kiss, kiss, kiss, kiss." Then Sach does his motorlips. Sach decides he will stay in Africa with Anatta. That is until Tarzan appears, pounding his chest and roaring. Sach: "Chief, save me, save me." Sach gets on board the ship and blows kisses: "Goodbye Anatta, kiss, kiss, kiss."

Finale: Slip narrates: "As the ship slowly steamed into the setting sun, the natives on the shore smilingly waved goodbye." The natives actually are waving them to get out of there. Slip concludes: "Yes sir, they really loved us in Africa." Slip puts his hat on smiling, and winks at us.

The over-used jungle setting in movies from that era is not one of my favorites to find Slip and Sach, but somehow Hall in any situation still manages to be funny. Nevertheless, there are plenty of laughs throughout this film, especially in the first half of the story. Surprisingly, the focus does not stay on Sach's newfound ability of smelling diamonds. However, this seems to be one of the weakest of the *Bowery Boys* productions made by the collaborative writing efforts of Ullman and Bernds and/or directed by Bernds.

Unfortunately, *Jungle Gents* is diminished somewhat by a number of inconsistencies. Just to name three of them, first off, who pays for this big trip? Secondly, there is the incongruity of mixing stock footage of African wildlife (Sach calls a giraffe "a tall peeping tom") in open fields intercut with the Boys cutting through a swath of heavy jungle brush. Thirdly, there is an obvious fake lion head, which is intercut with a real lion. These incongruities are jarring and diminish the movie's enjoyment. Sach Comedy Meter: 3.0 out of 4.0.

36. Bowery To Bagdad

Released January 2, 1955

The film opens with a Biblical-tone narration of the story of the stolen Aladdin's Lamp that came to be found in "Bagdad by the Hudson," New York City. Sach purchased it for Louie's birthday at a hockshop for two bits (a quarter).

When two thugs harass Louie to sell his store, Sach briefly attempts to scare them by meanly ordering them: "Get going!" However, when he realizes one of them is a big guy, Sach softens his approach.

Sach cleans the lamp. He wishes that he were strong to help Louie. Sach: "Sure getting tired of being pushed around. Everything I do is wrong." The genie appears, and the thugs observe this. Sach asks: "Are you any relation to Jeanie with the light brown hair?" Sach wishes for six giant malteds. Sach: "You make them better than Louie."

Sach's next wish is for big muscles: "[I want to be] big and strong and not afraid of anything so I can take care of those guys that are pushing Louie around... give me muscles, big fat muscles." His wish is granted. He twists a crowbar, growling "Slip Mahoney." He now can pull a door off its hinges, and he calls himself "a human house wrecker."

Two groups (the crooks and a pair of Arab men) are in pursuit of the lamp. The crooks are not hard-boiled–they are more comedic. The leader of the crooks keeps being hit on the head. Slip is derogatory as he labels the Arabs as crooks. His unfortunate stereotyping leads him to call them "those crooks with the towels on their heads."

Slip does not believe Sach that he has a magic lamp and that he is "having hallukinations." Then he rubs the lamp, and he realizes that it works. The genie agrees to fulfill a wish only when Slip are Sach are together. Slip calls Sach many insults, including "Monkey," "Mousy," and "Imbecilic Idiot."

Reminiscent of a scene from the Three Stooges, Sach mixes up the coffee with a non-edible for Slip. Sach: "Black coffee, naturally whoever heard of white coffee?" Instead, he mixes it up with the cup of black paint and turpentine that Louie was using to decorate his shop. Slip is enraged, and he throws the cream pie at him. Sach ducks and a gun moll, pretending to be a Southern belle, is hit instead. Slip: "Say you're sorry you ducked, stupid." Sach: "I'm sorry I ducked stupid." Slip hits Sach with a backhanded slap.

The moll tells Sach she's lonesome, and asks him to take her out. Sach is sweet on her, but Slip is suspicious and tells her he will have to chaperone him. Sach: "I don't need no chaperone." Slip removes his hat implying he will hit him. Sach smilingly agrees: "Ohp! Yes I do. I can't be trusted." Sach allows Slip to go along with him to the moll's penthouse.

Sach wears his upturned black cap at Louie's Sweet Shop, but when he goes to the gun moll's pad, he dresses up with a jacket and tie. At the penthouse, Sach asks Slip: "What's the matter with you, can't you see she wants to be alone, with me?" Then Sach looks at her and does his motorlips.

One of the best scenes is when Sach mambos with the moll. He seems well coordinated with good footwork, but then he pulls a curtain and he is tangled in it. When asked if he's alright, Sach resumes dancing: "Oh certainly. I can dance this way all day long, and then go to the hospital."

Sach's flamboyant and zany nature tends to enjoy the moment and go along with things that are happening. He never seems to have intuitions or sense danger lurking. When the moll holds Sach at gunpoint, Sach reaches out his hand: "How about another dance? I'll hold your gun." Moll: "Shut up." Sach: "I like you so much with your southern accent." Moll: "Well then shut up, you'all." Sach: "Well, that's the way you feel about it, hominy grits and black-eyed peas to you–you'all." The moll complains that Sach's moving around bothers her, and he expresses his nervousness by talking-back to her. Of course, the Boys and Louie have to rescue Sach from this situation.

The genie goes off to get drunk. Sach: "Oh he's gonna blame me. And I get drunk on rye bread."

When the Arabs run in with a knife directed at Sach, he responds: "Oh! Oh! Oh! Oh! Oh! Oh! That knife tickles. Why don't you use it where you need it the most?" Sach touches one of their beards. He then reveals the hiding spot of the lamp to the Arabs talking to the moll.

When a fight ensues between the crooks and the Arabs, Sach predictably moves away from the action, offering "Go ahead. Fight 'em with footwork." A punch makes the lamp pop into his hands, and he calls on the genie to help save him. Instead, the genie offers Sach an ancient Babylonian stratagem: "Scram!"

Sach hides in the closet so as to evade the crooks as he proclaims to himself: "What a mind, what a mind. I amaze myself." As he looks at the coats surrounding him, he makes a joke. Sach: "Boy I can have a ball in here if I was a moth–a moth ball." He laughs heartily.

Sach, left to his own devices, gets a top hat stuck on his head over his face and he goes out on a balcony high above the street not seeing the danger he is in. Slip comes to his aid. Slip helps remove the hat. Sach does not realize he is on the ledge. Sach declares: "Boy, fresh air. There's nothing like fresh air. Hey Chief, there's Venus and Mars, hello Mars. Oh!

I have had enough of this outside air, I'm going inside." However, as soon as he looks down and sees his perilous location, he screams in terror.

Even when in danger, Sach does not grasp his own situation. It is not always relevant to him. He tries to reduce the seriousness of the reality, and maybe he is being humorous for that reason. For instance, while Slip is holding onto Sach who is hanging over the ledge, Sach comments: "Hey Chief, look, a guy just went through a red light. HEY YOU SUNDAY DRIVER, THAT'S DANGEROUS!"

Slip calls on the genie: "Get us out of here, that's an order!" They are brought back to Bagdad, to the genie's home. The girls in the harem surround Sach and Slip. The magic lamp gets back to its rightful owner, but the genie does not know who to listen to. Slip agrees to give back the genie, if they could just be sent back to where they came from. The genie takes their wish literally, and they are back on the window ledge high above the street as the crooks shoot at them.

Finale: Slip and Sach are in Louie's Sweet Shop. The genie returns and gives them one more wish. Slip refuses Sach's desire to suggest a wish, telling him to stay out of it. Slip: "And I don't want you to goof this up, you meandering maniac." Sach: "Meandering maniac. Insults, insults, always insults. I wish I had the nerve to sock him in the chin." The wish is granted, and he knocks Slip out.

Sach: "Ooh boy, I did it! Oh I blew the last wish, I really did it!" Genie: "Yes, you certainly did!" Sach: "Genie, genie, where are you? Don't leave me now, I need protection. I just socked the Chief. Look at that poor helpless Chief. When he wakes up it's gonna be poor helpless me. I'm getting out of here!" Louie: "Sach, Sach where you going?" Sach: "Louie, if anyone wants me, I'm at Bagdad 8-243. Dancing girls here I come!"

Simply stated, *Bowery to Bagdad* is another one of Hall's best motion pictures. Sach Comedy Meter: 4.0 out of 4.0.

37. High Society

Released April 17, 1955

The Boys run a business at the Bowery Garage. Now the sign spells it with only one "R" in "Terence," Terence Aloysius Mahoney is General Manager, General Superintendent, General Treasurer and Horace Debussy Jones is General Help.

Sach supposedly is working under a car; however, Slip discovers the fake legs. Slip exclaims: "Goldbricking again." Slip tests the car, and it does not start. Actually, Sach is sleeping inside the car's motor. Sach does not respond to Slip screaming his name at the top of his lungs. Slip: "Get my baseball bat." Sach then wakes up. Sach: "Did I hear baseball? I'm a good catcher."

Sach drives the car backwards for he thinks "R" means right straight-ahead and he crashes it. Slip chases Sach out, and telling him not to show his ugly face. Sach bangs the tools down, and takes a sledgehammer and starts beating the damaged car. Just then the owner, Mr. Jones, walks in and sees Sach destroying his car.

The owner, in demanding to see the manager, leads Slip to don a disguise as the manager with a long Hasidic beard. Disrespectfully, Sach pulls the beard off right away, saying: "I wish to have my beard back, it cost me eighty-six box tops."

Mr. Jones recognizes the Jones name, and says he may have important news for him, which he will tell him in a day or two. Then Mr. Jones plots to pass off Sach as a relative who disappeared 20 years ago in order that Sach will get the fortune under his guardianship. This wild scheme then would entail charming the fortune away from Sach. It has to work because Mr. Jones flittered away his share of the fortune.

Back at the garage, Sach accidentally hoses down Mr. Jones. He realizes his mistake: "Ohp! Ohp!" Sach is told he is the blueblood grandson of the big financier Terwilliger Jones. Sach arrives dressed as Buster Brown/Little Lord Fauntleroy as Slip bought the clothes. Sach gives Terwilliger Jones III, nicknamed "Twig," a boxing lesson only to be knocked out by the kid.

Sach comes to dinner wearing a crazy striped suit. Twig asks if he prefers a cold plate. Sach: "I don't know, I never tried one. But I'm game. I'll do anything." He proceeds to chew the plate.

At a performance, a Liberace-like pianist plays an arrangement of "As the Dove Flies Softly." Sach asks: "This is a dove flying softly? It sounds more like an octopus dying madly. That guy can't play." Woman: "Do you play the piano?" Sach: "I don't know I haven't tried yet."

The performance begins as Twig takes his box of trained fleas and puts two up inside Sach's shorts. Then Twig accidentally drops the box releasing all the fleas. Sach is twisting and turning in the chair and going nuts scratching. Slip admonishes him: "I told you to change those socks....You're not paying attention." Quickly everyone is scratching madly. Sach is heard saying: "Ohp!" Then the pianist goes to accuse Sach, and he is scratching away too. This is a well-done scene, choreographed to perfection.

When Sach says he is homesick, tired of high society, and just wants peace of mind, Slip tells him: "You always think of yourself!"

Slip compliments himself: "I'm still in pretty good shape." Sach wisecracks: "So is a blimp." Slip makes a move that he wants to hit Sach for the remark, but he does not. Slip: "I only got one word for you: traitor, rat, spy, double-crosser." Sach misunderstands Slip's labels: "Stop building me up already. I don't want to hear anymore about it. Look, all of a sudden I get money, I lose all my friends. Money, money, wealth, wealth, it's a curse, especially if you don't have it."

Slip and Sach are sneakily searching for the birth certificate records that were obtained to connect Sach to the wealthy family. Sach pokes around alone on one side of the den. This is another example of how in the moment Sach is. One second he is on a mission searching for something, until a distraction comes along. A second later, he's forgetting himself and making noise. In this case it's turning a knob on and discovering a cabinet with a blaring television set.

The scene starts as he looks for his birth certificate behind framed wall pictures. Sach: "Not there. Not there. Not there. Oh father of our country, well. Ohp! There it is, a safe. Jimmy Valentine, get out of town. Wish I had some sandpaper, (examines his fingers) sharp enough anyway." He turns the knob and a television set goes on. A woman is loudly screaming as we see a couple fighting.

Sach opens the television cabinet fully. Sach: "Oh! tel-e-vision, oh I love it. I love it." Sach sits down. Sach: "Get your hands off her you villain. Why don't you pick on someone your own size." Slip: "Do you mind turning that thing off?" Sach: "Just a moment Chief." Sach: "Oh! Oh! Oh! Hopalong Skippity, my favorite cowboy and his horse Snicker." He laughs.

Slip: "I said TURN IT OFF!" Sach: "Okay, okay, okay." Sach turns the dial to see a flying bomber. Sach: "Captain Do Good." Sach laughs. Sach: "He screams." Slip walks over and slaps him over his head. Slip: (mockingly) "He screams, I TOLD YOU TO TURN IT OFF." Slip turns it off. Slip: "We're gonna take care of you later, it's lucky for you we gotta beat it, we'd have the whole house down here in a minute." Sach: "Goodbye, Captain Do Good."

They find the birth certificate, which differs from Sach's ancestry, so he is not the heir. Louie: "Well, in the first place, Sach's father wasn't named 'Pierpont,' it was 'Pete.' And in the second place, his mother name wasn't Gwendolyn, it was 'Gertie.'" However, Twig wants them to stay to get the goods on his conniving Uncle Stuyvesant.

One of Sach's admirable traits, though short-lived, is that he can be very strong-willed, as he puts up a fight to get his way. For instance, when Sach packs up to go home, he is insistent in his conviction. Slip hounds him with criticism. Slip: "In words of one syllable. You're a coward." Sach: "Oh! You gotta admit Chief, cowards live a lot longer." Louie: "I just can't believe that my boy Sachela's got a yellow streak." Sach: "Yellow. Louie, that's my favorite color." Slip: "All the time I thought we was blood brothers." Sach: "That's what I'm afraid of –the blood. Goodbye Chief."

Sach goes to shake Slip's hand, but Slip slaps Sach's hands. Slip: "Just remember, that only a rat deserves a sinking ship." Sach: "And just remember, only a stupid rat stays on one. I'm tired of this sob stuff. Going once, going twice, going three times." Sach walks out the door. Then he comes back in. Sach: "GONE!" Sach walks out again, slamming the door.

The niece, aware of the Uncle's swindle, asks: "You're not afraid of me?" Sach: "No, I'm afraid of me." She flatters him. Then, "Horace, tell me, do you believe in love at first sight?" Sach: "I certainly do. I'll never forget the first time I saw a hamburger with everything on it. Ahhhh!"

The niece amorously moves in on him, as Sach resists. Niece: "What can I say, I love you" Sach: "I hate you." Niece: "What?" Sach: "Oh I don't mean I hate you. I mean I can say I hate you just as well as I say I love you." Niece: "Horace, you said it." Sach: "What did I say? What did I say? What? What? What?" She passionately kisses him. Of course, Sach responds with prolonged motorlips. Sach stops for some air: "Nothing like this on the Bowery."

When Sach goes to initiate more kissing, she rebuffs him. Sach: "You're so fickle. Well, honey blossom, if you ever want another word with me. My number is Plaza-72956-02742-47255-87256." He walks out and shuts the door and then walks in again. Sach: "69." He then leaves and slams the door.

Slip realizes Sach has been kissing from the lipstick showing. Slip: "I don't want to sound pharmaceutical, but you're bleeding. There's only one girl in this house and she's a third-rate Jezebel." Sach shows that he can be very naïve at times. He tells Slip of his belief in the niece's love. Slip: "Didn't you know she was in with the crooks?" Sach: "Oh you're nuts, she's too beautiful."

As we have seen, Sach has the habit of taking insults or criticisms as compliments. Slip uses those moments to go further. For instance, when Twig enters the room: "Cousin Horace, your lipstick is on crooked." Sach: "Well, thank you." Slip: "If you look a little closer, you'll see that his head is on crooked too." Sach here knows he has been insulted as he briefly scowls at Slip. Sach: "What are you sore about, call Cleopatra and the four of us will go out together." With this wisecrack, Slip slaps Sach. Sach: "Ohp! Jealous."

Sach realizes the lawyer is part of the scheme too when the latter points a gun at him. He refers to him as "Super-Chief" because of the gun. Sach's ingenuity in avoiding something is apparent here as he delays the signing of the papers regarding the fortune by using various means, including splashing the pen's ink, and insisting he has to read it between the lines.

Oftentimes, Sach does dumb things after he did something smart. He stupidly throws the gun that Slip just grabbed out the window. Sach: "Oh! Ohp! Ohp! Ohp!" Then Sach sends a toy train across the floor, causing another gun to be dropped. Sach throws that gun out the window too, and then he uses a bow and arrow to shoot rubber darts. Slip is hit. Slip: "Next time call your shots William Tell." Sach: "Well I could have done better if you put an apple on your head."

Slip: "Hey Twig, where's the idiot?" Sach enters the room. Sach: "Somebody call me?"

Sach angers Slip when he takes the credit. Sach: "Guess I cleared up this situation." Slip chases him with a sword: "Come back for one second. I wanna take one slice out. A little stab." Sach: "Alright so you helped me." Slip continues to chase after Sach. Slip: "Well, that's different. Congratulations, come back. I don't wanna belt you. I just wanna raise your arm in victory. Congratulations." Sach shakes Slip's hand. Sach: "Congratulations." Slip slaps Sach over the head with his hat. Sach: "Uh, you sneak."

Finale: The sign at the garage says, "Aristocratic Bowery Garage, We cater to the 400 and cash customers…" It's the same as before for Slip, but Sach now is "General in charge of Bolts and Nuts." Sach is wearing a top hat, and he is using a magnifier. Sach: "What does this wrench doing with grease on it? Take this out and have it dry cleaned immediately." As at the beginning of this movie, Sach is ready to drive Twig's car out of the garage. This time Slip insists on doing it, and he crashes the car driving in reverse. Sach: "How stupid can one man be?" Slip: "When am I ever gonna ever learn to keep my big mouth shut?"

The flea-scratching scene in *High Society* is one of the funniest moments. There are humorous lines sprinkled throughout, including some vaudevillian lines. In addition, Sach does an impression of James Cagney but Slip calls him Bogie, and Slip does an impression of Edward G. Robinson. Sach Comedy Meter: 2.8 out of 4.0.

38. Spy Chasers

Released July 31, 1955

The music over the credits is a bit slower version of "The Gang's All Here," with some extra flourishes.

A girl (Princess from Truania) is following Sach down the street into Louie's Sweet Shop. Sach goes to sit down when Slip was talking to the

Sach's Comedy

Princess. Slip to Sach: "Not you, noodle face." Her father was dethroned. Sach responds: "Send him to the U.N. Yeah. He'll collect U. N. Employment Insurance." She explains: "General Dumbrowksi (Louie's brother) is in charge of the underground forces." Sach: "Underground? What's he building sewers?" Slip backhandedly slaps Sach. Sach screams in pain: "Ouuu!" Sach backhandedly slaps Slip repeatedly saying: "Stop it, stop it."

At the Consul General's office, Louie advises Sach: "Sachela, please whatever you do, watch your manners. Don't disgrace us in front of the King, you got it straight?" Sach: "Oh Louie, what are you worried about? You don't have to tell me anything more than five or six times." Sach is introduced to Lady Zelda, lady in waiting. Sach: "If she's waiting for me, I'm ready." Sach does his motorlips.

Sach sits in the King's chair, and grabs a metallic fruit bowl for a crown on his head. Sach: "Boy I feel just like a King. Bring on the dancing girls. Get me a thousand slaves, and give them all fans because I'm really warm. I'll be a great King. I'll treat my subjects equally. I'll be mean to every one of them." Slip: "If you pardon me, I'll endeavor to curtail my friend's maniacal outbursts." Slip hits Sach with a metal shovel and tells him to "get that silly-looking crown off."

Lady Zelda tells Sach: "I'm so weak and so helpless. I can't tell you what it means to have a strong, dominant man at my side." Sach looks around: "Somebody came in?" Lady Zelda: "You know, I'll gonna tell you something you may not believe. My movements are being watched." Sach: "I believe it." Sach does his motorlips.

Slip: "Sach we're going home now." Sach: "Oh I'm not leaving, just send over my laundry." Slip: "I said we're going home. Get moving!" Sach kisses her hand saying goodbye. Slip apologizes to Lady Zelda. Slip: "You'll have to ignore my friend. Before he was born, his mother was badly frightened by a Ferris wheel."

Slip says he is drafting the Boys since they are working for the King. Sach: "You can't draft me. I'm 12-Z." Slip: "What's that?" Sach: "A coward with flat feet." Slip tries to give them some Basic Training, using mops as rifles. However, Sach is uncooperative and says obnoxious things as if to intentionally annoy Slip.

In a plot to save the King, Louie hides an important coin in a wooden display chocolate candy bar (Try Rich Chocolate Covered PERKIES A Delicious Candy). Slip forces Sach to mind Louie's store. Sach tells Slip: "Oh! I'm not going to do any guard duty. I didn't have enough sleep last night. I only slept 12 hours."

Sach refuses to sell a little girl some candy since she does not have enough money. Sach childishly tells the girl, "Well, you can't have a penny's worth of that, and a penny's worth of that, and a penny's worth of that." The girl screams, and gets Slip's attention. Slip tells Sach to give her the candy. Sach gives her a bunch of candies including the Perkies sample with the hidden coin. Sach tells girl: "You want candy little girl? Oh boy, you'll get candy. Candy, I'll give everything in the store. You want candy, candy, want more, and eat it all at once so you get sick." Little girl: "You remind me of my big brother... and I hate him!" She waves her fingers at her ears and sticks her tongue out at him, and Sach does the same back.

When Slip returns, Louie's store is taken apart looking for the coin. The Boys and Louie go all over town in search of the girl. Sach comes back holding the little girl's hand. Sach: "Cause I'm brilliant. Well you see, I figured she must be living with her mother. So I went to where her mother lived, and sure enough, and there she was." Louie: "Sachela how did you know where her mother lived?" Sach: "Oh I knew it all the time. I guess maybe I forgot to tell you." Slip mockingly repeats Sach: "Just maybe I forgot to tell you." He goes to hit Sach, but then he does not.

Sach's Comedy

Slip: "I'm kind of a coin collector. You might say I'm a numerologist." Little girl: "You mean a numismatist." The Boys interrogate her, and Sach acts out how she is supposed to act stressed, fearful, and guilty under the hot lights. Little girl: "What a hamboat, get out of that chair. I'll show you how to do it." She sits in the chair and says: "I ain't talking." Louie simply brings in an ice cream cone and she gives the coin back. Little girl: "Goodbye Mr. Dumbrowski, Goodbye Mr. Mahoney, (to Sach) Goodbye Peasant."

Lady Zelda explains she told Sach: "I want to be alone with him." Zelda is asked: "What did he say?" Zelda: "He didn't say anything. He just went... (she does his motorlips)."

Another effort to hypnotize Sach follows. Zelda: "Look at my eyes...What do you see?" Sach: "Lots of mascara." Zelda: "No, no, no, no, my eyes, look at them again." Sach: "I see one green eye and one red eye. I don't know whether to stop or go ahead." She uses her necklace to put him in a trance.

Sach's food demands are extraordinary when he orders a hamburger at Nick's Place with everything on it. Sach: "What about the ice cream and the cake?" He adds, he wants it not on it... but under it.

Slip: "Wait until I get my hands on that Colonel Baxis." Louie: "Wait until I get my hands on that phony courier." Sach: "Wait till I get my hands on that Lady Zelda." Sach does his motorlips.

Sach is in a trance as he hears Zelda's voice tell him to hit Slip over his head, get the coin, and open the door to give his half of the coin to the men who appear. He does as directed. When Slip hits Sach's head with a pan, Slip asks: "Now what is the little voice tell you?" Sach: "What voice? All's I hear now is birds."

Oftentimes, Sach takes things literally, and he needs Slip to set him straight. For example: Slip says they are going to "Put a tail on him."

Sach: "On him, it would look good. On her, Uh-uh! Uh-uh!" Slip: "On you I'd like to put a jackass's tail. You know to put a tail on somebody in subterranean language means to follow them."

Lady Zelda: "Goodbye Darling." Sach: "Achantee. That's French for WOW!" Slip slaps Sach: "I told you to follow her, not to usurp her." Sach: "We went window shopping. If I had some money I would have bought her some windows."

Although the story is somewhat convoluted, the King was going back ten days too soon with the traitorous Colonel and Zelda as they kidnapped the Princess. A fight breaks out, and Sach is hypnotized by Zelda's jewelry. When he wakes up Sach gives fighting orders: "Get him Chief. . . murder the usher!"

As Sach starts to call the Police department, he is hypnotized several times by Zelda's jewelry until a gun, knocked into the fireplace, goes off when it gets hot. Sach awakes from the spell. As Sach grabs Lady Zelda to tell her she is under arrest, her dress comes off. This shocks Sach: "Ahh! Ahh! Ahh! Ahh! Ahh!"

Finale: The King gives medals to everyone. To Sach who makes him laugh, he is made a Royal Knight of Truania. Sach starts talking a silly speech. Slip makes fun of it, and Sach hypnotizes Slip. This makes Slip also give a silly speech. Sach: "Ohp! Ohp! Oh! The Chief is flipped. . . what am I going to do, Oh! No, Oh! This ought to do it. . ." Sach cracks a sugar bowl over Slip knocking him down.

As Sach goes into his own insane speech as follows, Chuck and Butch continue throwing cream pie pieces at him in order to shut him up. Sach: "Now that we got rid of Sir Blabbermouth, we can continue with the party. On your feet peasants, slaves, peons. A toast to me, to Horace Debussy Jones. Shall be King. King of Truania. You can mock me! You can destroy me! You can usurp my subjects! But I shall be King!"

Spy Chasers is a funny movie with Hall at his peak. Among the highlights is the scenes with the little girl. Sach Comedy Meter: 4.0 out of 4.0.

39. Jail Busters

Released September 18, 1955

The film opens at Louie's Sweet Shop where Slip gives an IOU for three banana splits. Louie suggests that the Boys get a job like Chuck who was promoted to reporter. Sach: "Louie, you said a n—a—s—t—y word!"

Sach talks about working at a newspaper. Sach calls out: "Copy boy–stop the presses, tear out the front page, I got an exclusive." Slip: "What is it?" Sach: "It's so exclusive I don't even know it myself." Slip: "I got an exclusive for you." Sach: "Yes?" Slip: "You're nuts!"

The Boys want to find out who beat up Chuck while he was doing an investigative story at a penitentiary. As suggested by a dishonest reporter, they purposely arrange to be sent to prison.

The reporter set them up since he is a gambler in need of money. Slip: "We do a caper. We get a real rap against us. We really go up the river." Sach gets it wrong. Sach: "Up the river. Where we're going fishing?" Slip: "Shut up." Sach humorously suggests to the reporter: "How about knocking off a pizza wagon, and eating all the pizzas?"

The Boys do a jewelry robbery, and they purposely leave behind evidence so they can be caught. This is one of the movie's best scenes. Sach tries to crack open the safe first by listening. Sach again remarks: "Jimmy Valentine, get out of town." He fails using his sense of hearing. Then he dumps a bag of tools, and he tries an eggbeater. Sach: "I'll beat it open."

Sach pokes around the store, leaving clues. Sach: "Beautiful fingerprints." He stamps the safe, and collects an armful of watches.

We are treated to another one of Hall's fine efforts at delivering laughs via a telephone conversation. The telephone rings. Sach nonchalantly answers it: "Hello. Yes. This is Potnick's Jewelry Store. No, I'm not Mr. Potnick. Who am I? I'm your friendly neighborhood burglar. I'm sorry Madame I'm busy robbing the store." He hangs up. Sach: "Get a load of these crazy earrings (puts them on)." We see he stamped the safe: "Sach was Here, Please Contact Sach... Phone Bowery 85425."

They enter prison, and the camera explodes when Sach's mug shot is taken. Although they were sentenced for 6 years, Sach (#41328) tells the Warden he will be in for 3 weeks as the Boys do not realize they were setup by the dishonest reporter.

Sach tells the jail psychologist: "You are a mental case if I ever saw one." Later, the psychologist goes crazy after the Boys aggravate him weaving baskets.

Slip says Sach went to nursery school last year. Slip calls out Sach for putting a round piece in a square hole. Sach explains: "I'm doing it the hard way." Slip: "I think your head is on the wrong way–upside down."

In the kitchen, Sach scrubs the lettuce leaves with soapsuds and hangs them to dry. Gus (Murray Alper) sees this and calls him: "A real mental giant." Sach: "Thank you for the compliment."

Sach causes havoc by allowing the toast to burn. Sticking a fork in the toaster shocks him. The warden comes to see why his lights are blinking only to be sprayed by Sach extinguishing the flames coming out of the toaster.

Slip says Sach is soft in the head. Sach fights back. Sach: "Just a moment Miss Mahoney, I've been taking your snide remarks from now on for two years, take off your hat. . . ." Sach begins to take his jacket off ready to punch. Another inmate calms Sach.

Sometimes Sach gets a chance to insult back. Gus: "I got something for you to do that don't require no brains." Sach: "Why don't you do it yourself?" In addition, when Slip directs Sach as to where to mop, Sach asks Slip what he is going to do. Slip says he is going to stand here and see that someone does not bother him. Sach: "You know something, if you did a little work, you might take off a little weight." Slip: "Just a minute, for your information, I dropped a lot of weight." Sach: "Yeah from your chin to your stomach." Slip goes to slap Sach. Sach picks up his pail and moves away to avoid Slip. Sach: "Ohp! Ohp! Ohp! I'm going, I'm going. He was a fat man for the FBI."

One of the convicts is being coddled with TV, wall to wall carpet, refrigerator, and a bar. Butch observes: "How do you like that guy leading the life of Riley?" Sach asks: "How could he be leading the life of Riley when his name is Lannigan?" Sach points to the name above the prison cell door.

The warden eventually discovers what's going on, and believes the Boys' claim about going to the prison to investigate Chuck's beating.

The obligatory fight scene comes with Sach atypically almost getting involved in the fighting. He picks a knife off the wall and starts to threaten one of the men involved in the brawl. However, when he realizes he only grabbed the handle and not the blade, he quickly runs and tells the guy: "Get another man." Yet, Sach is not wasted in this situation. He amusingly comes through and saves the day when he throws a rug over the hole in the floor, luring the three coddled convicts into the hole. He teases one guy by pinching his nose and runs away to get him to fall in the hole.

Finale: The warden is arranging for the Boys' formal release, he tells them to be a little patient. Slip: "What did that warden say?" Butch: "Just be patient." Slip: "But how patient can you be?" They turn around in the jail cell to reveal the considerable passage of time as they are all heavily bearded. As the finale fades, Sach pushes the ends of his moustache up. Unexpectedly and unrealistically, he seems to be amused by his plight.

This ending, though a neat twist visually, seems unfair to the Boys. Their trust of a reporter that the latter would arrange their caper with the editor and authorities is illogical. Although they broke the law only to get into prison to investigate the beating, they did not have any assurance that the authorities would know and accept their scheme as investigative journalism. Nonetheless, they find themselves aging in prison. This scheme of Slip's, though encouraged by a dishonest reporter, proves that Sach did not have a monopoly on stupidity. Slip had his share of unintelligent behavior.

Jail Busters seems to miss so many possible slapstick gags. When Slip moves towards Sach to hit him, the viewer is disappointed for he does not follow through with his threats. Overall, at times the production seems to fall flat and be tired. The all-male cast offers a story around hardened criminals, but it did not provide enough real conflict. Though Sach's humor is limited, most effective is the scene at the jewelry store. The delivery and timing of the telephone conversation is superb. Moments like this make Hall's Sach a real scream. Sach Comedy Meter: 2.5 out of 4.0.

40. Dig That Uranium

Released December 25, 1955

The Boys are having lunch at Louie's as Sach arrives with Shifty. The latter found wealth with uranium ore. Louie is conned into spending $500 for the claim and the equipment.

They head out to Panther Pass, Nevada. They first run for cover when they see bullets flying. Sach: "What's this, the western Fourth of July?" When Sach speaks incorrect English expected of an American Indian, the latter responds: "White man big square."

After Sach spills a drink on a tough, he is forced to have a drink. This chokes him up. Sach: "I just drank a volcano."

Sach, dressed in his nighties, gets repeatedly pushed out of the bed he shares with Slip, Chuck and Butch.

As usual, Sach is vulnerable to reveal secrets to attractive females. Sach tells one that Louie bought the deed to the mine. Of course, when she gets the information, she chases him away by saying her husband will be coming back soon.

The crooks play card games with Louie to con him out of his mine. Sach learns of this, and dutifully runs to tell Slip. Sach: "If he ain't losing, I'll eat my hat." Of course, Louie wins instead, and Slip punishes Sach by making him eat his cap. No, he does not eat his upturned baseball cap, but a captain's cap. Later he is wearing a tam (Tam o'Shanter). Sach seems to change caps often and not stick to his typical baseball cap.

The Boys go digging for uranium, and the Geiger Counter is not working. Slip calls Sach 'Geiger Head.' Slip explains that it is broke because it ran on AC ("Altercating Current"), and Sach, who is now wearing a coonskin hat, is using DC current ("Dirty and Crinkly"). However, a prospector bursts their bubble, and tells them they've been "flimflammed" as they bought a dead old silver mine.

Slip blames Sach for the latter's friend who conned him into buying the mine. Slip takes Sach off-camera to tell him a secret. The viewer hears the sound of slapping. Then we see Sach with an ice pack on his head, with everyone blaming him.

Sach gives a speech: "So they're gonna throw us out of our room and we gonna have to live out there in the desert with the rattlesnakes and the scorpions, and we haven't even got enough money to get back to the Bowery. But be happy, look at the bright side of things." Sach laughs, then moans and cries hysterically.

Sach makes Slip some eggs "over easy," and they wind up on Slip's eyes. Sach: "Yahhh! Oh! He's really got egg on his face."

The film's highlight is Sach's dream sequence. Moustached Louie is bartender in saloon. Slip and Sach are the Lone Disarrangers. They come in to rescue a girl from Pecos Pete and his partner, and they scare them away. Sach says: "Pick up your guns and git." They agree to a fair fight, just 2 against 2 which turns into a street shootout, 6 against 2. Slip alone pursues Pecos Pete. The woman tells Sach that one of them is hiding and is going to ambush Slip. Sach ricochets a bullet to hit the guy who was hiding. Slip: "Thanks partner." Then Slip fires one. Slip: "I got them with one of my slow bullets."

Sach is described by the prospector: "So much like Josephine (the burro); your nose, your brain. . . ." Sach: "Gee thanks!" The prospector says they found uranium, and that Sach was supposedly shot in the back while running for cover. Sach awakes stuck on the edge of a mountain. Slip and the Boys search for Sach, and they find a water bottle with the inscribed initials "N.W." Slip takes it to mean it belonged to Sach, the nitwit.

Slip and the Boys' sadness ceases when they hear Sach, and then spot him stuck below on the mountain ridge. Sach is calling "Oh Chiefy?" Slip: "What are you doing down there, you idiot? Stay right where you are." Sach: "Oh no. I might get out of here and go to a nightclub and do a hoe-down. What an idiot!" Slip is lowered down the mountain. Slip uses his hat to slap Sach over the head. Slip: "If I ever get you out of here alive, I'm gonna kill you."

The crooks ("Happiness Boys" to Sach) are disappointed when they realize that Sach was not killed. However, Sach suggests to them how they can eliminate them all. Sach: "Well, it's corny but it'll work. You gotta make it look like an accident, you see. If I was boss of this outfit, I would take these four fellows. Hit 'em all over the head. Put 'em in a car and drive it off a cliff. It wrecks the car, and believe me it doesn't help the bodies." The crooks like the idea. A delighted Sach exclaims: "See that,

Chief, he likes it!" Slip: "You and that big disposal that you call a mouth are going to be the death of us yet."

The crooks chase the Boys as the latter drive their jalopy backwards. Perhaps the only serious morally questionable moment in the *Bowery Boys* series occurs when the Boys save their own lives by moving a sign. This makes the crooks go over a cliff and their jeep explodes upon hitting the ground. Sach understates the intentional tragedy: "Oops! They blew a tire."

Finale: The Geiger Counter sensor indicates they finally found uranium in their mine. A group of American Indians appear and claims it as their reservation land. Sach is frightened: "Ooh! Awl, Awl, Awl, A scalper." The Boys learn that since the land is part of their reservation, any uranium found on it belongs to them in perpetuity.

Nevertheless, the Chief acknowledges their help in finding the uranium by offering a gift. The Chief's son translates: "My father, the Chief, is very grateful. In appreciation of what you have done, he would like to make you a gift of Spring Wild Flowers." Slip: "Anytime I want any spring wild flowers, I'll go and pluck 'em."

Chief's son: "My father wishes to know if Mountain Nose will accept Spring Wild-Flowers?" Sach: "Certainly, what have I got to lose?" Slip: "Nothing, absolutely nothing!" Son: "This is Spring Wild Flowers." Sach: "Who needs uranium, oh?" Slip: "This is Spring Wild Flowers and I turned it down." Slip faints. Sach turns and passionately kisses her. In one of the best last scenes, Sach turns to face the camera, and he does his motorlips and American Indian calls with his hands. Sach: "Wooo-wooo-wooo-wooo, wooo-wooo-wooo-wooo, wooo-wooo-wooo-wooo!"

Dig That Uranium flows better than some of the other *Bowery Boys* movies so that the adventure aspect keeps things going even when the comedy is sparse. The film's Western flavor and the presence of Sach alone make this a very enjoyable effort. In addition, it offers one of my favorite final shots with Sach. Sach Comedy Meter: 3.8 out of 4.0.

41. Crashing Las Vegas

Released April 22, 1956

The movie opens at Kate Kelly's Furnished Rooms where Sach is telling Slip how he sold the tires off the car for ten dollars. Slip: "How do we supposed to get around?" Sach: "We'll walk. We ain't got tires, but we got shoes." Slip: "You're a financial genius. You know something? I think if I gave you a million dollars, in about fifteen seconds you'd be filing a partition for bankruptcy."

Kate is being evicted. She has been managing the rooming house for 34 years, but now it is being sold out from under her. Slip tells Kate that he has been taking up a collection to help her cover the down payment on the property.

Sach wants Kate to make him scrambled eggs and a meatball sandwich with tamale sauce and raisins. Slip tells him to leave her alone, as he should make it himself. We see Sach's crazy cooking as he takes out a number of different items from the refrigerator. He empties a bag of sugar or coffee into a bowl. He adds what looks like leeks. He then pours milk over it. Then he gets shocked plugging in the mixer, but the jolt gave him the ability to add numbers up in his head.

The Boys go on a quiz show to help pay off the down payment. There's a funny spoof of game shows in *Live Like a King* TV show, sponsored by Grin Toothpaste. Sach knows the number that the wheel will stop at is number 47. He does his motorlips, next predicting the number would be 62. The winner is a bum named Joe Crumb who lives in the middle of Central Park. He says he is self-employed as a wine taster, and he wins a swimming pool erected anywhere, and a complete paint job on a yacht of any size.

Sach does his motorlips again. The next number that is called is predicted by Sach to be 87. Slip forces a man out of his seat so that he can win the prize of a trip to Las Vegas for 4 weeks for one person. Instead, Slip asks to change the prize to a trip for 1 week for four persons.

Slip tests Sach's predictive ability on the airplane. Slip: "Alright, alright, alright so you're a genius." Slip calls Sach "Mr. Clairvoyant." Sach: "Sticks and stones may break my bones, but words will never harm me." Slip asks: "Give me the dictionary, please. Are there words in here? And they'll never harm you?" Slip is ready to hit Sach with the book. Sach: "I'm gonna report you to the pilot."

When they enter the casino, Sach remarks: "We gotta get out of here, they're gambling in here. Slip: "In Las Vegas, it's against the law not to gamble."

Sach plays roulette. Repeatedly, Sach does his motorlips first and then picks a winning number. Some crooks think he has a system worked out when he wins nine times in row. Sach, known as "Eagle Beak" to Slip, manages to lose a million dollars when Slip calls him over from the table where he left his winning chips. Slip demands to see the money. Sach goes back to the table to show him the money only to see that the game continued after he walked away. Sach lost it all. Sach: "What are you squawking about? I only lost a quarter."

Sach is now a seasoned gambler, and he is wearing a beret, sunglasses and loud clothes. He falls for the sob story offered by a gun moll. She claims she lost $10,000 and needs to win money for her mother's operation and for her sister's schooling. Sach gambles and loses her last hundred dollars, and he quotes Confucius, saying "You can't win every ballgame." Sach: "Oh! What are you worried about? I know why I lost.

I didn't do (he does his motorlips). Sach: "So (does his motorlips)." He kisses her, and he loses her money at the table again.

Sach: "Anyone that doesn't adore me, I write 'em right out of my book."

When he goes back to the roulette table with his own money and motorlips, he wins six times. He goes to eat. Sach: "Well I feel a little hungry. So I think I'll have some onions smothered with a couple of steaks. Mmmmh! Escargots my favorite dish. I'll have some beef à la stroganoff. Then'll have some pizzas covered with more pizzas, and have some. . . ." Slip: "JUST A MINUTE!" Sach: "Wait a minute, I'm not through ordering yet." Slip: "You're through as far as I'm concerned. We got to get back to that roulette wheel and do a little more work."

Sach: "You know something Chief? I think I'll write a book, *How to Become a Millionaire in Three Easy Lessons.*" Slip: "You gonna write a book? Write a book. You couldn't even read one." Sach: "What's this? Chopped liver. How do you like that 'Dumbo Gets Drafted.'" Sach proceeds to pull out a comic book.

The hotel clerk tells Sach that he has become famous, as the morning paper has his picture in it. Sach: "Oh boy, how about that? My picture in the paper. But it's really not a very good picture of me. My eyelashes are much longer, and they should have put some highlights in my hair, and that would have done it." Clerk: "Mr. Jones, there's only one thing that would improve your looks." Sach: "What's that?" Clerk: "Plastic surgery." Sach: "Oh! thank you for the compliment. I'll pick it up the first thing in the morning."

When Sach goes missing, Slip thinks the crooked gamblers did this to make Sach talk. Actually, Sach goes with the gun moll in her convertible to her supposed penthouse on the twenty-first floor. She kisses him twice, but he does not react. He is more interested in eating. She keeps him from looking out the window. Her "husband" walks in and grabs Sach. In a struggle with Sach, the "husband" fakes falling out the window in the shuffle. They tell Sach that he is a cold-blooded murderer. Sach runs out scared and goes off.

The police are contacted since Sach is supposedly missing. Sach hides on the floor behind the back seat of a police car. He is frightened as he hears the radio transmission: "Attention all cars, be on the lookout for Horace DeBussy Jones, alias Sach, described as white male American, 6 feet, 154 pounds, large wide nose." Of course, Sach really thinks he's being hunted down for murder.

Sach returns to the hotel and hides in the closet where he goes into a dream. Sach and the Boys are all convicted for murder and sentenced to 99 years. The judge agrees to Slip's offer of a double or nothing wager. Judge: "Oh well, if you want to gamble, we must do it the legitimate way, this is Las Vegas you know. Bring in the wheel. You boys name the right number, and you will all go free." Sach does his motorlips, but he cannot think since seeing the gun moll distracts him. He wrongly predicts the number.

The judge gets the warden to give him another chance. Judge: "Yes, the electric chair doesn't work the first time, he'll let you try again." A sign reads: "Execution Chamber, 3 Chairs, No Waiting." Sach: "Gee, these things don't look very comfortable."

A game of musical chairs decides which of the four Boys will avoid the electric chair. Sach: "Ooooh! That's my favorite game." The same dance music is used here as in previous *Bowery Boys* movies. Slip loses and gets to throw the switch. Sach wakes up from the dream and tells the Boys he killed a guy, that he accidentally pushed a man out of the penthouse window.

Slip: "Now we gotta go out and look for a good liar–a, that is lawyer." Sach alone: "I'll plead insanity. Naah! No one can ever make a jury believe that I'm insane."

The gun moll and friends demand that Sach reveal his system of winning. They tell him they will go to the police. To settle things, Sach then gives the suitcase of winning money. Sach: "Chief is gonna be real happy when I tell him what I did with the money." Uncharacteristically, when Slip is told about it, he does not slap Sach. Slip just commits to getting the money back.

A crazy fight scene ensues with the money blowing out the window since Sach knocks the fan on. Sach gets electrocuted again when he touches the fan switch. Now he lost his power to predict numbers.

Finale: Kate arrives at the hotel. Sach uses his motorlips to help Slip figure her room number is #17. They enter a room. After a loud scream, Slip and Sach are thrown out. Sach: "Chief, I guess I ain't got my power back." Slip: "Well, I got mine back." For the last time ever in the series, Slip takes his hat and hits Sach several times on his head. Sach: "Ohp! Ohp! Ohp!"

There are many funny moments in *Crashing Las Vegas*, all driven by Sach. It is obvious that Gorcey is drunk throughout the film. His mugging is much more than usual. In addition, Gorcey seems to be handing the reins willingly to Hall as the latter seems to dominate the entire movie. Interesting how Hall could take a simple mannerism, such as his motorlips, and garner so many laughs from repeatedly doing this one thing so many times in this movie. In addition, Hall superbly makes the transitions back and forth from slapstick to the dramatic moments. Sach Comedy Meter: 4.0 out of 4.0.

42. Fighting Trouble

September 16, 1956

The credits change with this first film without Leo Gorcey. Hall is now the lead name. The first card reads: "Allied Artists Picture Corporation presents Huntz Hall and The Bowery Boys. The second card: "In Fighting Trouble." The third card reads: "Featuring Stanley Clements with…"

The character of Duke Covelesky (Stanley Clements) replaces Slip Mahoney (Leo Gorcey) for this movie until the end of the series.

Now the Boys are wearing suits and ties. They are six months behind in their rent at Kate Kelly's Furnished Rooms. The mail carrier tells Duke if he paid rent, he would not have to wash windows. Photographer Sach is dressed in a smock, and he shows Kate a photo of herself. Sach's radar lens camera moves around to find its subject. However, Sach blinds Duke with the flash when taking a photo.

Kate says that Sach: "has everything–a heart as big as the Bowery, has brains, is brilliant, and a hard worker." Sach adds: "and handsome too." Sach gets excited to see the lunch Kate made for him; namely, sardine sandwiches smothered with peanut butter.

Duke and Sach need money so they try to submit a photo in a contest, but the deadline passed. Instead, they are offered a job at a newspaper because no on else wanted it. Slip and Sach are assigned by the Editor to get a picture of a crook. Sach starts to take a picture as the crook aims a gun at the window, and Sach steps on a bulb. Consequently, he overreacts as he thinks he has been shot and is now dying.

Sach has a big ego in this film: "Well, I don't like to talk about myself, cause I'm what one would call a modest genius…I don't mind calling myself brilliant." Yet, Sach's ability does not match his ego as he cannot even count money correctly.

In a disguise as a French interior decorator, Sach searches the crook's apartment under a ruse of decorating. In the process, Sach wrecks the room right in front of a gun moll. Duke reassures: "He's the greatest decorator in the world." Sach snaps the picture of the crook when he comes home, but then ruins the film when he pulls it from the Editor's hand to say he will take it to develop. Sach's goofiness does not matter to Kate, as she says he's "still my star border." However, Duke sees him as a "knucklehead."

They try again when Sach disguises himself as a tough Chicago mobster named Handsome Hal. Again, the landlady has nothing but praise as she calls Sach: "devastating and handsome." The crook's club hostess asks him, "Something I can do for you?" Sach as Handsome Hal: "Yeah, wiggle." When Sach sees the attractive gun moll, he asks: "Where's she from?" Crook: "New York." Sach: "Nice territory New York." Then he does his usual motorlips.

Hall effortlessly spoofed the Chicago gangster with a germ phobia; however, these scenes are generally humorless and slow moving. Predictably, Sach is found out to be an imposter, the police arrive; and of course, he takes another picture of the crook. Again, he ruins the film by exposing it.

Finale: The Boys are demoted to hawking papers. Sach: "Well I got to say that Mr. Vance is a man of his word. He says we'd be his outside representatives. Extra, extra, read all about it, 'Horace Debussy Jones smashes counterfeiting ring single-handed.'" Duke hits Sach in his chest with a newspaper. Sach: "Double handed."

Fighting Trouble is the first film in which Huntz Hall received star billing, and it is disappointing. Stanley Clements' characterization lacks the low-key anger that Leo Gorcey brought to Slip. Although Duke will call Sach a host of denigrating names, Duke does not hit Sach, but just threatens to hit him. The chemistry between Sach and Duke is just not there. It seems as if they are simply going through all the motions, but the comedy payoff is miniscule. It makes little sense, except in an idiot-savant manner, that here Sach can convincingly pull-off an involved disguise, but he cannot properly handle a roll of film.

Although the music seems somewhat counter-productive to the mood, it was composed and conducted by Buddy Bregman. Hall's friendship with Bregman obviously had something to do with giving him an opportunity to work on the movie.

At times, *Fighting Trouble* tries to be a serious gangster film, though it falls flat since the characters are bumbling and lethargic. The uninteresting plot offers no danger or real conflict at all. Simply put, this film is a mess. Sach Comedy Meter: 1.5 out of 4.0.

43. Hot Shots

Released December 23, 1956

Sach and Duke catch Joey Munroe, a missing child star, trying to steal their car. Sach says to Joey: "Nobody's gonna hit you, especially me." Joey is a runaway, and he tells a story taken from a script that has him complaining that he's been beaten and made to steal. He complains that he is sick of not having fun and being used so that others like his uncle can make a lot of money.

Police detectives question the Boys, suspecting that they kidnapped Joey. Detective: "Who's the brains of this mob?" Sach: "Don't look at me." Detective: "I wasn't, I asked for the brains."

Sach is depicted as maternal-minded as he cares about Joey. At one point Sach insists: "Listen, there's nothing wrong with that kid. Too many people make him think he's a big shot. Won't you let him go to school like other kids and play hooky?" Duke: "That's the smartest thing you ever said."

As we have seen, Sach has a tendency to take everything literally.

Duke: "They don't know Duke Coveleske." Sach: "Oh would you like to meet him? Morley, this is Duke Coveleske."

Sach opens his safe as the Boys watch. Duke takes the piggy bank from him. Sach: "No please, not my life savings. I was gonna put my uncle through law school." Duke: "You mean when he gets out of Sing-Sing?" Sach: "How do you like that? A guy makes one mistake and everybody hates him."

The TV producer hires Sach and Duke. When they meet the secretary, a blonde bombshell, they both do the motorlips. She walks in carrying a serving tray: "This is all right with you, isn't it Mr. Jones?" Sach: "Oh! Oh! Yes! Yes!" Secretary: "The coffee, I mean." Sach: "Ohp! That's what I always wanted, a beautiful office with a gorgeous cup of coffee." She explains what all the desk buttons do in the office, and Sach goes goo-goo eyes. Sach turns on the A/C which makes the papers go flying all over the office.

Sach asks Duke: "How do you like your coffee?" Duke: "You know I take my coffee black. Sach: "Where am I going to get black cream?"

More of Sach's funny lines…He tells a soap sponsor: "Another thing, your soap is too slippery–put some sand in it." The secretary asks Sach for money to do a trick with an egg. Sach: "Now don't forget where you got it, for this is my mad money, and I might want to go mad."

When offered cigars from the TV producer, Sach takes them. Duke: "What do you think you're doing? You know you don't smoke cigars." Sach: "Are you kidding, I might get married some day." Duke: "What's that got to do with it?" Sach: "My wife may have a little boy." Duke: "Supposing she has a girl?" Sach: "So I'll put little dresses on the cigars." Producer to Sach: "Well I like the way you handle Joey." Sach: "Oh! Well that's simple, you see I happen to be an expert with children cause I was a child myself once."

A "Sach alone" scene has him grooming. Sach: "Wooh! You handsome devil, don't overdo it, give the homey fellows a chance." Sach continues: "Mirror, mirror on the wall who's the fairest of them all?" The mirror shatters, and he looks at the bright side. Sach: "At least I'll live another seven years."

At a gathering, Sach thinks he is pouring a drink into a planted wall box, but instead he pours it down a woman's back.

A very funny scene happens when a barelegged Sach is looking silly in his nightgown top and a bandanna. Sach is alone speaking to himself, looking at a banana and a pickle he is holding. Sach: "My favorite dish, banana and pickle. Wonder why this banana is so pretty and this poor little pickle is all full of warts?"

The bell rings at Sach's apartment. Joey has run away again and wants to stay with his newfound friend. Sach offers more laughs when he says: "But you'll have to forgive the way I look. You see, I washed my hair tonight and I can't do a thing with it."

Sach makes a mess knocking stuff over in order to get something for Joey to eat. Upstairs Duke hears noise. Duke says to himself: "I don't know. My good friend, egghead." Much of the humor in these scenes comes from Sach mothering Joey, with the boy even falling asleep in Sach's arms.

When Joey is held for ransom, Sach's clumsiness is evident as he tries to climb up a wall to find him. After climbing a ladder, Sach goes on a ledge carrying a crowbar. This results in his pants falling down.

Sach is able to make us laugh even with a scene where he is hiding in the limited space of a closet. Duke opens the closet door, and Sach bops Duke with a bat. Sach: "What are you doing down there, I'm sorry Duke, I lost my head." Duke attempts to bat him back to retaliate. In attempting to deflect Duke's anger, Sach picks up a ball and glove from the closet shelf. With clenched teeth, Duke gets ready to hit him with the bat. Sach: "Oh, we're playing ball?" Duke: "Yeah we're playing." Sach pitches the ball to Duke, as Duke is ready to swing at him.

Finale: Duke starts to say to Joey: "If that paper-headed imbecile ever shows up." Sach walks in: "Am I being paged?" The TV show's summer replacement for Joey is a young girl named Annie. Sach asks her: "Are those guns loaded?" She responds by squirting water in their faces. Sach: "Ohp! Ohp! Ahh! Ahh!" Duke: "Wet bullets." Sach: "They were loaded."

Hot Shots is a below-average entry that still has Sach offering some very funny bits, but not enough to sustain interest throughout some rather dull stretches. Duke fails to counterbalance and offset Sach's comedy since Stanley Clements is a weak substitute for gruff Slip. The best moment is seeing Sach after he just washed his hair. Sach Comedy Meter: 2.0 out of 4.0.

44. Hold That Hypnotist
Released February 24, 1957

The Boys clean up Mrs. Kelly's apartment after Sach overheard her talking to her doctor. Actually, he is a hypnotist. Sach in an apron washes the floor by pouring water on the floor from a bucket. Duke slips and flips over. Sach and Duke start to fight, engaging in some fake fencing. Sach tells Mrs. Kelly he is going to cook French scrambled eggs using eggs from "French chickens."

Sach often takes things literally. Here Sach wants to find out if Mrs. Kelly's doctor is legitimate, so he calls the operator. Sach: "Could you tell me if Dr. Noble's a phony?" Then the Boys go to a reception offered by the hypnotist. An attractive hostess carrying a tray of food asks Sach: "Anything look good to you?" Sach: "Well, what did you have in mind?

I, I, I mean a what's that?" Hostess: "That's caviar." Sach: "Ooh! I don't like caviar." Duke: "It's expensive." Sach: "Ooh then I like it (Sach tastes it). Mmmh, real bad."

Duke is supposed to be hypnotized, but instead Sach is regressed to August 23, 1682. In a gambling game of slaviarsh with Blackbeard the pirate, Sach is Algy the tax collector for the American colonies. What's funny is that Sach inadvertently wins the game three times in a row, without knowing how to play. Blackbeard plays one more game wagering his treasure map. When Algy-Sach looks over and sees a girl's leg as she pulls up her dress exposing her thigh, he blurts out "yipes." Unknowingly, saying that means he is the first one to triple-ootz Blackbeard and win. Blackbeard accuses him of cheating. A sword fight ensues as cowardly Algy-Sach runs for cover under a table in fear.

Back in current time, the Boys are in a library researching the facts. Sach reads with the page upside down. Duke asks if he can really read that way. Sach: "Certainly, that's what you get from working in a printing shop. This is the only way I can read."

Sach is hypnotized to find the location of Blackbeard's treasure. At first attempt, Sach has trouble getting sleepy. After many cups of coffee, Sach gets sleepy. Sach laments: "Is it my fault coffee makes me sleepy?"

When he sees swimsuit-clad girls, Sach does not react with his usual motorlips. Why he did not follow the pattern from other movies is not known, but it is a lost opportunity for a predictable laugh.

The Doctor's assistant arrives, clad in a black bathing suit, Duke tells Sach: "Put those eyes back in your head or they'll fall out." Sach: "Well I always want the black bathing suit filled." When Sach spills the beans about the treasure, Duke kicks Sach in the legs. They watch her put her stockings on, and Sach's eyes are popping out. Duke: "Hey, what happened? You haven't said nothing." Sach: "No, but I've been thinking quite a bit."

With the use of earrings, Sach is placed under hypnosis. This time he regresses much further back to Mark Antony from Ancient Rome. When he is moved further ahead again to be Algy in 1682, Sach reveals the location of the treasure. In order to find the treasure himself, the hypnotist double-crosses the Boys by hypnotizing Sach to guard the Boys under gunpoint.

The hypnotist's female assistant breaks the spell by the sudden shock of a kiss. As in other *Bowery Boys* movies, Sach stupidly throws the gun away. Duke: "You idiot!" Also as seen earlier, there is the sight gag of Sach taking an endless number of tools from a small box.

The last thing Sach finds in the box is a comic book on Blackbeard, and he realizes everything he recounted came from when reading that issue. When Duke promises not to hit Sach, he then proceeds to act like he is going to hit him. Sach: "Wait a minute, wait a minute, you promised not to lay a hand on me." Duke: "I won't, but didn't say nothing about a pick." Sach runs as Duke chases him with a pick.

Sach finds the treasure chest, and a skeleton rises out of it. The chest is empty, but then as they leave the cave, Sach steps on the inside cover to reveal diamonds. The Doctor and his cohorts arrive and fight the Boys.

Finale: A costume party celebration is held with Sach in prehistoric garb dancing with the Doctor's assistant. The police arrive to confiscate the pirate treasure since they reveal it was jewelry stolen from a Fifth Avenue store some six years ago.

Sach goes into a trance from the earrings. Duke worries: "Well I hope he don't come back as Cochise." Duke tells the Doctor's assistant: "I guess you'll just have to do what you did in the office again." She replies: "Well if I must, I must." She kisses Sach. Duke: "Hold it, he's out of it." Sach: "I am not." He grabs the assistant and kisses her passionately.

Sach's wig flies off. Duke: "Well, he finally blew his top." Sach looks at the camera and does his motorlips.

The usual enjoyment that comes from Sach reacting with his motorlips is not enough to make this movie worthwhile. However, though arguably, this is among one of the better of the seven movies made without Gorcey. The scene with Blackbeard the Pirate playing the game of slaviarsh is one of the highlights of *Hold That Hypnotist*. Sach Comedy Meter: 3.0 out of 4.0.

45. Spook Chasers

Released June 2, 1957

The film opens at Clancy's Café. "The Special Today–Irish Stew." Sach asks Duke for help with a puzzle; what has ten letters, and it runs, jumps, and has twenty legs? Duke says it is two basketball teams. Sach answers: "Very smart, but who won?"

Sach says he is going to leave Clancy's, complaining: "I'll take my IOUs somewhere else." Sach wants "a 104-letter word for an island off the coast of Malaya." Sach explains: "Well that's including the population." Duke's coffee is spilled. Sach makes a connection: "Ohp! Ohp! I got the island, Java."

When a customer (a real estate agent) complains that the coffee is ice cold, Sach puts his finger in it: "I agree its cold, but it's not ice cold." He then proceeds to take the heartbeat of the customer.

A real estate agent and his female companion (Darlene Fields, cover photo) dump a ghost-haunted, run-down house on Mike Clancy. The sign outside the house reads "Cedar Crest, No Peddlers." Sach gets it wrong: "Well, that let's me in, I don't own no bicycle." The usual cowardly Sach is scared to go in the house first since the door squeaks.

Inside the cobwebbed entrance hall, Sach observes: "This looks like a spooks-do-it-yourself kit."

There is a "Sach alone" scene with him picking up various objects and commenting. When the clock cuckoos, Sach, tries to catch it, even throwing white paint on it. Unexplained are Sach's wardrobe changes. In the scene with the cuckoo clock and onwards at the house, he is dressed like an artist; beret, smock over trousers and shirt with tie. In the previous scene, when he arrived at the house, he was wearing a white construction hat, knickers and a striped T-shirt. At the opening in Clancy's, he was wearing his upturned black cap. Apparently, we cannot be sure this is a wardrobe error, so we assume Sach found the artist clothing at the mansion and changed into it. This is something that is not at all far-fetched for Sach to do.

We see Sach's stream of consciousness best when he is all alone. When solitary Sach is at the kitchen table, he says: "I'm no good. All I do is get in everybody's hair. I think I'll end it all. (He picks knife up). Not that way, it's too drastic. Think I'll jump off that sink. Sink. Drip. Boy, if I could fix this drip, I'd be the hero of the day."

Reminiscent of a sequence, years earlier, when Curly from the Three Stooges rewired the electric and plumbing, Sach twists pipes out, and pulls wires out of the pipes. He stops to look at the wire, and pulls it across his fingers: "Let me see 14, 44, the stock market is going up a little."

Sach tells Mike: "Your drip will no longer drip." The result is that electrical sparks are coming out of the sink. Sach: "Behold…what are you worrying about, at least I fixed the drip, ha, ha, ha, sparkling water." The stove explodes, and water is coming out of the telephone. Duke goes to hit him and then chases him. Sach: "Don't get excited Dukey…."

Sach is always doing or saying something funny–at times it leads to some positive outcome. Here he runs through the living room and slides on a tea wagon. He crashes into a wall knocking money out of a compartment. This scene reminds one of Lou Costello finding money in a moose's head in *Hold That Ghost* (1941).

Sach knocks bottles and things out of the cabinets, messing everything up. Duke: "You sneak, looking for money on your own?" Sach: "Who's looking for money? I was looking for mustard for my sandwich. I demand an apology." Duke asks: "I apologize?" Sach thinks he did: "Thank you!" Sach finds a quarter in a large pot, throws the pot, and it lands over Duke's head. "A quarter, goody, goody." Duke yells at him. Sach waves his hand back at Duke, meaning get out of here. Then Sach proceeds to stuff his mouth with food, again waving his hand.

Back at the real estate office Sach starts to spill the beans about the money they found in the mansion. Sach: "Well you see I was running through the living room and accidentally." Duke interrupts and threatens him. Duke: "And accidentally opened his big mouth too wide. Don't do it again or I'll disconnect your jaw!"

Oftentimes, Sach is at ease in getting friendly with females. He also pays no mind to their lack of interest in him. For example, a female assistant politely says: "I hope we meet again." Sach: "Oh! I'll be back every five minutes if you want me too." She responds: "No thank you." Sach: "You know something? You're terribly attractive." Sach places a cigar band on her finger. Sach: "For you. Don't ever take it off."

Sach: "Gee you look beautiful in that dress." She responds: "You like it?" Sach: "Yeah!" She adds: "Just a little thing I picked up in Paris." Sach: "When are you going to get back and pick the rest of it up?" Sach does his motorlips.

The threat of violence is never carried out by Duke, but is always played for laughs. Sach comes into Clancy's wearing a miner's helmet, carrying a shovel and pick. Sach: "Fellows, look what I have got in case we have to do any digging, and in case we have to dig very deep. How do I look?" Duke "I'll show you how you look. . . ." Duke goes to hit him with the shovel. Sach: "Wait a minute. It's against the law to hit a miner."

Sach can make you laugh with just some of his silly dancing. At the woman's apartment, the same dance tune is played as in previous *Bowery Boys* movies. Sach: "They're playing our tune. What is it?" She answers: "When I Hear Music, I Just Have to Dance." He goes to dance alone. She asks: "What'd you doing?" Sach: "I took a dancing lesson once and want to see if I remember it ... I remember. Now I'm ready for you." He dances, but does not lead. Sach: "Oh! there's something wrong?" She offers her hand so he can lead. Sach: "Oh! Vi-e-nna, I love these waltzes." Sach dances over to the couch.

Sach: "Got any black bulbs? (She turns off the lamp). That's black enough." She pours some lemonade. Sach: "Oh I'm crazy about lemonade, especially if you use lemons." They do the old routine of switching the glasses. Sach got the bad one, and he spits it out. Sach choking: "Sure that's lemonade?" She insists: "Why, of course, I made it myself." Sach: "Your lemons are a little pickled." He changes his mind after the second drink. Sach: "It's not bad." She kisses him, and he knocks the lamp and the lights go out.

Sach, when given a chance (and perhaps with a Mickey Finn), easily loses his head around the opposite sex. In this case, he is wooed into revealing how he found the money in the mansion.

Sach tells the agent what a gentleman farmer is: "A man who milks a cow with spats and kid gloves on."

He tells Duke that he gave away the secret and that he is tired. Duke threatens: "When I get through with you, [you] won't be tired."

There are the usual haunted mansion hi-jinks. In the "Sach alone" scene here, he is oblivious to the disappearance from the adjoining bed of Blinky, one of the background bennies from the last remaining *Bowery Boys* movies.

Sach is alone as he talks to himself while going through his luggage: Sach: "See if I got everything? My toothpaste. My electric razor. I won't need that there's no electricity. More toothpaste. My military brushes in case I go to war. My painting palette, sponge and makeup in the morning. Instant shaving cream. Instant coffee. What else I got here? Let me see. Oop! Shoelaces, some hollow bar. Everything's here. Oop! and my pajamas. And now for a goodnight's sleep."

A hairy ghost sneaked under the covers in the adjoining bed. Sach goes to sleep in that bed supposedly with Blinky: "Move over, move over, Blinky, you need a shave and a manicure. No it couldn't be." Next Sach looks to see a ghost. He is chased by the ghost and runs into another ghost, trying to grab him.

A chase and a fight ensue. Of course, Sach stays on the sidelines making comments. Sach: "'Little Spookco,' if he was only human, I'd put him in the heavyweight division." He laughs when a ghost knocks someone out. Then he realizes "Oop! Ooh! That was Duke."

The police arrive. Detective: "And who are the Halloween kids?" The ghosts are unveiled as the real estate agent and his assistant. They were trying to get the house back. The gangsters had stolen money hidden there in the mansion, again reminiscent of Abbott & Costello's *Hold That Ghost*. The detective removes the ghost hoods, and tries to take off Sach's face. Sach: "Wait a minute, wait a minute, what are you trying to do, disfigure me? That's me." Detective: "If that's you, you need a mask."

A ghost goes downstairs, and passes them. They mistakenly think Sach is fooling around. Duke: "You idiot, I'm going to give it to you in a minute!" Sach comes behind them: "Did you call?" The Boys scream and run out the front door. Sach does his "Aahhh! Aahhh! Aahhh!" He runs into the closed door. The movie could have ended well here.

Finale: A celebration party is held for the hero of the hour. Two beautiful women pose for pictures with Sach: "Make me about 500 of them, I want to give them out to my friends." Blinky declares mockingly: "Bravest man in the world? What a show-off!" When the photographer asks him to pose with Mike Clancy, Sach insists: "I'm not gonna hug him." Photographer: "Just shake his hand." Sach: "Oh! That's different. Limburger."

When a "ghost" arrives, everyone runs away. Sach thinks it is Duke. Sach: "Well, I suppose you've been invited, you might as well have some cake." He pushes the cake in the ghost's face, and he pulls the hood off and sees another scary face. Sach screams and runs. Duke removes the mask, and says mockingly: "Bravest man in the world. Ha, ha, ha, ha, ha!"

Spook Chasers is a nearly adequate blend of laughs and mild chills. Though Stanley Clements' Duke is not as entertaining as Leo Gorcey's Slip, there is still an average amount of Sach comedy moments. Sach Comedy Meter: 2.5 out of 4.0.

46. Looking For Danger

Released October 6, 1957

At Clancy's, the cash register alarm goes off, and Sach comes out with a shotgun. Sach has wired the register, the cuckoo and other things due to a wave of café robberies. He rigged it so that by hitting various keys, different crime prevention methods are unleashed. For instance, hit the $1 key, and a net drops over the person entering the store. Sach tells them not to ever hit the "No Sale" key, though he never specifies why.

A War Department official arrives to trace a missing aluminum pot that was taken by Duke and not returned. Duke says Clancy was the mess sergeant. Clancy: "I don't have any pot." Sach touching Clancy's stomach: "Oh, I wouldn't say that."

To answer the question of "what happened to the pot," Duke tells the story of their military service. The flashback shows the Allies arriving in Casablanca. Sach: "I cut myself six times peeling potatoes and never got the Purple Heart." Sach is trying to nap, and wonders why he cannot find the desert. Sach: "It's all in my shoes." Inside his headgear-camouflage is a dish with food. Sach starts to eat it and he is told to fall in. He slams Duke's foot with his rifle.

Duke and Sach are forced to volunteer on a mission to disguise as Nazi soldiers to get a message to the Sultan. Major: If you are to die, "they will stand you up in front of a stone wall and the officer will offer you a blindfold and your last cigarette." Sach: "Major, you better get another guy for the job." Major: "Why?" Sach: "I don't smoke."

They were given a ring used by the underground, and are told if they find the other half, they found a friend. Sach: "Isn't this exciting. We might win medals. And get our pictures in the paper." Duke: "Yes, the German paper." Sach: "What's the difference? I love publicity."

From the play on names, regiments and the German accents, this film makes fun of the Nazis long before *Hogan's Heroes*.

At the Palace of Sidi-Omar, Duke and Sach seek the audience of the Sultan. Sach sees the Sultan's next bride, with face veiled, sitting next to him. Sach: "Tell the princess to pull up the shades so we can all get a peek." However, it is explained that it is certain death except for the Sultan and his other wives to see her face. Sach: "Other wives, this we can do?" Duke explains that this is the local custom. We have only one wife. Duke: "We call it monotony." Duke offers an occasional malaprop here.

The Sultan says "You may call me Sidi-Omar." Sach: "I'll do better than that, I'll call you Sidney." The Sultan introduces his assistant: "I withhold no secret from Hassan. He's my right arm." Sach: "What do you need with three arms?" Sultan: "You're among friends, gentlemen. We know you're Americans." Sach: "Now he tells me, I got a sore throat from that German accent."

What is happening is that the Boys were delivering a letter saying that Americans are going to liberate the Sultan and his people. However, Sidi Omar is really collaborating with the Nazis and does not want American help or liberation, as revealed by the harem girl. Consequently, the message that Sach and Duke are offering is one that will hurt American forces. The harem girl is an American spy that tells them she will come up with a plan to trap the Nazis.

Sach: "When you're free, we'll really live it up!" Sach to Hasson: "Listen, if you got any bubbles? I'd love a bubble bath." Music plays as Sach is asked: "Perhaps native dancing would amuse you?" Sach: "Forget the perhaps. Bring on the girls." Sach changes the music to a record by The Hepcats. Sach dances jive, a girl joins him, and then others join in. Sach shows Duke a note given to him. Sach thinks it's "love at first sight." Earlier, Sach accidentally pulled the veil and dress off a seated girl. The Sultan angrily orders: "Off with their heads."

The Sultan gives them a message to bring back, and asks the disposition of their troops. Sach misunderstands the question: "The disposition of our troops? Well, they're lonesome and they all like a few dates."

The harem girl grabs Sach from the palace hall. Girl: "There's no time to waste." Sach: "Who's wasting?" He misunderstands her remark as he starts kissing her arms and getting amorous. She reads the message the Sultan gave them, and realizes that it is a plot to mislead the Americans. This is one of the rare moments in all of the *Bowery Boys* series when a female is portrayed in a positive light, here helping the Boys fight the bad guys.

Sach's Comedy

Sach dresses up as a harem girl, and the guards chase after him. Sach: "It's no use Dukey, we're trapped like rats." Duke: "Thanks to you." Sach: "You're welcome."

They are arrested. When he hears Morse code, Sach: "I know what they're saying. I went to radio school." Duke: "What's it saying?" Sach: "Dot, dot, dot, dot, dot and a dash."

Back home, Clancy thinks they are celebrating in luxury; then we cut to see them in a prison cell waiting for the axe. Duke and Sach are forced to interrogate each other. Duke hitting Sach and asking him, "Who is the Hawk?" However, when Sach hits Duke, it is done more forcefully. Sach delivers the most laughs interrogating a Nazi, hitting him maniacally. The Nazi pleads repeatedly, "I don't know!" Sach gives a speech as if he is campaigning to be a Sultan: "A chicken in every pot and a dancing girl in every tent."

They get the guard drunk so they can escape. Sach: "I got a little dizzy watching him drink." The other Boys arrive disguised as Nazi soldiers to free them, and to stop the plot. Sach: "A secret passage. I'm crazy about secret passages."

By the end, this movie attempts to offer us a new characterization for Sach; namely, as a hero Saber fighting with the Sultan. After knocking him out, Sach notes: "That ends the hassle in the castle."

Finale: The film returns from the flashback. Government agent: "Can you tell me what happened to the pot?" Sach: "Is there anyway we can pay the army for the pot?" The agent says it costs $4.38. So Clancy tells him to help himself. The hitting of the cash register key of "No Sale" leads to an explosion causing a pot with a plant growing in it to fall off the shelf onto the government agent's head. Sach (looking at the camera): "Well he got the pot!"

At times, the many differences and some twists in the *Bowery Boys* formula may seem unsettling. Sach is not as idiotic as in the other *Bowery Boys* movies. In addition, the female lead is not working with the bad guys as is usual in all the other movies in the series. Although this is an average spy film spoof, the changes in the characters undermine the usual comedy elements.

A funny moment of slapstick comes early on as Sach and Duke are both disguised as Nazis. Sach is asked to give his name and regiment to another Nazi arresting Duke. The result is that as Sach leaves, he knocks the whole tent over onto the Nazi.

Probably the best comedy moment in the disappointing *Looking for Danger* comes from the double meaning of the word pot. Perhaps the writers offered viewers the best joke here. The movie's ending is funniest when the viewer understands it as a play on a word, and then at the time of the movie's release, viewers knew about Hall's arrest for possession of pot. The dialogue could refer to the government searching for and wanting Hall's marijuana. Sach Comedy Meter: 2.0 out of 4.0.

47. Up In Smoke

Released December 22, 1957

Early on in the movie, Sach is physically stretching the bacon at Clancy's, and then cutting it into four slices. Sach goes to the bank with $90 which is the money raised by the Boys to help a child suffering from polio. A patron offers Sach a ride; however, the car breaks down. Sach is taken to a phony horse betting room where he is conned out of the money.

Sach: "Go on hit me, I deserve it." Duke: "No Sach, I don't want to hit you, cause if I did I'd be held for murder!" Sach: "You mean you're mad at me?" Duke (shouting): "I won't be, if you get out of here and never come back....Now beat it, I never want to see that ugly face again."

Sach's Comedy

Sach pouts: "I can take a hint...ugly." Sach packs alone: "...Holler at me no more.... I ain't staying anywhere where I'm not wanted."

The Devil (a.k.a. "Mr. Bub") enters. He offers Sach an opportunity to revenge the bookmakers. Sach signs a contract with his blood. Mr. Bub promises to give him sure winners, in exchange for his soul. However, the bookmakers will not take his bet without money. To raise money, Sach gets conned by a car salesman, winds up in jail, and Duke bails him out. However, the way this is played, there is little humor here.

As agreed, he continues to receive a betting tip each day from Mr. Bub disguised as a monkey, skeleton, etc. Sach writes a letter and burns it as the way to get a message back to Mr. Bub. When Sach is seen talking to a monkey who Sach says is Mr. Bub, Duke thinks Sach has gone crazy. A psychiatrist works to find Sach's unconscious mind. Duke: "With Sach it'll be easy. The only mind's he's got is unconscious." Instead, Sach drives the psychiatrist to lay on the couch, and Sach does the questioning.

The crooks intimidate Sach and Duke to find out how Sach gets his winning tips. Sach sees the new waitress at Clancy's, the bookmakers' girl, for which he does his motorlips. Sach takes the waitress to the track. When he looks through a telescope, he sees a girl pass. Sach: "Wow! Get a load at that Filly, I wish I had a bet on her." The day's winning tip from Mr. Bub is 'Rubber Check,' and it comes inside a soda pop bottle.

Sach schemes to call the deal off. If Mr. Bub's tip loses, Sach can nullify the contract. The jockey riding 'Rubber Check' is tied up, and then Sach rides the horse to make it lose. Observer: "Hey, that jockey looks a little long-legged, doesn't he?" Nevertheless, Sach fails at losing. "Rubber Check" wins.

In preparing to fulfill his bargain and go with Mr. Bub to hell, Sach gives away his bowling ball and bean shooter to Duke. Duke sadly refuses, but greedily asks: "How about that electric blanket? You won't be needing that where you are going!" When the jockey gets unbound, "Rubber Check" is disqualified because of the unauthorized rider. A delighted Sach tells Mr. Bub he lost. Sach: "I'm a free man. My soul's my own. (To Mr. Bub) Oh don't be chicken, read the contract, read the contract. . . . And I want some of my blood back."

Finale: The bookmakers are now eating at Clancy's since they lost all their money. Sach: "Who needs money when you got friends. On second thought, I wish I had friends with money." Mr. Bub now works serving at Clancy's. Mr. Bub: "After thousands of years of faithful service they made me turn in my horns. . . . Might help if I can find new clients." Sach (looking at the bookmakers): "There's three of them over there for you. And believe me, they deserve you. Tell them Sach sent you." Then Mr. Bub is observed with one horn back. Duke: "Boy they're gonna like those guys down there." Sach: "I'm sure glad that nobody down there likes me anymore. O, such a little Devil!"

Up in Smoke offers little humor although Sach dominates this interesting take-off of the Faust story. Zany Sach seems lost, and this likeable fantasy is played semi-seriously. Unlike the previous film, *Looking for Danger*, we are back again with the usual and standard slant of the female characters always assisting the crooks. Sach Comedy Meter: 2.0 out of 4.0.

48. In the Money
Released February 16, 1958

Sach delivers a hot corned beef sandwich from Mike Clancy's to a travel agency: "98 cents not including the tip." While waiting for the busy agent, Sach eats the sandwich. When Sach tries to take payment, the agent punches Sach's finger. Sach: "You ruined it, now I'll have to play the piano with my elbow!"

Sach gets a secret job from the patron at the agency as a bodyguard for a dog named Gloria on a trip to England. The patron is actually a diamond smuggler, using the dog to hide the jewels. A smuggler tells his cohorts that Sach: "hasn't got a brain in his head or anywhere." The unquestioning Sach accepts the generous offer as he is given $500 for new clothes, $300 for old debts, $2,000 salary advance, and the balance to be paid when he arrives in London.

Although Sach tells the Boys about the trip, he does not tell them that Gloria is a dog. The Boys sense Sach is in danger, so they stowaway on the ship. Consequently, they are caught and are stuck working on the deck.

Sach's loyalty to his employer means he tells the Boys very little; they believe he's minding a woman. Sach describes his duties. Sach: "Holding Gloria by scruff of neck, giving a bath once a day, feeding her a bowl of food under her bed in case she gets hungry during the night. . . ." Initially, the Boys think he has lost his mind. However, they all laugh when they realize that he is just minding a dog.

The smugglers make Sach think that a snooping police Inspector is a dognapper. Sach offers some lame comical responses to Duke's comments regarding the sights of London. A sight gag has their hotel room being foggy.

They take the dog to a veterinarian named Rufus B. Smedley since they think she has gallstones. Sach goes nuts when he hears that the doctor is going to X-ray the poodle. Sach is hysterical: "Can't stand to see her suffer!" The doctor is ready to give Sach a needle. However, the doctor discovers that there are concealed diamonds under a false fur.

Sach calls Scotland Yard: "Scotland Yard, no answer, maybe they are all out in the yard." When Gloria gets lost, they search the hotel for her. Sach absurdly calls inside a vase for the dog. As usual during the obligatory fight scenes, Sach never fights as he just gives directions. The Boys are caught up in the unfunny chase between smugglers and Scotland Yard for the dog and the diamonds.

Sach goes into the wrong room, and he is forced out on the window ledge of the hotel. He tells the woman to come to his funeral. He finds a dog in another room in which that woman insists is her dog. Precariously back out on the building's ledge, Sach is in danger, but he cannot resist commenting about something else. He asks the woman, "you haven't got an eight story ladder in there, have you?...Ohhh! Look at that guy, he's driving on the left hand side of the street. You English drivers!"

Sach also cannot tell the difference between diamonds and glass as he thinks he is walking on some broken glass in the hotel's hallway. Sach: "Lucky I'm not walking around here without shoes." However, it is diamonds. At gunpoint, the crooks demand the Boys hand over the diamonds. It is Duke, not Sach, who saves the day as Duke drops the diamonds so he can kick the gun out of the smuggler's hand. Sach's ineptness is obvious as when he gets the gun and accidentally fires it near his own foot.

Finale: The newspaper headline reads: "Scotland Yard Honors Americans with Cracking Smuggling Ring." Gloria is presented with a special token of appreciation; namely, one large dog bone. Sach: "Hey wait a minute. Now wait a minute Gloria, we're in this thing together. Half of that thing is mine. Here's your half, take it." The guests laugh. Sach eats the bone and pets Gloria: "You're a wonderful puppy."

In the Money shows Sach being clueless about the job he is hired for. Not only is Sach clueless, but more so is Duke. By comparison, with the forty-one movies with Slip, and the seven movies with Duke, the differences are obvious. One of the things is that if Sach got a job that the Boys did not know about, Slip would have found a way to know what Sach was up to more quickly.

At the very least, Slip would have bullied Sach to find out. Duke never tries to really dominate Sach or go as far as Slip would. Duke calls Sach names, such as "lamebrain," and though he threatens Sach, he does not hit him nor have the control or "leash" on Sach as Slip had. Therefore, this difference in the relationship between Slip and Sach vs. Duke and Sach accounts for part of the reason why truly funny moments are non-existent in these movies.

As in the other movies, here Sach wears many hats; including a beret, a deerstalker (this time correctly), and his upturned cap.

Unfortunately, there is so little good comedy moments found in this ridiculous plot of Sach unknowingly smuggling diamonds that are hidden on a poodle headed to England. This is a disappointing finale to the *Bowery Boys* series. Sach Comedy Meter: 2.0 out of 4.0.

Summary of Sach Comedy Meter Ratings:
(Out of a maximum score of 4.0):

1. *Live Wires* (1946)–1.0

2. *In Fast Company* (1946)–1.5

3. *Bowery Bombshell* (1946)–2.0

4. *Spook Busters* (1946)–3.0

5. *Mr. Hex* (1946)–2.5

6. *Hard Boiled Mahoney* (1947)–2.5

7. *News Hounds* (1947)–2.5

8. *Bowery Buckaroos* (1947)–2.0

9. *Angels' Alley* (1948)–2.5

10. *Jinx Money* (1948)–2.0

11. *Smugglers' Cove* (1948)–2.0

12. *Trouble Makers* (1948)–2.5

13. *Fighting Fools* (1949)–2.8

14. *Hold That Baby!* (1949)–3.0

15. *Angels in Disguise* (1949)–2.0

16. *Master Minds* (1949)–4.0

17. *Blonde Dynamite* (1950)–2.5

18. *Lucky Losers* (1950)–3.5

19. *Triple Trouble* (1950)–2.5

20. *Blues Busters* (1950)–3.5

21. *Bowery Battalion* (1951)–2.0

22. *Ghost Chasers* (1951)–2.0

23. *Let's Go Navy!* (1951)–3.0

24. *Crazy over Horses* (1951)–2.5

25. *Hold That Line* (1952)–2.0

26. *Here Come the Marines* (1952)–2.0

27. *Feudin' Fools* (1952)–2.0

28. *No Holds Barred* (1952)–3.0

29. *Jalopy* (1953)–3.0

30. *Loose in London* (1953)–3.0

31. *Clipped Wings* (1953) –3.0

32. *Private Eyes* (1953)–3.8

33. *Paris Playboys* (1954)–4.0

34. *The Bowery Boys Meet the Monsters* (1954)–4.0

35. *Jungle Gents* (1954)–3.0

36. *Bowery to Bagdad* (1955)–4.0

37. *High Society* (1955)–2.8

38. *Spy Chasers* (1955)–4.0

39. *Jail Busters* (1955)–2.5

40. *Dig That Uranium* (1956)–3.8

41. *Crashing Las Vegas* (1956)–4.0

42. *Fighting Trouble* (1956)–1.5

43. *Hot Shots* (1956)–2.0

44. *Hold That Hypnotist* (1957)–3.0

45. *Spook Chasers* (1957)–2.5

46. *Looking For Danger* (1957)–2.0

47. *Up in Smoke* (1957)–2.0

48. *In the Money* (1958)–2.0

APPENDIX

Interview Transcript
NBC Television–February 5, 1963

The Tonight Show Starring Johnny Carson.

This interview with Huntz Hall is the earliest that is known to exist. The only surviving material is the audio taped by Phil R. Gries, Archival Television Audio, Inc. Gries provided the following transcript of that rare audio.

Gries: "Almost all of *The Tonight Show Starring Johnny Carson* episodes from 1962 to 1971 were wiped (original quad tapes erased). However, the audio survives as recorded off the air on ¼" reel to reel audiotape, direct line, at the time of the original broadcast."

Please note that the interview from the show ends abruptly. Gries said that he could not recall why but noted that this could be perhaps because only "the goodbyes" were left before the show ended.

Johnny Carson: "Many of you will remember him as one of the Dead End Kids. A lot of them will remember him as one of the zany Bowery Boys. But, I'll introduce him by his real name. Ladies and gentleman, say hello to Huntz Hall."

Huntz Hall: "Do you like the hat? You know, I came to New York. Everything is so British, you know, like *Beyond the Fringe*, and *Stop the World, You* [sic] *Want to Get Off*. So I put this on."

JC: "Huntz, it just doesn't seem to be you though. I don't know why?"

HH: "I told Sherlock Holmes it wouldn't work."

JC: "Hey, it's good to have you on the show. This is your first trip, isn't it?"

HH: "That's right."

JC: "How did you get away with that nutty stuff? That's funny stuff though. I mean the old slapstick type of humor. You're still playing all over television in the *Bowery Boys* series."

HH: "Yeah. We have 48 of them now on television, just released. Allied Artists Television Corporation just released them."

JC: "Do you guys get anything out of the television or is that in somebody else's hands? It's none of my business, but…"

HH: "We get a piece."

JC: "Oh you do."

HH: "Most actors get a pension; a pension plan. How much money you make a year. That's the Screen Actors Guild."

JC: "So you get a certain amount out of it."

HH: "Well, when you're 65 they give you a pension."

JC: "Well, it's like I was reading earlier in the show. Retire at 50 if you got $495 a month, and you can retire."

HH: "I told them, I'll shoot them double or nothing." (AUDIENCE LAUGHTER)

JC: "What are all the fellas doing who were in the series, *Dead End Kids* and *The Bowery Boys*? You ever keep in touch with them?"

HH: "Oh! Yeah."

JC: "There was Billy Halop, Gorcey, Leo Gorcey."

HH: "Billy's in the furniture business. He builds old furniture for people who live in the slums." (AUDIENCE LAUGHTER)

JC: "How about Gorcey? What's he doing now?"

HH: "He's a rancher."

JC: "Leo Gorcey, the rancher?"

HH: "Yeah. He's in the ranch business. He's got 2,300 acres of land up in Los Molinos, California.[92] He moved out of L.A. because he couldn't stand the traffic. It's the truth. He couldn't stand the traffic. He says, 'I'm moving.' He went to Northern California."

JC: "Got a ranch and went into the cattle business?"

HH: "The money, the ranch, four pencils. He's got konometers[93] in his house. Adding machines."

JC: "He's loaded now?"

HH: "That's his hobby, MONEY (AUDIENCE LAUGHTER). Nothing but money."

JC: "On a rainy day, everybody needs a hobby."

HH: "He takes care of the church. He does their books. He goes to church every Sunday."

JC: "You're putting me on now."

HH: "No! It's the truth. Like one time in the Valley, when he lived in North Hollywood, he took up the collection…you know for the church. He was like bookkeeping everything. He helped the priest. But, on Sunday when he took up the collection he used to walk down the aisle. There were actors there. And, they would go in their pocket and they would take out a buck to put in the basket. 'What are you doing? Put a fin in. You worked last week (AUDIENCE LAUGHTER). What's a matter here with the money?' That's the way he used to do it."

JC: "You do it well. You do a good impersonation of him."

HH: "He loves guns. He's got a big gun collection. Outside the church, he built a safe for the priest to take the money with his gun and everything. He thinks he's Jungle Jim. He goes out and hides the money (AUDIENCE LAUGHTER). He puts the money in the safe. The cement safe. And, all of a sudden in the middle of mass, when they're doing the offering, they hear gun shots that you won't believe. Pop! Pop! Pop! Pop! Six gun shots. People automatically run out of the church. Maybe people are shooting at them. And, there he was standing. And, there was a snake, like a garter snake, about this long, laying on the safe. And, he had shot it. Everybody looked and he says, 'He was trying to get near the money.'"(AUDIENCE LAUGHTER).

JC: "He was trying to get near the money! That's a funny story (AUDIENCE APPLAUSE). Extortion in church and then shooting the snakes outside."

HH: "And Gabe's in the show with Phil."

JC: "Gabe Dell."

HH: "He's in *Wonderful Town*. Bobby owns a piece of a club, and Bernard Punsley is a doctor. He did my nose job" (AUDIENCE LAUGHTER).

JC: "What is it, a special tonight? Watch *The Tonight Show*, friends. You went in to business. Somebody said you went into the construction business."

HH: "I wanted to go into business. I said, I had my acting and everything. So I wanted to become a business man. Some friend of mine came to me and says, I have a friend who's in the construction business. Go in and talk to him. So, I went in and he said, 'Look Huntz, we want you in the organization. And what we're gonna do…You go out and plug our product and we're gonna go on television with it, and you'll be the sponsor.' It was putting up siding on houses. Alright, I thought, I was going to do television. He said you'll have to go around and look at the pictures. So I said, 'great.' He took me into a house...the first house we went to. 'And, Mr. Hall's going to be with the advertising end of the business. He's going to be on television.' We are going to take your house and we are going to show it before and after. And, all of a sudden, from nowhere...you know I come from a family of 16 kids. 13 boys, 3 girls."

JJ: "You do?"

HH: "Yeah. 16 children in my family."

JC: (ASTONISHED, WHISTLE).

HH: "I saw eight kids. I saw food being taken out of their mouths. And this guy was going with a pitch and everything. He had him. And here he is and he's gonna do this. And, he had the man for like $7,200 for the deal. And I flipped. And, I screamed. I got up and said 'You're kidding.' I looked at the guy and said, 'He's robbing you out and out. He's a thief.'"

JC: "This is your partner."

HH: "He's a crook. You pick up a phone. Call SEARS. You get it for $12! (AUDIENCE LAUGHTER) I walked out. He sold the deal!"

JC: "And that was the end of your business affiliation?"

HH: "I said I can't take it. I got deathly ill."

JC: "They had a lot of pretty good rackets going on out there in California."

HH: "Oh yeah. Suede shoe boys. I couldn't wear suede shoes. That's why I got out of it."

JC: "We used to do commercials out there. One year what was very popular was this type of 'not siding.' It was something they sprayed on your house. It was like 'maltex' or something. I'm making up a name, and they would come on and they would pitch. And, they would spray this on your house and it would last forever. And the first rain, it would float off your house. And, by that time they're out of the state. A real racket."

Endnotes:

1. An example of this would be David Cook's 1,200-plus page *A History of Narrative Film*.
2. On Sundays, WPIX-TV Channel 11 broadcast Abbott & Costello movies from 11:30 a.m. to 1 p.m. This overlapped WNEW-TV Channel 5's airing of Gorcey & Hall's films from 12 noon to 1 p.m.
3. *Los Angeles Times,* October 14, 1990.
4. "News of the Screen," *New York Times,* April 21, 1937.
5. *New York Times,* May 30, 1937.
6. "Goldwyn Puts Poker Lesson in *Dead End*," *Chicago Daily Tribune,* June 18, 1937.
7. "Not So Dead End," 1944.
8. *Los Angeles Times,* March 4, 1938.
9. "Leg Art: Hollywood's New Crisis," *New York Times,* May 30, 1937.
10. Gorcey, Leo. *An Original Dead End Kid Presents Dead End Yells, Wedding Bells, Cockle Shells, and Dizzy Spells.* New York: Vantage, 1967.
11. "Local Boys Make Good in Films," *New York Times,* August 22, 1937.
12. *Washington Post,* September 25, 1937.
13. *Los Angeles Times,* March 4, 1938.
14. *Los Angeles Times,* November 30, 1938.

15. "'John Alden' of 'Dead End,'" *Pittsburgh Press,* September 1, 1938.
16. *Los Angeles Times,* January 27, 1939.
17. *Los Angeles Times,* January 27, 1939.
18. *Washington Post,* January 23, 1940. Additions in 1944 reprint.
19. *Washington Post,* June 14, 1939.
20. *Washington Post,* October 8, 1944.
21. *Washington Post,* November 26, 1939.
22. *Washington Post,* June 18, 1938.
23. *Washington Post,* June 15, 1938.
24. *Washington Post,* June 15, 1938.
25. John R. Franchey, *New York Times,* "Victims of Café Society," January 21, 1940.
26. *Washington Post,* Sept. 6, 1939.
27. *Washington Post,* July 16, 1940.
28. *Washington Post,* July 27, 1940.
29. *Washington Post,* September 16, 1940.
30. *Chicago Daily Tribune,* November 28, 1944.
31. "Looking at Hollywood with Hedda Hopper," *Chicago Tribune,* 1944.
32. *Chicago Daily Tribune,* August 1, 1938.
33. *Los Angeles Times,* June 18, 1941.
34. *Los Angeles Times,* October 6, 1939.
35. *Los Angeles Times,* October 25, 1941.
36. *Los Angeles Times,* December 24, 1941.
37. Tom Weaver, *Eye on Science Fiction: 20 Interviews with Classic Science Fiction and Horror Filmmakers.* McFarland, 2003.
38. *Washington Post,* November 25, 1942.

39. *Washington Post,* January 23, 1940.

40. David A. Cook, *A History of Narrative Film.* W. W. Norton & Co., 1981.

41. *Los Angeles Times,* July 24, 1941.

42. "Dead End Kid Dippy Didn't Sing, He Almost Didn't Talk," *Chicago Daily Tribune,* December 17, 1967.

43. *Los Angeles Times,* September 2, 1967.

44. Leonard Getz, *From Broadway to the Bowery: A History & Filmography of the Dead End Kids, Little Tough Guys, East Side Kids and Bowery Boys Films.* McFarland, 2006.

45. Tom Weaver, *Eye on Science Fiction: 20 Interviews with Classic Science Fiction and Horror Filmmakers,* McFarland, 2003.

46. Boyd Magers and Mike Fitzgerald. *Western Clippings* website.

47. *New York Times,* "Victims of Café Society," January 21, 1940.

48. *Washington Post,* August 15, 1951.

49. *Los Angeles Times,* December 16, 1952.

50. *Los Angeles Times,* December 20, 1952.

51. *Chicago Daily Tribune,* December 27, 1953.

52. *Washington Post,* April 2, 1953.

53. *Washington Post,* January 20, 1955.

54 *Los Angeles Times,* July 14, 1955.

55 *Chicago Daily Tribune,* September 1, 1955.

56 *Los Angeles Times,* July 26, 1956.

57 *Troy Record,* July 24, 1971.

58 *Chicago Daily Tribune,* April 19, 1959.

59 Eight of Hall's fifteen siblings died before adulthood.

60 *Chicago Daily Tribune,* May 30, 1964.

61   *Chicago Daily Tribune*, December 17, 1967.

62   *Lodi News-Sentinel*, February 23, 1971.

63   *Chicago Tribune*, September 12, 1971.

64   Folsom, Tom. *The Mad Ones: Crazy Joe Gallo and the Revolution at the Edge of the Underworld*, Weinstein Books, 2009, p. 11.

65   Hall appeared on Merv Griffin's shows three times: December 29, 1967; January 31, 1968; and June 2, 1971.

66   Woodson, Michelle. "Shiftless and Idol: An interview with Huntz Hall—A former 'Bowery Boy' talks about the past and present generations of slackers." *Entertainment Weekly*, June 3, 1994.

67   *Los Angeles Times*, September 28, 1966.

68   Florabel Muir, *The News and Courier* (Charleston, NC), January 14, 1967.

69   "Whatever ? happened," *Chicago Tribune*, May 21, 1967.

70   *Chicago Tribune*, December 17, 1967.

71   *Los Angeles Times*, January 9, 1968.

72   *Chicago Tribune*, October 3, 1971.

73   *Los Angeles Times*, October 17, 1970.

74   *Los Angeles Times*, April 18, 1971.

75   *Chicago Tribune*, January 8, 1971.

76   *Los Angeles Times*, July 1, 1971.

77   *Chicago Tribune*, July 30, 1972.

78   *Los Angeles Times*, July 7, 1974.

79   *Chicago Tribune*, May 31, 1976.

80   *Los Angeles Times*, April 11, 1976.

81   *Los Angeles Times*, June 16, 1977.

82   *Chicago Tribune*, October 13, 1977.

83 *Los Angeles Times*, November 7, 1977.

84 *Los Angeles Times*, June 9, 1982.

85 *Los Angeles Times*, September 23, 1982.

86 *Los Angeles Times*, October 2, 1982.

87 *Los Angeles Times*, September 22, 1983.

88 *Los Angeles Times*, July 6, 1988.

89 *Los Angeles Times*, October 14, 1990.

90 *Chicago Daily Tribune*, February 14, 1946.

91 *Los Angeles Times*, October 14, 1990.

92 Gorcey lived in Los Molinos, California at 207 Mary Lee Ranch from 1956 until his death in 1969. It is nearly 500 miles north of Los Angeles. In the 1960s, Hall lived in Hollywood at 7719 Hampton Avenue, apartment #17.

93 Hall meant comptometer. A konometer measures airborne dust.

Selected Bibliography:

Interviews with Rev. Gary R. Hall by Jim Manago (April 2013–February 2014)

Interviews with Huntz Hall by Johnny Carson (February 5, 1963), by Richard Lamparski (1965), by Tom Snyder (March 19, 1979), and by David Letterman (February 22, 1983).

"Actor Huntz Hall Sued for Divorce." *Los Angeles Times*, May 9, 1944, 5.

"An Evening with the Bowery Boys." *Los Angeles Times*, June 9, 1982.

Associated Press. "Retrial." *Washington Post*, February 27, 1949.

Beck, Marilyn. "An 'East Side Kid' defends Nureyev." *Chicago Tribune*, October 13, 1977, a2.

Broeske, Pat H. "In Search of...Huntz Hall." *Los Angeles Times*, October 14, 1990.

"Cagney, O'Brien Stars Underworld Story Full of Action." *Washington Post*, November 26, 1938, X18.

Chicago Daily Tribune, September 1, 1956, 6.

Churchill, Douglas W. "Leg Art: Hollywood's New Crisis." *New York Times*, May 30, 1937, 123.

"Collegiate Opus Shown: *Zis Boom Bah*." *Los Angeles Times*, October 25, 1941.

"Count Basie Puts 'Em in Aisles." *Los Angeles Times*, October 6, 1939.

"*Crime School*." *Washington Post*, June 15, 1938, X14.

"*Crime School* Perfect Vehicle for Youths." *Washington Post*, June 18, 1938, X16.

Crosby, John. "Not Required: Panel People Now Don't Think at All." *Washington Post*, August 15, 1951, B13.

"Dead End Kids Prove Nemesis to Humphrey Bogart." *Los Angeles Times*, March 4, 1938.

"East Side Kids Score in *Bowery Blitzkrieg*." *Los Angeles Times*, July 24, 1941.

"Editor TV Times." *Los Angeles Times*, April 18, 1971.

"Feast Planned for Orphans." *Los Angeles Times*, December 24, 1941.

Folsom, Tom. *The Mad Ones: Crazy Joe Gallo and the Revolution at the Edge of the Underworld*. Weinstein Books, 2009.

Franchey, John R. "Victims of Café Society." *New York Times*, January 21, 1940.

"Friars Roasting." *Los Angeles Times*, January 8, 1968.

"Friends to Honor Late Actor Garfield." *Los Angeles Times*, September 22, 1983.

Getz, Leonard. *From Broadway to the Bowery: A History & Filmography of the Dead End Kids, Little Tough Guys, East Side Kids and Bowery Boys Films*. McFarland, 2006.

Goldsborough, Robert. "Whatever ? happened." *Chicago Tribune*, May 21, 1967, E4.

"*Hit the Road* Amusing New Dead End Kids Feature." *Los Angeles Times*, June 18, 1941.

Gorcey, Leo. *An Original Dead End Kid Presents Dead End Yells, Wedding Bells, Cockle Shells, and Dizzy Spells*. New York: Vantage, 1967.

Hayes, David and Brent Walker. *The Films of the Bowery Boys*. Secaucus: Citadel, 1982.

"Hollywood Parade." *Chicago Daily Tribune*, September 3, 1957.

Hopper, Hedda. "A Former 'Dead End Kid' Regrets Every Penny He Made From the Play's Hollywood Career." *Washington Post*, January 23, 1940, 11.

Hopper, Hedda. "Looking at Hollywood." *Chicago Daily Tribune*, November 25, 1942, 18.

Hopper, Hedda. "In Hollywood." *Washington Post*, October 8, 1944, 56.

Hopper, Hedda. "Looking at Hollywood." *Chicago Daily Tribune*, November 28, 1944, 19.

Selected Bibliography

Hopper, Hedda. "Looking at Hollywood." *Chicago Daily Tribune*, February 14, 1946, 26.

Hopper, Hedda. *Los Angeles Times*, December 16, 1952.

"Huntz Hall, Dead End Kid, Fined in Row." *Los Angeles Times*, July 14, 1955.

"Huntz Hall Thankful The Bowery Boys Died." *Lodi News-Sentinel*, February 23, 1971.

"Huntz Hall–Still A Dead End Kid." *Los Angeles Times*, July 1, 1971.

" 'John Alden' of 'Dead End.' " *Pittsburgh Press*, September 1, 1938.

Kaufman, Michael T. "Huntz Hall, Perpetual Youth in Bowery Films, Dies at 78." *New York Times*, February 2, 1999, B9.

" 'Kids' Have Light Brush with Police." *Los Angeles Times*, November 30, 1938.

Kilgallen, Dorothy. *Washington Post*, January 20, 1955, 47.

Kilday, Greg. "Challenged *Valentino*." *Los Angeles Times*, November 7, 1977.

Kramer, Carol. "New York Today: Non-Reminiscences of a Dead End Kid." *Chicago Tribune*, July 30, 1972, w1.

Los Angeles Times, January 18, 1955.

Los Angeles Times, April 12, 1955.

Los Angeles Times, April 6, 1960.

Los Angeles Times, October 17, 1970.

Los Angeles Times, July 7, 1974.

Los Angeles Times, January 19, 1975.

Los Angeles Times, June 16, 1977.

Los Angeles Times, September 23, 1982.

Los Angeles Times, October 5, 1987.

Los Angeles Times, July 6, 1988.

Los Angeles Times, October 14, 1990.

"Marines Host Screen Event." *Los Angeles Times*, July 26, 1956.

Michaels, Ken. "Say, isn't that Huntz Hall over there?" *Chicago Tribune*, September 12, 1971, h36.

"Moving Day for Musical Chairs." *Los Angeles Times*, January 18, 1955.

Muir, Florabel. *The News and Courier* (Charleston, South Carolina), January 14, 1967.

O'Brian, Jack. "Sammy-Mai Rift Rumors Afloat." December 28, 1966, B11.

"Original Kids Add Pepper to Water-Front Drama, with Sylvia Sidney." *Washington Post*, September 25, 1937, 8.

Parish, James. *The Great Movie Series*. Cranbury, New Jersey: A. S. Barnes and Co., Inc., 1971.

Parsons, Louella O. "Close-Ups and Long Shots of the Motion Picture Scene." *Washington Post*, June 14, 1938, 18.

Parsons, Louella O. "Close-Ups and Long Shots of the Motion Picture Scene." *Washington Post*, May 17, 1939.

Parsons, Louella O. "Close-Ups and Long Shots of the Motion Picture Scene." *Washington Post*, September 6, 1939, 16.

Parsons, Louella O. "Close-Ups and Long Shots of the Motion Picture Scene." *Washington Post*, July 16, 1940, X8.

Parsons, Louella O. "Close-Ups and Long Shots of the Motion Picture Scene." *Washington Post*, July 27, 1940, 4.

Parsons, Louella O. "Close-Ups and Long Shots of the Motion Picture Scene." *Washington Post*, September 12, 1940, 10.

Prelutsky, Burt. "The Charmer in the Dell." *Los Angeles Times*, April 11, 1976.

Pryor, Thomas M. "Local Boys Make Good in Films." *New York Times*, August 22, 1937, X3.

Roat, Richard. *Hollywood's Made-to-Order Punks: The Dead End Kids, Little Tough Guys, East Side Kids and the Bowery Boys*. BearManor Media, 2009.

Saints and Sinners 24-hour Milkathon." *Los Angeles Times*, December 20, 1952.

Scott, Vernon. *Chicago Tribune*, September 2, 1967.

Scott, Vernon. "Bombs Away: The Celluloid on the Shelves." *Chicago Tribune*, October 3, 1971, g7.

Shaffer, George. "Goldwyn Puts Poker Lesson in 'Dead End,' Young New Actors to Illustrate Roles." *Chicago Daily Tribune*, June 18, 1937, 23.

Siskel, Gene. "Tempo/Movies: Won Ton Ton can't save bad script." *Chicago Tribune*, May 31, 1976, a9.

Smith, Cecil. *The Troy Record*, July 24, 1971, 26.

Special to the *New York Times*. "News of the Screen." *New York Times*, April 21, 1937.

Special to the *New York Times*. "Huntz Hall, Arrested: Former 'Dead End Kid' Accused in Marijuana Case." *New York Times*, October 30, 1948, 32.

Special to the *New York Times*. "Huntz Hall, Actor, Cleared." *New York Times*, April 19, 1949. 28.

Stitt, Tom. "Letter to 'Sound Off, Sports Fans.'" *Chicago Tribune*, January 8, 1971, c3.

Terry, Clifford. "Dead End Kid Dippy Didn't Sing–He Almost Didn't Talk." *Chicago Tribune*, December 17, 1967, h7.

Terry, Clifford. "Holiday Bookings Bring a Flood of New Films." *Chicago Tribune*, December 17, 1967, h7.

"The Bowery Boys Top Stage Show at Regal Theater." *Chicago Daily Tribune*, December 27, 1953, f10.

Tinée, May. "'Dead End' Kids Succeed Again in Crime Film: 'Little Tough Guy.'" *Chicago Daily Tribune*, August 1, 1938, 17.

"TV Mailbag: Is Huntz Hall living?" *Chicago Daily Tribune*, May 30, 1964, D2.

United Press International. "Held." *Washington Post* and *Times Herald*, February 17, 1959, A11.

Walters, Larry. "Radio TV Gag Bag." *Chicago Daily Tribune*, April 19, 1959, G60. *Washington Post*, November 26, 1938, x18.

Weaver, Tom. *Eye on Science Fiction: 20 Interviews with Classic Science Fiction and Horror Filmmakers*, McFarland, 2003.

Winchell, Walter. *Washington Post*, April 2, 1953, 33.

"Wives Team Up, Divorce Former Dead End Kids." *Los Angeles Times*, May 15, 1953.

Woodson, Michelle. "An interview with Huntz Hall–A former 'Bowery Boy' talks about the past and present generations of slackers." *Entertainment Weekly*, June 3, 1994.

Award:

Blue Ribbon Award, New York Theatre Critics Circle, *A Walk in the Sun*, 1945, Hall played Private Carraway.

Credits:

The film dates are for U.S. general release.

Feature Films:

> *"The greatest gangster thriller that ever exploded from the screen!"*
> *Dead End* (1937) D: William Wyler.

Sylvia Sidney, Joel McCrea, Humphrey Bogart, Wendy Barrie, Claire Trevor, Allen Jenkins, Marjorie Main, Billy Halop, Huntz Hall, Bobby Jordan, Leo Gorcey, Gabriel Dell, Bernard Punsly, Charles Peck, Minor Watson, James Burke, Ward Bond, Elisabeth Risdon, Esther Dale, George Humbert, Marcelle Corday, Charles Halton, Robert E. Homans, Bill Dagwell, Wade Boteler, Jerry Cooper, Kath Ann Lujan, Gertrude Valerie, Tom Ricketts, Charlotte Treadway, Al Bridge, Maude Lambert, Bud Geary, Frank Shields, Lucile Browne, Mickey Martin, Wesley Girard, Esther Howard, Gilbert Clayton, Earl Asam, Mona Monet, Donald M. Barry, Sidney Kibrick, Larry Harris, Norman Salling.

Film adaptation of Sidney Kingsley's play about the inhabitants of a New York City slum. Laborer McCrea is torn between rich Barrie and down-to-earth Sidney. A dangerous, legendary gangster Bogart returns to find that his beloved mother has renounced him and his former girlfriend is now a prostitute. A gang of neighborhood toughs populate the streets. Screenplay written by Lillian Hellman. Produced by Samuel Goldwyn and Merritt Hulburd. Filmed at Samuel Goldwyn Studios, 7200 Santa Monica Boulevard, West Hollywood, California.

Songs:
"Boo Hoo" (composed by Carmen Lombardo; John Jacob Loeb;

Edward Heyman) (sung by Huntz Hall)

"The Prisoner's Song" (Guy Massey) (performed on kazoo by Bobby

Jordan and sung by Hall and the boys)

"Girl of My Dreams" (Sunny Clapp)

Academy Award Nominations
(Picture) Samuel Goldwyn Productions.

(Supporting Actress) Claire Trevor.

(Cinematography) Gregg Toland.

(Art Direction) Richard Day.

Music by Alfred Newman, (Edward B. Powell).

Released on August 27.

(93 minutes/Western Electric Mirrophonic Recording/video/laserdisc/DVD)

Samuel Goldwyn Productions/United Artists

Crime School (1938) D: Lewis Seiler.

Humphrey Bogart, Gale Page, Billy Halop, Bobby Jordan, Huntz Hall, Leo Gorcey, Bernard Punsley [Punsly], Gabriel Dell, George Offerman Jr., Weldon Heyburn, Cy Kendall, Charles Trowbridge, Spencer Charters, Donald Briggs, Frank Jacquet, Helen MacKellar, Al Bridge, Sibyl Harris, Paul Porcasi, Frank Otto, Ed [Edward] Gargan, James B. Carson, John Ridgely, Harry Cording, Hally [Hal E.] Chester, Ethan Laidlaw, Vera Lewis, Clayton Moore.

Bogart becomes the warden of a reformatory and tries to clean out the corrupt administrators running the facility; he receives help from a group of boys recently sent there. Hall is Richard 'Goofy' Slade. Screenplay by Crane Wilbur and Vincent Sherman, from a story by Wilbur. Produced by Bryan Foy. A remake of the 1933 film *The Mayor of Hell*.

Songs:
"Rain, Rain, Go Away!" (traditional, composer unknown) (sung by Huntz Hall)

"Put On Your Old Grey Bonnet" (Percy Wenrich; Stanley Murphy)

Music by Max Steiner, (Leo F. Forbstein, Hugo Friedhofer, George Parrish).

Released on May 28. (86 minutes/DVD)

Warner Bros.-First National

> *"Here again... to jolt you from your seats!"*
> *Little Tough Guy* (1938) D: Harold Young.

Robert Wilcox, Helen Parrish, Marjorie Main, Jackie Searl, Peggy Stewart, Helen MacKellar, Ed [Edward] Pawley, Olin Howland, Pat C. Flick, Billy Halop, Huntz Hall, Gabriel Dell, Bernard Punsly, Hally [Hal E.] Chester, David Gorcey, Edward Gehman, Robert Homans, Eleanor Hanson, Charles Trowbridge, Selmer Jackson, Buster Phelps, George Billings, Ben Taggart, William Ruhl, Hooper Atchley, Jason Robards [Sr.], Tom London, Harry Hayden, Paul Dubov, J. Pat O'Malley, Samuel S. Hinds (voice).

Halop becomes a criminal after his father is condemned for a murder he didn't commit. Halop forms a gang that includes Hall (as Carl "Pig" Adams), Dell, Punsly, Gorcey, and Chester. A rash of lawless activity sees them trapped by police. Screenplay by Gilson Brown and Brenda Weisberg, from a story by Weisberg. Produced by Ken Goldsmith.

Music by Charles Previn, (Charles Henderson, Hans J. Salter, Frank Skinner).

Released on July 22.

(80 minutes/Western Electric Mirrophonic Recording/video/DVD)

Universal

"The saga of America's dirty-faced kids... and the breaks that life won't give them!"

Angels with Dirty Faces (1938) D: Michael Curtiz.

James Cagney, Pat O'Brien, Humphrey Bogart, Ann Sheridan, George Bancroft, Billy Halop, Bobby Jordan, Leo Gorcey, Gabriel Dell, Huntz Hall, Bernard Punsley [Punsly], Joe Downing, Edward Pawley, Adrian Morris, Frankie Burke, William Tracy, Marilyn Knowlden, William Worthington, Earl Dwire, Oscar O'Shea, Harris Berger, William Pawley, John Hamilton, Mary Gordon, Vera Lewis, Robert Homans, John Harron, George Offerman Jr., Harry Hayden, Dick Rich, Steven Darrell, Joe A. Devlin, Frank Coghlan Jr., Dick Wessel, Dave Durand, Charles Trowbridge, Lane Chandler, Jack Perrin, Sonny Bupp, St. Brendan's Church Choir [The Robert Mitchell Boy Choir].

Tough gangster Cagney revisits his old neighborhood to find a group of slum boys idolizing him and his illegal exploits. Slowly seeing himself as a bad influence, Jimmy decides to do something about it. Hall plays Crab. Screenplay by John Wexley and Warren Duff (with uncredited contributions by Ben Hecht and Charles MacArthur), from a story by Rowland Brown. Produced by Samuel Bischoff. Portions filmed at Sing Sing Penitentiary, Ossining, New York.

Songs:
"Angels with Dirty Faces" (Maurice Spitalny; Fred Fisher)

"In My Merry Oldsmobile" (Gus Edwards; Vincent Bryan)

"The Sidewalks of New York" (instrumental) (Charles Lawlor)

"Shuffle Off to Buffalo" (instrumental) (Harry Warren)

"From Me to You" (instrumental) (Fabian Andre; Wayne King; Nat Conney)

Academy Award Nominations
(Actor) James Cagney.

(Director) Michael Curtiz.

(Writing—Original Story) Rowland Brown.

National Board of Review Award
(Acting) James Cagney.

New York Film Critics Circle Award
(Actor) James Cagney.

Music by Max Steiner, Hugo Friedhofer, Leo F. Forbstein. Released on November 24. (97 minutes/computer color version/video/laserdisc/DVD) Warner Bros.-First National

> "I am a fugitive... I am hunted by ruthless men! I am shunned by decent women! I am doomed to hide forever!"
> *They Made Me a Criminal* (1939) D: Busby Berkeley.

John Garfield, Claude Rains, Ann Sheridan, May Robson, Gloria Dickson, Billy Halop, Bobby Jordan, Leo Gorcey, Huntz Hall, Gabriel Dell, Bernard Punsley [Punsly], Robert Gleckler, John Ridgely, Barbara Pepper, William [B.] Davidson, Ward Bond, Louis Jean Heydt, Frank Riggi, Cliff Clarke [Clark], Dick Wessel, Raymond Brown, Sam Hayes, Robert Strange, Arthur Housman, Sam McDaniel, Clem Bevans, Doris Lloyd, Irving Bacon, John Harron, Ronald Sinclair.

Boxer Garfield fears he has killed a man in a brawl, so he flees westward and finds refuge at Robson's desert ranch. Hall is Dippy, one of several delinquents undergoing rehabilitation at the spread. Screenplay by Sig Herzig, from a novel by Bertram Millhauser and Beulah Marie Dix. Produced by Hal B. Wallis. A remake of the 1933 film *The Life of Jimmy Dolan*. Portions filmed in Palm Desert, California.

Songs:
"M-O-T-H-E-R, a Word That Means the World to Me" (Theodore Morse; Howard Johnson)

"By a Waterfall" (Sammy Fain; Irving Kahal) (sung and whistled by Huntz Hall)

"Cowboy from Brooklyn" (instrumental) (Harry Warren)

"The Whip" (instrumental) (Abe Holzmann)

"Spirit of Independence" (instrumental) (Holzmann)

Music by Max Steiner, Leo F. Forbstein, (Hugo Friedhofer). Released on January 28. (92 minutes/RCA Sound/video/laserdisc/DVD) Warner Bros.

"The right road… or the 'last mile'… which way are they headed?"
Hell's Kitchen (1939) D: Lewis Seiler, E.A. Dupont.

Margaret Lindsay, Ronald Reagan, Stanley Fields, Billy Halop, Bobby Jordan, Leo Gorcey, Huntz Hall, Gabriel Dell, Bernard Punsley [Punsly], Frankie Burke, Grant Mitchell, Fred [Frederic] Tozere, Arthur Loft, Vera Lewis, Robert Homans, Charley Foy, Raymond Bailey, Clem Bevans, George Irving, Ila Rhodes, Lee Phelps, Jimmy O'Gatty, Don Turner, Joe A. Devlin, Jimmie Lucas, Jack Kenney, Sol Gorss, Cliff Saum, Charles Sullivan, Jack Gardner, Max Hoffman Jr., Dick Rich, Tom Wilson, Reid Kilpatrick, George O'Hanlon, Jack Mower, Ruth Robinson, George Offerman Jr.

Reagan befriends a gang of wayward teens when they are placed in a brutal youth shelter. Hall plays Bingo. Screenplay by Crane Wilbur and Fred Niblo Jr., from a story by Wilbur. Produced by Mark Hellinger and Bryan Foy. A remake of the 1933 film *The Mayor of Hell.*

Song:
"Auld Lang Syne" (traditional melody; lyrics by Robert Burns) (sung by

Stanley Fields, Huntz Hall, and boys)

Music by (Heinz Roemheld). Released on July 8. (81 minutes/DVD) Warner Bros.

The Angels Wash Their Faces (1939) D: Ray Enright.

Ann Sheridan, Billy Halop, Bernard Punsley [Punsly], Leo Gorcey, Huntz Hall, Gabriel Dell, Bobby Jordan, Ronald Reagan, Bonita Granville, Frankie Thomas, Henry O'Neill, Eduardo Ciannelli, Berton Churchill, Bernard Nedell, Dick Rich, Jack [Jackie] Searl, Margaret Hamilton, Marjorie Main, Minor Watson, Cyrus [Cy] Kendall, Grady Sutton, Aldrich Bowker, Robert Strange, Egon Brecher, Sibyl Harris, Frank Coghlan Jr., Frankie Burke, John Hamilton, John Ridgely, William Hopper, Elliott Sullivan, Charles Trowbridge, John Harron, Howard Hickman, Lee Phelps, Jack Clifford, Tom Wilson, Edward Keane, Max Hoffman Jr., Wendell Niles.

A district attorney's son (Reagan) strives to smash an arson racket and gets help from the Dead End Kids (including Hall as Huntz). Screenplay by Michael Fessier, Niven Busch, and Robert Buckner, from a story by Jonathan Finn. Produced by Max Siegel. A follow-up to the 1938 film *Angels with Dirty Faces*.

Songs:
"A-Tisket A-Tasket" (instrumental) (traditional, composer unknown)
"In a Moment of Weakness" (instrumental) (Harry Warren)
Music by Adolph Deutsch, Leo F. Forbstein, Ray Heindorf.
Released on August 26.
(84 minutes/RCA Victor Sound)
Warner Bros.-First National

> "Call the riot squad! Because the Dead End Kids and the Little Tough Guys are battling for control of the gutter!"
> *Call A Messenger* (1939) D: Arthur Lubin.

Billy Halop, Huntz Hall, Robert Armstrong, Mary Carlisle, Anne Nagel, Victor Jory, Larry [Buster] Crabbe, El Brendel, Jimmy Butler, George Offerman Jr., Hally [Hal E.] Chester, William 'Billy' Benedict, David Gorcey, Harris Berger, Jimmy O'Gatty, Cliff Clark, John Hamilton, J. Anthony Hughes, Kay Sutton, James C. Morton, Sherwood Bailey, Joey Ray, Ruth Rickaby, Frank Mitchell, James Farley, Frank O'Connor, Lyle Moraine, Payne Johnson, Jack Gardner, Kernan Cripps, Russ Powell, Wilson Benge, Louise Franklin.

Juvenile hoodlum Halop takes a job with a messenger service in order to escape reform school. He tries to steer his sister away from gangster Crabbe. Hall plays Pig.

Screenplay by Arthur T. Horman, from a story by Sally Sandlin and Michael Kraike. Produced by Ken Goldsmith.

Song:
"When You and I Were Young, Maggie" (instrumental) (composer unknown)

Music by (Hans J. Salter).

Released on November 3.

(65 minutes/Western Electric Mirrophonic Recording)

Universal

On Dress Parade (1939) D: William Clemens, (Noel Smith).

Billy Halop, Bobby Jordan, Huntz Hall, Gabriel Dell, Leo Gorcey, Bernard Punsley [Punsly], John Litel, Frankie Thomas, Cissie [Cecilia] Loftus, Selmer Jackson, Aldrich Bowker, Douglas Meins, William Gould, Don [Donald] Douglas, Eddie Acuff, Creighton Hale, John Hamilton, John Harron, William Hopper, George Offerman Jr., George Reeves, John Ridgely, Dick Simmons.

At a military school, non-conformist Gorcey defies discipline with near-tragic results, ostracizing him from his fellow cadets. Hall is Cadet Johnny Cabot. Screenplay by Tom Reed and Charles Belden. Produced by Bryan Foy. Portions filmed at Warner Ranch, Calabasas, California.

Songs:
"How Dry I Am" (instrumental) (traditional, composer unknown)

"The Battle Cry of Freedom" (instrumental) (George Frederick Root)

"My Buddy" (instrumental) (Walter Donaldson)

"Home on the Range" (Daniel E. Kelley; Brewster M. Hickey) (sung by Huntz Hall)

"You're in the Army Now" (traditional, composer unknown)

Music by (Howard Jackson).

Released on November 18.

(62 minutes/DVD)

Warner Bros.

> "He lives to kill and kills to live!"
>
> *The Return of Doctor X* (1939) D: Vincent Sherman.

Humphrey Bogart, Rosemary Lane, Wayne Morris, Dennis Morgan, John Litel, Lya Lys, Huntz Hall, Charles [C.] Wilson, Vera Lewis, Olin Howland, Cliff Saum, Creighton Hale, John Ridgely, Joseph Crehan, Glenn Langan, DeWolf [William] Hopper, Ian Wolfe, Jack Mower.

Horror opus with Bogart as Marshall Quesne, an executed criminal who has been brought back to life—but murders to obtain the fresh blood he needs to maintain his undead existence. Hall is Pinky. Screenplay by Lee Katz, from a story by William J. Makin. Produced by Bryan Foy.

Music by (Bernhard Kaun).

Released on December 2.

(62 minutes/DVD)

Warner Bros.-First National

> "Hold everything... the gang's here again! Fists fly and jaws crack! As the 'Kids' and the 'Guys' join forces to round up a racket ring in the rowdiest, roughest, fastest, funniest package of dynamite entertainment."
>
> *You're Not So Tough* (1940) D: Joe May.

Billy Halop, Huntz Hall, Gabriel Dell, Bernard Punsly, Bobby Jordan, Nan Grey, Rosina Galli, Henry Armetta, Eddy Waller, Harry Hayden, Joe King, Arthur Loft, Cliff Clark, Evelyn Selbie, Joe Whitehead, Harry Humphrey, Don Rowan, Hally [Hal E.] Chester, Harris Berger, David Gorcey, Ralph Dunn, Kernan Cripps, Eddie Phillips,

Ralph Lapere, Marty [Martin] Faust, Frank Bischell, Heinie Conklin, Harry Strang, Ed Piel Sr., Spade Cooley.

Halop and his cohorts are satisfied to ride the rails and promote crap games to make money—until trouble with the law paroles them into jobs at a California farm. While there, Halop takes on the responsibility of helping the matronly owner when she comes into conflict with a produce packing company. Hall is Halop's sidekick, Albert—also known as Pig. Screenplay by Arthur T. Horman and an uncredited Brenda Weisberg, from the story "Son of Mama Posita" by Maxwell Aley. Produced by Ken Goldsmith. Portions filmed in Salinas Valley, California.

Music by Hans J. Salter.

Released on July 26.

(71 minutes/Western Electric Mirrophonic Recording)

Universal

> "Their first action-packed serial… the gang's all here… on the most thrilling man-hunt ever imagined!"

Junior G-Men (1940/serial) D: Ford Beebe, John Rawlins.

Billy Halop, Huntz Hall, Gabriel Dell, Bernard Punsly, Ken Lundy, Kenneth Howell, Roger Daniel[s], Phillip Terry, Russell Hicks, Cy Kendall, Ben Taggart, Victor Zimmerman, Edgar Edwards, Gene Rizzi, Florence Halop, Harris Berger, Hally [Hal E.] Chester, Donald Curtis, George Eldredge, Ralph Peters, Jean Brooks, Lane Chandler, Kenneth Harlan, Ethan Laidlaw, Tom London, Pierce Lyden, David Sharpe, Tom Steele.

Chapters:
1. Enemies Within
2. The Blast of Doom
3. Human Dynamite
4. Blazing Danger
5. Trapped by Traitors
6. Traitor's Treachery
7. Flaming Death
8. Hurled Through Space
9. The Plunge of Peril
10. The Toll of Treason
11. Descending Doom
12. The Power of Patriotism

A gang of street toughs join the FBI in pursuing a violent, subversive group who have kidnapped a scientist—father to one of the boys. Hall plays Gyp. Screenplay by George H. Plympton, Basil Dickey, and Rex Taylor. Produced by Saul A. Goodkind and Henry McRae. Portions filmed at Metropolitan Airport, Los Angeles, California.

Music by Charles Previn.

Released on July 19.

(240 minutes/Western Electric Mirrophonic Recording)

Universal

"Fighting their way up to the skies! The gang from across the tracks demand the right to win their wings!"

Give Us Wings (1940) D: Charles Lamont.

Billy Halop, Huntz Hall, Gabriel Dell, Bernard Punsly, Bobby Jordan, Wallace Ford, Anne Gwynne, Victor Jory, Shemp Howard, Milburn Stone, Harris Berger, William 'Billy' Benedict, James Flavin, Addison Richards, Etta McDaniel, Paul White, Milton Kibbee, Ben Lewis, Ethan Laidlaw, Tom Steele, Jimmy Wakely, Johnny Bond, Dick Reinhart.

The Little Tough Guys (including Hall as Pig) get involved with a disreputable crop dusting outfit when they want to become flyers. Screenplay by Arthur T. Horman and Robert Lee Johnson, from the story "Men of Dust"/"Crop Dusters" by Eliot Gibbons. Produced by Ken Goldsmith.

Songs:
"Come on Down" (Dick Reinhart)

"On a Blue Ridge Mountain Trail" (Johnny Bond; Johnny Marvin)

"Fur Away" (composer unknown)

"Reuben, Reuben" (composer unknown)

"Swing Your Partner" (composer unknown)

"Happy Jubilee" (composer unknown)

Music by Charles Previn, Hans J. Salter.

Released on December 20.

(62 minutes/Western Electric Mirrophonic Recording)

Universal

> *"Adopted... by a dame! The gang meets a new boss... and she's truthful, tender... and tough!"*
>
> Hit the Road (1941) D: Joe May.

Gladys George, Barton MacLane, Billy Halop, Huntz Hall, Gabriel Dell, Bernard Punsly, Bobs Watson, Evelyn Ankers, Charles Lang, Shemp Howard, Walter Kingsford, Eily Malyon, Edward Pawley, John Harmon, Charles R. Moore, Hally [Hal E.] Chester, Jess Lee Brooks, Charles Sullivan, Ernie Stanton, Lee Moore, Kernan Cripps.

When mob violence affects a gang of youths, they are packed off to a ranch. However, the boys cannot escape the gangsters—who now threaten their new guardian's family. Hall is Pig. Screenplay by Robert Lee Johnson and Brenda Weisberg, from a story by Johnson. Produced by Ken Goldsmith.

Music by Hans J. Salter.

Released on June 27.

(61 minutes/Western Electric Mirrophonic Recording/video)

Universal

Bowery Blitzkrieg (1941) D: Wallace Fox.

Leo Gorcey, Bobby Jordan, Huntz Hall, Key[e] Luke, Warren Hull, Charlotte Henry, Bobby Stone, Donald Haines, Sunshine Sammy Morrison, David Gorcey, Martha Wentworth, Jack Mulhall, Eddie Foster, Dennis Moore, Tony Carson, Pat Costello, Dick Ryan, Minerva Urecal.

Some crooks try to persuade Leo Gorcey to throw an upcoming prizefight. Hall plays Limpy in his first entry in the East Side Kids series. Screenplay by Sam Robins and an uncredited Carl Foreman, from a story by Brendan Wood and Don Mullahy. Produced by Sam Katzman.

Song:
"Jeanie with the Light Brown Hair" (Stephen Foster) (sung by Huntz Hall)

Music by Johnny Lange, Lew Porter.

Released on September 8.

(62 minutes/Glen Glenn Sound/video/DVD)

Banner/Monogram

Mob Town (1941) D: William Nigh.

Dick Foran, Anne Gwynne, Billy Halop, Huntz Hall, Gabriel Dell, Bernard Punsly, Darryl Hickman, Samuel S. Hinds, Victor Kilian, Truman Bradley, John Butler, John Sheehan, Peter Sullivan, Dorothy Darrell, Beatrice Roberts, Cliff Clark, Paul Fix, Will Wright, Eva Puig, Dorothy Vaughan, Edward Emerson, Rosina Galli, Mary Kelley, Dick Rich, Bob Gregory, Claire Whitney, Terry Frost, John Kellogg, Clara Blore, Harris Berger, Duke York, Hally [Hal E.] Chester, Joe Recht, Eddie Dew, Pat Costello, Riley Hill.

A policeman (Foran) tries to keep some street boys from getting into serious trouble, but he cannot reach the younger brother (Halop) of a man he arrested. Hall is Pig. Screenplay by Brenda Weisberg and Walter Doniger. Produced by Ken Goldsmith.

Music by Hans J. Salter.

Released on October 3.

(70 minutes/Western Electric Mirrophonic Recording)

Universal

"Each chapter a cargo of death-defying thrills!"
   Sea Raiders (1941/serial) D: Ford Beebe, John Rawlins.

Billy Halop, Huntz Hall, Gabriel Dell, Bernard Punsly, Hally [Hal E.] Chester, Joe Recht, William Hall, John McGuire, Mary Field, Edward Keane, Marcia Ralston, Reed Hadley, Stanley Blystone, Richard Alexander, Ernie Adams, Jack Clifford, Richard Bond, Morgan Wallace, Eddie Dunn, Dick Curtis, John Merton, Jack Mulhall, Paul Newlan, House Peters Jr., Tom Steele, Duke York, Forrest Taylor.

Chapters:
1. The Raider Strikes
2. Flaming Torture
3. The Tragic Crash
4. The Raider Strikes Again
5. Flames of Fury
6. Blasted from the Air
7. Victims of the Storm
8. Dragged to Their Doom
9. Battling the Beast
10. Periled by a Panther
11. Entombed in a Tunnel
12. Paying the Penalty

A naval scourge known as the Sea Raider is sinking Allied ships, which prompts a gang of patriotic youths to ferret out this enemy villain. Hall plays Toby Nelson. Screenplay by Clarence Upson Young and Paul Huston. Produced by Henry MacRae. Duke York was Huntz Hall's stunt double.

Music by Charles Previn, Milton Rosen.

Released on October 14.

(229 minutes/Western Electric Mirrophonic Recording/DVD)

Universal

Spooks Run Wild (1941) D: Phil Rosen.

Bela Lugosi, Leo Gorcey, Bobby Jordan, Huntz Hall, Sunshine Sammy Morrison, David [Dave] O'Brien, Dorothy Short, David Gorcey, Donald Haines, Dennis Moore, P.J. Kelly, Angelo Rossitto, Guy Wilkerson, Rosemary Portia, Slim Andrews, Pat Costello, George Eldredge, Joe Kirk, James Sheridan.

The East Side Kids (with Hall as Glimpy) stumble onto a New England mansion that houses a mysterious Mr. Nardo (Lugosi), who may or may not be the Monster Killer. Story and screenplay by Carl Foreman and Charles R. Marion. Additional dialogue by Jack Henley. Produced by Sam Katzman.

Music by Johnny Lange, Lew Porter, (Milan Roder).

Released on October 24.

(69 minutes/Glen Glenn Sound/video/DVD)

Banner/Monogram

Zis Boom Bah (1941) D: William Nigh.

Grace Hayes, Peter Lind Hayes, Mary Healy, Huntz Hall, Jan Wiley, Frank Elliot[t], [Richard] Skeets Gallagher, Benny Ruben [Rubin], Ed [Eddie] Kane, Leonard Sues, Roland Dupree, Betty Compson, Lois Landon, Si Jenks, Bill Lawrence.

Wishing to re-connect with her estranged son, entertainer Grace Hayes strikes upon the idea of producing a theatrical show at his college. Hall appears as Skeets Skillhorn, who does a dance in drag. Choreography by George King. Screenplay by Harvey Gates and Jack Henley, from a story by Connie Lee and Gates. Produced by Sam Katzman.

Songs:
"Put Your Trust in the Moon" (Charles R. Callender; Joan Baldwin)

"It Makes No Difference When You're in the Army" (Johnny Lange; Lew Porter) (sung by Huntz Hall)

"Miss America" (Lee Ellon; Earl Hammand)

"I've Learned to Smile Again" (Neville Fleeson)

"Good News Tomorrow" (Fleeson)

"Annabella" (Lange; Porter) (danced by Peter Lind Hayes and Huntz Hall, reprised by Huntz Hall)

"Zis Boom Bah" (Elaine Cannon)

Music by Johnny Lange.

Released on November 7.

(62 minutes/DVD)

Monogram

Mr. Wise Guy (1942) D: William Nigh.

Leo Gorcey, Bobby Jordan, Huntz Hall, Billy Gilbert, Guinn [Big Boy] Williams, Douglas Fowley, Joan Barclay, Warren Hymer, Ann Doran, Jack Mulhall, Gabriel Dell, Sidney Miller, David Gorcey, Bobby Stone, Dick Ryan, Benny Rubin, Bill Lawrence, Sunshine Sammy Morrison, Joe Kirk, Stanley Blystone, Kit Guard, Frank O'Connor, Charles Sullivan.

The East Side Kids (including Hall as Glimpy Stone) are accused of a truck robbery and sent to reform school. Learning that the same gang has framed an innocent Fowley for theft and murder, the boys break out to clear both themselves and the falsely-condemned man. Screenplay by Sam Robins, Harvey Gates, and Jack Henley; from a story by Martin Mooney. Produced by Sam Katzman and Jack Dietz.

Music by Johnny Lange, Lew Porter.

Released on February 20.

(70 minutes/Western Electric Mirrophonic Recording/video/DVD)

Banner/Monogram

> "Those East Side shock troops deliver a 'kiss' to Hitler's and Hirohito's henchmen over here… and smash a giant spy ring."

Let's Get Tough! (1942) D: Wallace Fox.

Leo Gorcey, Bobby Jordan, Huntz Hall, Gabriel Dell, Tom Brown, Florence Rice, Robert Armstrong, David Gorcey, Sunshine Sammy Morrison, Bobby Stone, Sam Bernard, Philip Ahn, Jerry Bergen, Pat Costello, George Eldredge, Patsy Moran, Beal Wong, Jack Cheatham, Moy Ming.

The East Side Kids' mischief leads them to uncover a secret Japanese Black Dragon Society operating against America. Hall is Glimpy. Screenplay by Harvey Gates, from his story "I Am an American." Produced by Sam Katzman and Jack Dietz.

Music by (Johnny Lange, Lew Porter, Milan Roder)

Released on May 29.

(62 minutes/Glen Glenn Sound/video/DVD)

Banner/Monogram

"The gang takes over the law."
Tough As They Come (1942) D: William Nigh.

Billy Halop, Paul Kelly, Helen Parrish, Ann Gillis, Huntz Hall, Bernard Punsly, Gabriel Dell, Virginia Brissac, John Gallaudet, Giselle Werbiseck [Gisela Werbisek], Jimmie [Jimmy] Butler, John Eldredge, Theresa Harris, Clarence Muse, Mala Powers, James Flavin, George Offerman Jr., Antonio Filauri, Dick Hogan, Frank Faylen.

Legal student Halop takes a job with a finance company to make ends meet, but discovers their dishonest practices threaten the livelihood of a struggling cab driver. Hall plays Albert, nicknamed Pig. Screenplay by Lewis Amster and Brenda Weisberg, from a story by Amster and Albert Bein. Produced by Ken Goldsmith.

Music by Hans J. Salter, (Frank Skinner).

Released on June 5.

(61 minutes/Western Electric Recording)

Universal

"Yeah man! Even the jeeps are jivin'!...when these music-makers swing out with an Army band and get hep with a host of U.S. Oh! Honeys!"
Private Buckaroo (1942) D: Edward F. Cline.

The Andrews Sisters [Patty, Maxene, Laverne], Dick Foran, Joe E. Lewis, Ernest Truex, Jennifer Holt, Shemp Howard, Richard Davies, Mary Wickes, Donald O'Connor,

Peggy Ryan, Huntz Hall, Susan Levine, The Jivin' Jacks and Jills [Dorothy Babb, Roland Dupree, Joe Geil, Jane McNab, Jean McNab, Dolores Mitchell, Tommy Rall, Robert Scheerer], Harry James and His Music Makers (with vocalist Helen Forrest), Eddie Acuff, Wade Boteler, George Chandler, Jimmy Conlin, Pat Flaherty, Bess Flowers, Grace Hayle, Robert Emmett Keane, Sidney Miller, Addison Richards.

The Andrews Sisters join Harry James in putting on a USO show for the troops. Hall plays Corporal Anemic, who gives James pointers on how to blow a bugle. Choreography by John Mattison. Screenplay by Edmund [Edmond] Kelso and Edward James, from a story by Paul Gerard [Girard] Smith. Produced by Ken Goldsmith.

Songs:
"Three Little Sisters" (Vic Mizzy; Irving Taylor)

"Six Jerks in a Jeep" (Sid Robin)

"Steppin' Out Tonight (That's the Moon, My Son)" (Art Kassel; Sammy Gallop; Norman Litman)

"Don't Sit Under the Apple Tree (with Anyone Else But Me)" (Samuel Stept; Lew Brown; Charles Tobias)

"Johnny, Get Your Gun Again" (Gene DePaul; Don Raye)

"We've Got a Job to Do" (Vickie Knight)

"I Love the South" (composer unknown)

"You Made Me Love You" (James V. Monaco; Joseph McCarthy)

"Private Buckaroo" (Allie Wrubel; Charles Newman)

"Nobody Knows the Trouble I've Seen" (traditional 19th century American spiritual, composer unknown)

"The Flight of the Bumblebee" (Nikolai Rimsky-Korsakov)

"The Good Old South" (Lester Lee; Dan Shapiro; Jerry Seelen)

"Ma, I Miss Your Apple Pie" (Carmen Lombardo; John Jacob Loeb)

"I'm [We're] in the Army Now" (composer unknown)

"James Session" (Harry James)

"Concerto for Trumpet" (composer unknown)

Music by Harry James, Jack Matthias, Vic Schoen.

Released on June 12.

(68 minutes/Western Electric Mirrophonic Recording/video/DVD)

Universal

> "America's youthful heroes… smashing the Axis spies of the skies… in new amazing adventures!"
> Junior G-Men of The Air (1942) D: Ray Taylor, Lewis D. Collins.

Billy Halop, Gene Reynolds, Lionel Atwill, Frank Albertson, Richard Lane, Huntz Hall, Gabriel Dell, Bernard Punsly, Frankie Darro, David Gorcey, Turhan Bey, John Bleifer, Edward [Eddie] Foster, John Bagni, Noel Cravat, Paul Phillips, Eddy Waller, Paul Bryar, Frederick Burton, Jack Arnold [Vinton Hayworth], Mel [Melville] Ruick, Jay Novello, Angelo Cruz, Lynton Brent, Pat O'Malley, William 'Billy' Benedict, Ken Lundy, Guy Kingsford, Wen Wright, Jimmy O'Gatty, Joey Ray, Bill Moss, Bill Hunter, Kathryn Adams.

Chapters:
1. Wings Aflame
2. The Plunge of Peril
3. Hidden Danger
4. The Tunnel of Terror
5. The Black Dragon Strikes
6. Flaming Havoc
7. The Death Mist
8. Satan Fires the Fuse
9. Satanic Sabotage
10. Trapped in a Blazing Chute
11. Undeclared War
12. Civilian Courage Conquers

Gangsters are really Black Dragon saboteurs who are ready to cripple America by introducing a gasoline additive that will ruin engines. A band of youths (including Hall as Bolts Larson) are out to stop the enemy agents. Screenplay by Paul Huston, George H. Plympton, and Griffin Jay; additional dialogue by Brenda Weisberg. Produced by Saul A. Goodkind and Henry MacRae.

Music by (Milton Rosen).

Released on June 30.

(225 minutes/Western Electric Recording/DVD)

Universal

"Compared to the East Siders, a gorilla is a house pet! Wait'll you see them slug it out to a finish with Maxie Rosenbloom! And what a finish!"

Smart Alecks (1942) D: Wallace Fox.

Leo Gorcey, Bobby Jordan, Huntz Hall, Gabriel Dell, Maxie Rosenbloom, Gale Storm, Roger Pryor, Sammy Morrison, Stanley Clements, David Gorcey, Bobby Stone, Herbert Rawlinson, Walter Woolf King, Sam Bernard, Dick Ryan, Joe Kirk, Marie Windsor, Betty Sinclair, Tiny Jones.

A need for baseball uniforms leads Leo Gorcey, Huntz Hall (as Glimpy) and the gang into taking dishonest jobs to earn money. When Jordan is severely beaten, the boys go after the crooks. Screenplay by Harvey H. Gates. Produced by Sam Katzman and Jack Dietz.

Song:
"When You and I Were Young, Maggie" (J.A. Butterfield; George W. Johnson) (played by Huntz Hall on the harmonica and danced by Sammy Morrison)

Music by Edward J. Kay. Released on August 7. (60 minutes/Glen Glenn Sound/video/DVD) Banner/Monogram

Credits

> "They're the 'Bridge Gang'—the screen's rowdiest rascals in a smashing story of crime and terror in the seething shadows of New York's famous landmark!"
>
> *'Neath Brooklyn Bridge* (1942) D: Wallace Fox.

Leo Gorcey, Bobby Jordan, Huntz Hall, Gabriel Dell, Noah Beery Jr., Marc Lawrence, Ann Gillis, Dave O'Brien, Sunshine Sammy Morrison, Stanley Clements, Bobby Stone, Jack Raymond, Betty Wells, Dewey Robinson, Patsy Moran, Jack Mulhall, Bud Osborne, J. Arthur Young, Betty Sinclair, 'Snub' Pollard, Franklyn Farnum.

A young woman's abusive boyfriend winds up dead, with suspicion for the murder centered on Jordan. The East Side Kids (including Hall as Glimpy) find a witness who can identify the real killer. Story and Screenplay by Harvey Gates. Produced by Sam Katzman and Jack Dietz.

Music by Edward [J.] Kay.

Released on November 20.

(61 minutes/Glen Glenn Sound/video/DVD)

Banner/Monogram

> "Two boys from far-flung worlds learn... shoulder to shoulder... what America is fighting for!"
>
> *Junior Army* (1942) D: Lew Landers.

Freddie Bartholomew, Billy Halop, Huntz Hall, Bobby Jordan, Boyd Davis, William Blees, Richard Noyes, Joseph Crehan, Don Beddoe, Charles Lind, Billy Lechner, Peter Lawford, Robert O. Davis [Rudolph Anders], Bernard Punsly, Wally Albright, Johnny Duncan, Tom London, Kenneth MacDonald.

Wayward Halop ends up at military school, where he and the young cadets uncover a band of Nazi saboteurs. Hall plays Bushy Thomas. Screenplay by Paul Gangelin, from a story by Albert Bein. Produced by Colbert Clark.

Music by Morris Stoloff.

Released on November 26.

(70 minutes)

Columbia

> "The Kids and the Guys clean up the toughest town's toughest racketeers!"
>
> *Mug Town* (1942) D: Ray Taylor.

Billy Halop, Huntz Hall, Grace McDonald, Bernard Punsly, Gabriel Dell, Edward Norris, Virginia Brissac, Tommy Kelly, Dick Hogan, Jed Prouty, Murray Alper, Paul Fix, Lee 'Lasses' White, Syd Saylor, Sid Melton, June Bryde [Gittelson], Ralph Dunn, Napoleon Simpson, William Hall, Matt Willis, Ernie Adams, Paul Dubov, William Forrest, Danny Beck, William Gould, John Sheehan, Dan Seymour, John Bagni, Jack Marvin, Joline Westbrook, Evelyn Cook, Dorothy Cordray, Clara Blore, Eddie Parker, Johnny Walsh, Napoleon Simpson.

The Kids (including Hall as Pig) end up in a flophouse where they meet a sick boy. After the lad dies, Halop and the gang try to console the mother—but run into a batch of truck racketeers. Screenplay by Brenda Weisberg, Lewis Amster, Harold Tarshis, and Harry Sucher; story by Charles Grayson. Produced by Ken Goldsmith.

Music by Hans J. Salter, (Frank Skinner).

Released on December 18.

(60 minutes/Western Electric Recording)

Universal

> "Those tenement terrors are in for the scrap of their lives!"
>
> *Kid Dynamite* (1943) D: Wallace Fox.

Leo Gorcey, Huntz Hall, Bobby Jordan, Gabriel Dell, Pamela Blake, Benny Bartlett, Sunshine Sammy [Morrison], Bobby Stone, Dave Durand, Vince Barnett, Daphne Pollard, Charles Judels, Dudley Dickerson, Henry Hall, Minerva Urecal, Wheeler Oakman, Margaret [Marguerita] Padula, Jack Mulhall, Kay Marvis, Ray Miller, Mike Riley's Orchestra, Marion Miller, 'Snub' Pollard, Lafe McKee.

A misunderstanding causes Gorcey and Jordan to become bitter rivals, a situation complicated by a boxing match, crooked gamblers, and Jordan's desire to marry Gorcey's sister. Huntz Hall plays Glimpy McGleavey. Screenplay by Gerald J. Schnitzer, from the *Saturday Evening Post* magazine story "The Old Gang" by Paul Ernst. Additional dialogue by Morey Amsterdam. Produced by Sam Katzman and Jack Dietz.

Song:
"Comin' Thro' the Rye" (traditional Scottish melody; lyrics by Robert Burns)

Music by Edward [J.] Kay.

Released on February 5.

(73 minutes/Glen Glenn Sound/video/DVD)

Banner/ Monogram

Keep 'Em Slugging (1943) D: Christy Cabanne.

Bobby Jordan, Huntz Hall, Gabriel Dell, Norman Abbott, Evelyn Ankers, Elyse Knox, Frank Albertson, Don Porter, Shemp Howard, Samuel S. Hinds, Mary Gordon, Milburn Stone, Joan Marsh, Joseph Crehan, Wade Boteler, Paul McVey, Joe King, Minerva Urecal, Arthur Hoyt, Cliff Clark, Alice Fleming, Dorothy Vaughan, William Gould, Mira McKinney, Janet Shaw, Dave Durand, Jimmie Dodd, Dick Chandlee, Ernie Adams, Milton Kibbee, Fern Emmett, Harry Holman, Johnny Walsh, Budge Patty, Lew Kelly, Ben Erway, Anthony Warde, Joey Ray, Peter Michael, Harriet Vine, Frank O'Connor, Caroline Cooke, Rex Lease, Howard M. Mitchell, Robert Spencer, Jack C. Smith, Roy Brent, Jane Frazee, Robert Paige, Sidney Kibrick.

Department store shipping worker Jordan is framed for jewel theft, prompting the Kids (including Hall as Pig) to expose the gang responsible for hijacking store shipments and fingering Bobby. Screenplay by Brenda Weisberg, from a story by Edward Handler and Robert Gordon. Produced by Ben Pivar.

Music by (Hans J. Salter, Frank Skinner, Ralph Freed).

Released in March.

(60 minutes/Western Electric Recording/video)

Universal

"Anything goes, everything happens in the funniest hit the tenement terrors have ever made!"

Clancy Street Boys (1943) D: William Beaudine.

Leo Gorcey, Huntz Hall, Bobby Jordan, Noah Beery Sr., Lita [Amelita] Ward, Benny Bartlett, Rick Vallin, [William] Billy Benedict, J. Farrell McDonald [MacDonald], Jan Rubini, Martha Wentworth, Sammy Morrison, Dick Chandlee, Eddie Mills, George DeNormand, Jimmy Strand, Johnny Duncan, Bernard Gorcey, Gino Corrado, Symona Boniface.

Leo Gorcey and his pals try to make a good impression on visiting "Uncle" Pete (Beery), a rich Texan. This includes dressing Hall (as Glimpy Freedhoff) in drag and presenting him as Leo's 'sister' Annabelle. Screenplay by Harvey Gates. Produced by Sam Katzman and Jack Dietz. Filmed at Hal Roach Studios, Culver City, California.

Songs
"Happy Birthday to You" (Mildred J. Hill; Patty Hill) (sung by Huntz Hall and the gang)

"One O'Clock Jump" (instrumental) (Count Basie)

"Home on the Range" (Daniel E. Kelley; Brewster M. Higley)

Music by Edward [J.] Kay.

Released on April 23.

(66 minutes/Glen Glenn Sound/video/DVD)

Banner/Monogram

"You'll yell with glee when these happy-go-lucky hooligans invade the shivery domain of the man of a thousand horrors! It's chill-arious!"

Ghosts on the Loose (1943) D: William Beaudine.

Leo Gorcey, Huntz Hall, Bobby Jordan, Bela Lugosi, Ava Gardner, Rick Vallin, Sammy Morrison, [William] Billy Benedict, Stanley Clements, Bobby Stone, Minerva Urecal, Wheeler Oakman, Peter Seal, Frank Moran, Jack Mulhall, Bill Bates, Kay Marvis, Robert F. Hill, 'Snub' Pollard.

Helping out newlywed relatives of Glimpy (Hall), the East Side Kids go to the wrong house...one filled with sinister Lugosi and his Nazi spies. Screenplay by Kenneth Higgins. Produced by Sam Katzman and Jack Dietz.

Songs:
"Drink to Me Only with Thine Eyes" (R. Melish; Ben Jonson) (played on the organ by Bill Bates and sung by Huntz Hall and the Kids)

"Bridal Chorus (Here Comes the Bride)" (instrumental) (Richard Wagner)

"The Wedding March" (instrumental) (Felix Mendelssohn-Bartholdy)

Music by (Edward [J.] Kay).

Released on July 30.

(65 minutes/Glen Glenn Sound/video/laserdisc/DVD)

Banner/Monogram

"From police blotter to social register in 10 easy lessons!"
      Mr. Muggs Steps Out (1943) D: William Beaudine.

Leo Gorcey, Huntz Hall, Gabriel Dell, [William] Billy Benedict, Joan Marsh, Bobby Stone, Bud [Buddy] Gorman, Dave [David] Durand, Jimmy Strand, Patsy Moran, Eddie Gribbon, Halliwell Hobbes, Stanley Brown, Betty Blythe, Emmett Vogan, Nick Stuart, Noah Beery [Sr.], Lottie Harrison, Kay Marvis.

Serving a court sentence to find work, Gorcey is hired as a chauffeur in a rich woman's offbeat household. When the other East Side Kids (including Hall as Glimpy Freedhoff) are rung in as additional servants for a party, they are blamed for stealing a valuable necklace. Screenplay by William X. Crowley [William Beaudine] and Beryl Sachs. Produced by Sam Katzman and Jack Dietz.

Music by Edward J. Kay.

Released on October 29.

(63 minutes/RCA Sound)

Banner/Monogram

> "It's their fight of fights! They've got the toughest guys in town on the run!"
> *Million Dollar Kid* (1944) D: Wallace Fox.

Leo Gorcey, Huntz Hall, Gabriel Dell, [William] Billy Benedict, Louise Currie, Noah Beery Sr., Iris Adrian, Herbert Hayes [Heyes], Robert Grieg [Greig], Johnnie [Johnny] Duncan, Stanley Brown, Patsy Moran, Mary Gordon, Al Stone, Dave [David] Durand, Jimmy Strand, Bud [Buddy] Gorman, Pat Costello, Bobby Stone, Bernard Gorcey.

The East Side Kids help out a millionaire by trying to reform his son, who has turned to street crime. Hall is Glimpy McCloskey. Screenplay by Frank H. Young. Produced by Sam Katzman and Jack Dietz.

Music by Edward [J.] Kay.

Released on February 28.

(65 minutes/RCA Sound/video/DVD)

Banner/Monogram

> "Follow 'em for fun… and thrills aplenty while the Kids put a hoodoo on the hoodlums!"
> *Follow The Leader* (1944) D: William Beaudine.

Leo Gorcey, Huntz Hall, Gabriel Dell, [William] Billy Benedict, Joan Marsh, Jack LaRue, Mary Gordon, J. Farrell MacDonald, Dave [David] Durand, Bobby Stone, Jimmy Strand, Bud [Buddy] Gorman, Gene Austin, The Sherrill Sisters [Doris, Grace], Sammy Morrison, Bernard Gorcey, Bryant Washburn, Marie Windsor.

Muggs and Glimpy (Leo Gorcey, Hall) return from war service to discover one of their former cohorts is in jail charged with robbery. When murder follows, the East

Side Kids get together and find the deadly thugs who framed their pal. Screenplay by William X. Crowley [William Beaudine] and Beryl Sachs, from the story "East Side of the Bowery" by Ande Lamb. Produced by Sam Katzman and Jack Dietz.

Songs
"Now and Then" (Gene Austin)

"All I Want to Do Is Play the Drums" (Sammy Stern)

Music by Edward [J.] Kay.

Released on June 3.

(64 minutes/Glen Glenn Sound)

Banner/Monogram

Block Busters (1944) D: Wallace Fox.

Leo Gorcey, Huntz Hall, Gabriel Dell, [William] Billy Benedict, Fred Pressel, Jimmy Strand, Bill Chaney, Roberta Smith, Noah Beery Sr., Harry Langdon, Minerva Urecal, Jack Gilman, Kay Marvis, Tom Herbert, Bernard Gorcey, Charlie Murray Jr., Robert F. Hill, Jimmy Noone and His Orchestra, The Ashburns.

The East Side Kids regret taking a French boy onto their baseball team when he turns out to be a showoff. Glimpy (Hall) strikes out at the plate while taking 'practice swings' and crashes a masquerade party with Muggs (Leo Gorcey). Screenplay by Houston Branch. Produced by Sam Katzman and Jack Dietz.

Music by (Edward J. Kay).

Released on July 22.

(60 minutes/Glen Glenn Sound)

Banner/Monogram

"Wuxtra! Wuxtra! It's a case of moider and you're the victim! You'll die laffing as the sidewalk sockers blast the tenement terror!"
                             Bowery Champs (1944) D: William Beaudine.

Leo Gorcey, Huntz Hall, Gabriel Dell, Bill [William 'Billy'] Benedict, Bobby Jordan, Jimmy Strand, Bud [Buddy] Gorman, Evelyn Brent, Ian Keith, Thelma White, Frank Jacquet, Anne Sterling, Wheeler Oakman, Fred Kelsey, Bill [William] Ruhl, Kenneth MacDonald, Betty Sinclair, Francis Ford, Eddie Cherkose, Joe Bautista, Bernard Gorcey, Jack Mulhall.

Muggs (Leo Gorcey) has a chance to rise from copy boy to reporter when he and the East Side Kids (including Hall as Glimpy) get involved with a murder case. Screenplay by Earle Snell, with additional dialogue by Morey Amsterdam. Produced by Sam Katzman and Jack Dietz.

Song:
"Hotcha Chornia Brown" (Sam H. Stept; Bud Green)

Music by (Edward J. Kay). Released on November 25. (62 minutes)
   Banner/Monogram

"Paramount's merriest musical in Technicolor!"
                             Bring on the Girls (1945) D: Sidney Lanfield.

Veronica Lake, Sonny Tufts, Eddie Bracken, Marjorie Reynolds, Johnny Coy, Peter Whitney, Alan Mowbray, Grant Mitchell, Porter Hall, Thurston Hall, Lloyd Corrigan, Spike Jones and His City Slickers, Joan Woodbury, Andrew Tombes, Frank Faylen, Huntz Hall, William Moss, Norma Varden, Yvonne De Carlo, Sig Arno, Jimmy Conlin, Veda Ann Borg, Walter Baldwin, James Millican, Jimmie Dodd, Doris Dowling, William Haade, Louise LaPlanche, Kay Linaker, Jerry Maren, Noel Neill, George Turner, Dave Willock, Grant Withers.

Rich boy Bracken joins the navy so he can get away from gold-digging women, but he becomes the matrimonial target of cigarette girl Lake. Huntz Hall is a sailor. Choreography by Danny [Daniel] Dare. Screenplay by Darrell Ware and Karl Tunberg, from a story by Pierre Wolff. Produced by Fred Kohlmar.

Songs:
"You Moved Right In" (Jimmy McHugh; Harold Adamson)
"Uncle Sammy Hit Miami" (McHugh; Adamson)
"Bring on the Girls" (McHugh; Adamson)
"How Would You Like to Take My Picture?" (McHugh; Adamson)
"If It Could Happen" (McHugh; Adamson)
"I'm Gonna Hate Myself in the Morning" (McHugh; Adamson)
"True to the Navy" (McHugh; Adamson)
"Egyptian-ella" (Walter Doyle; Sonny Tufts)
"Chloe" (Neil Moret; Gus Kahn)
"The Preacher and the Bear" (Joe Arzoma)
Music by Robert Emmett Dolan, (Phil Boutelje, Joseph J. Lilley, Victor Young).
Released on February 23.
(92 minutes/Western Electric Recording/Technicolor)
Paramount

> "Thrills... adventure... as exciting as the city in which they're located!"
> Docks of New York (1945) D: Wallace Fox.

Leo Gorcey, Huntz Hall, [William] Billy Benedict, Gloria Pope, Carlyle Blackwell Jr., Betty Blythe, Cy Kendall, George Meeker, Joy Reese, Pierre Watkin, Patsy Moran, Bud [Buddy] Gorman, Mende Koenig, Maurice St. Clair, Leo Borden, Betty Sinclair, Charles King.

Glimpy (Hall) finds a valuable necklace beside a dead body, plunging the East Side Kids into dangerous intrigue involving murderous foreigners. Screenplay by Harvey Gates. Produced by Sam Katzman and Jack Dietz.

Music by Edward J. Kay.
Released on February 24.
(61 minutes/DVD)
Banner/Monogram

> *"It's gala-gala with girls, gaiety and that Goldwyn glamour!"*
> *Wonder Man* (1945) D: [H.] Bruce Humberstone.

Danny Kaye, Virginia Mayo, Vera-Ellen, Donald Woods, S.Z. Sakall, Allen Jenkins, Edward Brophy, Steve Cochran, Otto Kruger, Richard Lane, Natalie Schafer, Huntz Hall, Virginia Gilmore, Ed [Edward] Gargan, Alice Mock, Gisela Werbisek, The Goldwyn Girls [Jane Allen, Deannie Best, Katherine {Karin} Booth, Alma Carroll, Loretta Daye, Gloria Delson, Phyllis Forbes, Karen X. Gaylord, Ellen Hall, Carol Haney, Virginia Kepler, Dorothy Koster, Georgia Lange, Janet Lavis, Mary Meade, Martha Montgomery, Mary Moore, Margie Stewart, Doris Toddings, Ruth Valmy, Chili Williams, Mary Jane Woods], Albert Ruiz, Willard Van Simmons, Luis Alberni, Maurice Cass, Byron Foulger, Jack Norton, Charles Irwin, Frank Orth, Cecil Cunningham, Chester Clute, James Flavin, Mary Field, Eddie Kane, Leon Belasco, Ray Teal, Eddie Acuff, Noel Cravat, Maureen Cunningham, Eddie Cutler, Franklyn Farnum, Bess Flowers, Grant Mitchell, Cathy O'Donnell, Sarah Selby.

Kaye stars as twins, one of whom is murdered and comes back as a spirit to spur his brother into finding the killer. Comedy with Huntz Hall as Mike, a sailor. Choreography by John Wray. Story by Arthur Sheekman; adapted for the screen by Eddie Moran and Jack Jevne. Screenplay by Don Hartman, Melville Shavelson, and Philip Rapp. Produced by Samuel Goldwyn. Filmed at Samuel Goldwyn Studios, West Hollywood, California.

Songs:
"So in Love" (David Rose; Leo Robin)

"Bali Boogie" (Sylvia Fine)

"Palpably Inadequate" (Fine)

"The Patter" (Fine)

"The Opera Sequence" (Fine)

"Otchi Tchorniya Number" (Fine)

Academy Award
(Special Effects) John Fulton; Arthur W. Johns.

Academy Award Nominations
(Sound Recording) Samuel Goldwyn Studio Sound Department, Gordon Sawyer, Sound Director.

(Music—Song) "So in Love" (David Rose; Leo Robin).

(Music—Scoring of a Musical Picture) Louis Forbes, Ray Heindorf.

Music by (Ray Heindorf, Heinz Roemheld, Louis Forbes, David Rose).

Released on June 8. One of the 33 top-grossing films of 1944-45.

(98 minutes/Western Electric Recording/Technicolor/video/laserdisc/DVD)

Beverly Productions/Samuel Goldwyn/RKO Radio

Mr. Muggs Rides Again (1945) D: Wallace Fox.

Leo Gorcey, Huntz Hall, [William] Billy Benedict, Johnny Duncan, Bud [Buddy] Gorman, Mende Koenig, Minerva Urecal, Nancy Brinckman, Bernerd [Bernard] Thomas, George Meeker, John H. Allen, Pierre Watkin, Milton Kibbee, Frank Jaquet, Bernard Gorcey, I. Stanford Jolley, Michael Owen, Betty Sinclair, Forrest Taylor.

Muggs (Leo Gorcey) is banned from horseracing due to false testimony from gangsters, but he and the East Side Kids catch a break when one of the crooks reforms and implicates his former cronies. Glimpy (Hall) poses as a fortune-teller during the carnival sequence. Screenplay by Harvey Gates. Produced by Sam Katzman and Jack Dietz.

Music by (Edward J. Kay).

Released on July 15.

(63 minutes/Glen Glenn Sound)

Banner/Monogram

> *"You won't know whether to kiss 'em… or kill 'em!"*
> *Come Out Fighting* (1945) D: William Beaudine.

Leo Gorcey, Huntz Hall, [William] Billy Benedict, Gabriel Dell, June Carlson, Amelita Ward, Addison Richards, George Meeker, Johnny Duncan, Bud [Buddy] Gorman, Fred Kelsey, Douglas Wood, Milton Kibbee, Pat Gleason, Robert Homans, Mende Koenig, Patsy Moran, Davison Clark, Meyer Grace, Alan Foster, Betty Sinclair, Henry Hall.

The East Side Kids undertake to "toughen up" a boy whose police-commissioner father thinks is not manly enough. However, the Kids are caught in a gambling raid while trying to steer their young charge away from criminals. Glimpy (Huntz Hall) steps in when Muggs (Gorcey) almost starts a fight at the commissioner's office. Screenplay by Earle Snell. Produced by Sam Katzman and Jack Dietz.

Music by Edward [J.] Kay.

Released on September 29.

(62 minutes/Western Electric Mirrophonic Recording)

Banner/Monogram

> *"They fought best when it was hopeless!"*
> *A Walk in the Sun* (1945) D: Lewis Milestone.

Dana Andrews, Richard Conte, George Tyne, John Ireland, Lloyd Bridges, Sterling Holloway, Norman Lloyd, Herbert Rudley, Richard Benedict, Huntz Hall, James Cardwell, George Offerman Jr., Steve Brodie, Matt Willis, Chris Drake, Alvin Hammer, Victor Cutler, Jay Norris, John Kellogg, Danny Desmond, Anthony Dante, George Turner, Robert Horton. Narrated by Burgess Meredith. Vocals by William Gillespie.

Credits

During World War II, an American sergeant (Andrews) takes control of his platoon in Italy after they suffer a series of deaths. On the verge of attacking a Nazi stronghold, each of the men thinks about his past and what led up to this point. Hall plays Private Carraway, who talks about his sister's record collection as his comrades prepare to capture a farmhouse and blow up an enemy bridge. Screenplay by Robert Rossen, from the 1944 novel by Harry Brown. Produced by Lewis Milestone and Samuel Bronston. Portions filmed at 20th Century-Fox Ranch, Calabasas, California. Earl Robinson and Millard Lampell.

Songs:
"It Was Just a Little Walk in the Sun"

"This Is the Story of One Little Job"

"Waiting"

"These Are the Men of the Texas Division"

"Trouble"

New York Theatre Critics Circle Award
(Blue Ribbon) Huntz Hall.

National Board of Review Award Nomination
(Best Picture) Lewis Milestone.

British Academy of Film and Television Arts Award Nomination 1952 (Best Film from Any Source—USA).

Music by Frederic Efrem Rich [Freddie Rich].

Released on December 25.

(117 minutes/Western Electric Recording/Rated TV-14/video/laserdisc/DVD)

Lewis Milestone Productions/20th Century-Fox

> *"They'll short-circuit your funnybone!"*
>
> *Live Wires* (1946) D: Phil Karlson.

Leo Gorcey, Huntz Hall, Mike Mazurki, Bobby Jordan, [William] Billy Benedict, William Frambes, Claudia Drake, Pamela Blake, John Eldredge, Patti Brill, Bernard Gorcey, Billy [Bill] Christy, Nancy Brinckman, Robert E. [Emmett] Keane, Earle Hodgins, Gladys Blake, William Ruhl, George Eldredge, John Indrisano, Pat Gleason, Frank Marlowe, Rodney Bell, Charles Sullivan, Henry Russell, Steve Taylor, Beverly Hawthorne, Jack Chefe, Malcolm McClean.

While working for the district attorney, Slip Mahoney (Leo Gorcey) learns that his former employer is a wanted racketeer with plans to skip the country. Hall begins playing his Sach Jones character in this initial entry of the Bowery Boys series. Screenplay by Tim Ryan and Joseph Mischel, from a story by Jeb [Dore] Schary. Produced by Lindsley Parsons and Jan Grippo.

Song:
"The Right Sort of Man" (composer unknown).
Music by Edward [J.] Kay.
Released on January 12.
(64 minutes/Western Electric Mirrophonic Recording/DVD)
Monogram

> *"Fast, furious and funny... those riotous rascals are on the loose again!"*
>
> *In Fast Company* (1946) D: Del Lord.

Leo Gorcey, Huntz Hall, Jane Randolph, Judy Clark, Bobby Jordan, [William] Billy Benedict, Douglas Fowley, David Gorcey, Marjorie Woodworth, Charles D. Brown, Paul Harvey, Luis Alberni, Mary Gordon, Bernard Gorcey, George Eldredge, William Ruhl, Dick Wessel, John Indrisano, Frank Marlowe, Judy Schenz, Charles Coleman, Stanley Price, Marcel De la Brosse, Walter Soderling, Lee Phelps, Jack Cheatham, Fred Aldrich, Mike Donovan, Wheeler Oakman, Paul Picerni, Harry Strang.

Slip (Leo Gorcey) and the Bowery Boys (including Hall as Sach) become cab drivers for an injured independent who is being targeted by the ruthless manager of a major taxi company. Screenplay by Edmond Seward, Tim Ryan, Victor Hammond, and Ray Schrock; from a story by Martin Mooney. Produced by Lindsley Parsons and Jan Grippo. Music by Edward [J.] Kay.

Released on June 22.

(61 minutes/DVD)

Monogram

> "Hey girls, he's dynamite! When Leo gets his love wires crossed, look out!"
> *Bowery Bombshell* (1946) D: Phil Karlson.

Leo Gorcey, Huntz Hall, Bobby Jordan, [William] Billy Benedict, David Gorcey, Teala Loring, Sheldon Leonard, Dawn [Daun] Kennedy, James Burke, Vince Barnett, [William] 'Wee Willie' Davis, William Ruhl, Emmett Vogan, Bernard Gorcey, Milton Parsons, Lester Dorr, William Newell, Eddie Dunn, Buddy Gorman, Nancy Brinckman, Charles Sullivan.

A photograph taken during a bank robbery may implicate an innocent Sach (Hall), so Slip (Leo Gorcey) attempts to destroy the picture's negative before the police see it. Screenplay by Edmond Seward, from a story by Victor Hammond. Tim Ryan provided additional dialogue. Produced by Jan Grippo and Lindsley Parsons.

Song:
"I Love Him" (Lou and Ruth Herscher)

Music by Edward [J.] Kay. Released on July 20. (65 minutes/Western Electric Mirrophonic Recording/DVD) Monogram

> "The fun's getting fearocious! Mad doctors! Haunted houses! Gorillas!"
> *Spook Busters* (1946) D: William Beaudine.

Leo Gorcey, Huntz Hall, Douglass Dumbrille, Bobby Jordan, Gabriel Dell, [William]

Billy Benedict, David Gorcey, Tanis Chandler, Maurice Cass, Vera Lewis, Charles Middleton, Chester Clute, Richard Alexander, Bernard Gorcey, Charles Millsfield, Arthur [Art] Miles, Tom Coleman.

Sach (Hall) falls into the hands of a mad scientist when the Bowery Boys are sent to "exterminate" some ghosts in a haunted mansion. Screenplay by Edmond Seward and Tim Ryan. Produced by Jan Grippo.

Music by Edward J. Kay.

Released on August 24.

(68 minutes/Western Electric Mirrophonic Recording/video/DVD)

Monogram

> "The kid's got hex-appeal… he's hypnotic and she's exotic! There's bedlam in the Bowery as Leo and his rough-house rascals get all hex-cited about a beautiful gal and a heckling hypnotist!"

Mr. Hex (1946) D: William Beaudine.

Leo Gorcey, Huntz Hall, Bobby Jordan, Gabriel Dell, [William] Billy Benedict, David Gorcey, Gale Robbins, Ben Weldon [Welden], Ian Keith, Sammy Cohen, Bernard Gorcey, William Ruhl, Danny Beck, Rita Lynn, Joe Gray, Eddie Gribbon, Meyer Grace, Gene Stutenroth [Roth], John Indrisano, Jimmy Aubrey, Dewey Robinson, Knox Manning.

Slip (Leo Gorcey) discovers a way to hypnotize Sach (Hall) into becoming a formidable prizefighter. Trouble comes when crooked managers use their own hocus-pocus to strengthen their boxer on the eve of a high-stakes bout. Screenplay by Cyril [Cy] Endfield, from a story by Jan Grippo. Produced by Jan Grippo. Louis Herscher

Songs:
"A Love Song to Remember"

"One Star-Kissed Night"

Music by Edward J. Kay.

Released on December 7.

(63 minutes/Western Electric Mirrophonic Recording/video/DVD)

Monogram

"They're tip-top snoopers in the tip-toe racket!"
Hard Boiled Mahoney (1947) D: William Beaudine.

Leo Gorcey, Huntz Hall, Bobby Jordan, Gabriel Dell, Betty Compson, [William] Billy Benedict, David Gorcey, Teala Loring, Dan Seymour, Byron Foulger, Patti Brill, Pierre Watkin, Danny Beck, Bernard Gorcey, Carmen De Antonio [D'Antonio], Noble Johnson, Bill [William] Ruhl, Ted Pavelec, Pat O'Malley, Jack Cheatham, Bob Faust, 'Snub' Pollard.

The Bowery Boys enter their own world of *film noir* when Slip and Sach (Leo Gorcey, Hall) are mistaken for detectives and go on a search for a woman; their caper leads to a dangerous blackmailer. Screenplay by Cyril [Cy] Endfield with additional dialogue provided by Edmond Seward and Tim Ryan. Produced by Jan Grippo.

Music by Edward J. Kay.

Released on May 10.

(63 minutes/Western Electric Sound/video/DVD)

Monogram

News Hounds (1947) D: William Beaudine.

Leo Gorcey, Huntz Hall, Bobby Jordan, Gabriel Dell, [William] Billy Benedict, David Gorcey, Christine McIntyre, Tim Ryan, Anthony Caruso, Bill Kennedy, Ralph Dunn, Nita Bieber, John Hamilton, Terry Goodman, Robert Emmett Keane, Bernard Gorcey, Buddy Gorman, Russ Whiteman, Emmett Vogan Jr., John H. Elliott, Leo Kaye, Emmett Vogan [Sr.], Meyer Grace, Gene Roth.

Would-be reporter Slip (Leo Gorcey) and his photographer Sach (Hall) delve into the story of racketeers fixing sports events. Screenplay by Edmond Seward and Tim Ryan, from a story by Seward, Ryan and George Cappy. Produced by Jan Grippo.

Music by Edward J. Kay.

Released on September 13.

(68 minutes/Western Electric Recording/DVD)

Monogram

Bowery Buckaroos (1947) D: William Beaudine.

Leo Gorcey, Huntz Hall, Bobby Jordan, Gabriel Dell, [William] Billy Benedict, David Gorcey, Julie Gibson, Russell Simpson, Minerva Urecal, Jack Norman [Norman Willis], Iron Eyes Cody, Bernard Gorcey, Rosa Turich, Chief Yowlachi[e], Sherman Sanders, Billy Wilkerson, Jack O'Shea, Cathy Carter, Bud Osborne, 'Snub' Pollard, Suzanne Ridgeway.

Slip (Leo Gorcey) is passed off as a deadly gunfighter when the Bowery Boys head west to clear Louie Dumbrowski (Bernard Gorcey) of a murder charge. Sach (Hall) loses the map to a gold mine because it washes off his back! Screenplay by Tim Ryan, Edmond Seward and Jerry Warner. Produced by Jan Grippo.

Songs:
"Louie, the Lout" (Eddie Cherkose)

"Two Gun Tillie" (Edward J. Kay; Cherkose)

"Oh Susanna" (Stephen Collins Foster) (sung by a banjo-playing Huntz Hall)

"Trail to Mexico (Bury Me Not on the Lone Prairie)" (instrumental) (traditional, composer unknown)

"Beautiful Dreamer" (Foster)

"Camptown Races" (Foster)

"Little Brown Jug" (Joseph E. Winner)

"Listen to the Mockingbird" (Alice Hawthorne [Septimus Winner])

"She'll Be Comin' 'Round the Mountain When She Comes" (traditional, composer unknown)

Music by Edward [J.] Kay.

Released on November 22.

(66 minutes/Western Electric Recording/video/DVD)

Monogram

> "The Bowery Boys make it rough on racketeers!"
> *Angels' Alley* (1948) D: William Beaudine.

Leo Gorcey, Huntz Hall, Gabriel Dell, [William] Billy Benedict, David Gorcey, Frankie Darro, Nestor Paiva, Rosemary La Planche, Geneva Gray, Bennie [Benny] Bartlett, John Eldredge, Nelson Leigh, Tommy [Thomas] Menzies, Mary Gordon, Richard [Dick] Paxton, Buddy Gorman, Robert Emmett Keane, John H. Elliott, William Ruhl, Dewey Robinson, Wade Crosby, Meyer Grace.

Slip (Leo Gorcey) and his mother welcome cousin Jimmy (Darro) into the household. Jimmy is a recently-released convict whose misfortunes may lead him to commit more crimes if Slip cannot turn him around. Sach (Hall) takes umbrage when Slip assumes all the credit for capturing the car thieves who employed Jimmy. Screenplay by Edmond Seward, Tim Ryan and Gerald Schnitzer. Produced by Jan Grippo.

Music by Edward [J.] Kay.

Released on March 7.

(67 minutes/Western Electric Recording/DVD)

Monogram

> "They're crammed with cash!...And flooded with fun!"
> *Jinx Money* (1948) D: William Beaudine.

Leo Gorcey, Huntz Hall, Gabriel Dell, Sheldon Leonard, Donald MacBride, Betty Caldwell, [William] Billy Benedict, David Gorcey, John Eldredge, Ben Welden, Lucien Littlefield, Bernard Gorcey, Benny Bartlett, Benny Baker, Ralph Dunn, Wanda

McKay, Tom Kennedy, William Ruhl, Stanley Andrews, George Eldredge, William Vedder, Mike Donovan, Gertrude Astor.

The Bowery Boys get involved with a cache of money won by a gambler—who soon turns up murdered. The Boys hide the cash and two more killings occur. Sach (Hall) has the only clue to find the murderer, "the umbrella with the hand". Screenplay by Edmond Seward, Tim Ryan and Gerald Schnitzer; adapted from a story by Jerome T. Gollard. Produced by Jan Grippo.

Music by Edward [J.] Kay.

Released on June 27.

(68 minutes/Western Electric Recording/DVD)

Monogram

Smugglers' Cove (1948) D: William Beaudine.

Leo Gorcey, Huntz Hall, Gabriel Dell, Martin Kosleck, Paul Harvey, Amelita Ward, [William] Billy Benedict, David Gorcey, Jacqueline Dalya, Bennie [Benny] Bartlett, Eddie Gribbon, Andre Pola [Hans Schumm], Gene Stutenroth [Roth], Emmett Vogan, Buddy Gorman, John Bleifer, William Ruhl, George Meader, Leonid Snegoff.

Slip (Leo Gorcey) thinks he has inherited a house; when he goes to look it over, he and the Bowery Boys (including Hall as Sach) discover it is the headquarters of smugglers. Screenplay by Edmond Seward and Tim Ryan, from the *Bluebook* magazine story by Talbert Josselyn. Produced by Jan Grippo.

Music by Edward [J.] Kay.

Released on October 10.

(66 minutes/Western Electric Recording/DVD)

Monogram

Credits

"It's moider! You'll almost die laughing... when these keyhole watchers tangle with a killer!"

Trouble Makers (1949) D: Reginald Le Borg.

Leo Gorcey, Huntz Hall, Gabriel Dell, Frankie Darro, Lionel Stander, John Ridgely, Helen Parrish, Fritz Feld, [William] Billy Benedict, David Gorcey, Benny Bartlett, Cliff Clark, Charles La Torre, Bernard Gorcey, William Ruhl, David Hoffman, Buddy Gorman, John Indrisano, Maynard Holmes, Pat Moran, Charles Coleman, Tom Coleman, Ken Lundy, Herman Cantor.

Slip (Leo Gorcey) and Sach (Hall) become bellboys in a hotel after they witnessed a murder and do what they can to close in on the killer. Hall's stunt double was Carey Loftin. Screenplay Edmond Seward, Tim Ryan, and Gerald Schnitzer; from a story by Schnitzer. Produced by Jan Grippo.

Music by Edward [J.] Kay.

Released on January 2.

(69 minutes/Western Electric Recording/DVD)

Monogram

Fighting Fools (1949) D: Reginald Le Borg.

Leo Gorcey, Huntz Hall, Gabriel Dell, Frankie Darro, Lyle Talbot, [William] Billy Benedict, David Gorcey, Benny Bartlett, Bert Conway, Evelynn [Evelyn] Eaton, Bernard Gorcey, Teddy Infuhr, Ben Welden, Dorothy Vaughan, Sam Hayes, Bill Cartledge, Paul Maxey, Stanley Andrews, Frank Moran, Anthony Warde, Ralph Peters, Tom Kennedy, Eddie Gribbon, Martin Mason, Robert Wolcott, Meyer Grace, Frank Hagney, Bert Hanlon, Buddy Gorman, Roland Dupree, Johnny Duncan, Mike Donovan, Jack Mower, John Indrisano.

Sach (Hall) is dispatched to find a kidnapped boy, held by gangsters as a control over a prizefighter (managed by Slip). The crooks demand that the boxer take a dive during an important match. Screenplay by Edmond Seward, Gerald Schnitzer, and Bert Lawrence. Produced by Jan Grippo.

Music by Edward [J.] Kay.

Released on March 17.

(69 minutes/Western Electric Recording/DVD)

Monogram

> "Leo is a 'little mother' now! The whole gang is diaper-daffy…when the infant heir to millions turns up in their washing machine!"
>
> *Hold That Baby!* (1949) D: Reginald Le Borg.

Leo Gorcey, Huntz Hall, Gabriel Dell, Frankie Darro, Anabel Shaw, John Kellogg, Edward Gargan, [William] Billy Benedict, Bennie [Benny] Bartlett, David Gorcey, Ida Moore, Florence Auer, Bernard Gorcey, Pierre Watkin, Torben Meyer, Fred Nurney, Frances Irvin, Emmett Vogan, Meyer Grace, Max Marx, Jody & Judy Dunn, William Ruhl, Lin Mayberry, William J. O'Brien, Danny Beck, Cay Forester, Herbert Patterson, John O'Connor, Harold Noflin, Roy Aversa, Buddy Gorman, Robert Cherry, Angi O. Poulos, Robert Strauss.

Slip and Sach (Leo Gorcey, Hall) find an abandoned baby and trace it back to a desperate mother who is trying to keep her unscrupulous aunts from pilfering the infant's fortune. Screenplay by Charles R. Marion and Gerald Schnitzer. Produced by Jan Grippo.

Music by Edward [J.] Kay.

Released on June 26.

(64 minutes/Western Electric Recording/DVD)

Monogram

> "It's their funniest fightin-est film!"
>
> *Angels in Disguise* (1949) D: Jean Yarbrough.

Leo Gorcey, Huntz Hall, Gabriel Dell, Mickey Knox, Jean Dean, [William] Billy Benedict, David Gorcey, Bennie [Benny] Bartlett, Bernard Gorcey, Richard Benedict,

Joseph [Joe] Turkel, Pepe Hern, Edward Ryan, Ray Walker, Rory Mallinson, Marie Blake, William Forrest, Don [C.] Harvey, Herbert Patterson, Roy Gordon, Jane Adams, Jack Mower, Lee Phelps, John Morgan, Tristram Coffin, William J. O'Brien, Carl Sklover, Dorothy Abbott, Tom Monroe, Jack Gargan, Peter Virgo, Doretta Johnson, Wade Crosby.

Slip and Sach (Leo Gorcey, Hall) go up against the Loop Gang, a bunch of criminals who have killed a policeman. Screenplay by Charles R. Marion and Gerald Schnitzer, with additional dialogue by Bert Lawrence. Produced by Jan Grippo.

Music by Edward J. Kay.

Released on September 25.

(63 minutes/Western Electric Recording/DVD)

Monogram

"The chills will electrify you when the Bowery Boys meet the monster."
Master Minds (1949) D: Jean Yarbrough.

Leo Gorcey, Huntz Hall, Gabriel Dell, Alan Napier, Jane Adams, [William] Billy Benedict, Bernard Gorcey, Glenn Strange, Bennie [Benny] Bartlett, David Gorcey, Skelton Knaggs, William Yetter [Sr.], Minerva Urecal, Chester Clute, Pat Goldin, Robert Coogan, Kit Guard, Whitey Roberts, Harry Tyler, Anna Chandler, Stanley Blystone, Tim O'Connor, Kent Odell.

A toothache seemingly gives Sach (Hall) the power to foretell the future. He becomes a carnival sensation and the target of a mad doctor who wants to transplant Sach's brain into a werewolf-like monster named Atlas. Story and screenplay by Charles R. Marion, with additional dialogue by Bert Lawrence. Produced by Jan Grippo.

Music by Edward J. Kay.

Released on November 27.

(64 minutes/Western Electric Recording/DVD)

Monogram

"The escort bureau's goofiest gigolos! They're professional Romeos…to a gang of glamorous gun-girls!"

Blonde Dynamite (1950) D: William Beaudine.

Leo Gorcey, Huntz Hall, Adele Jergens, Gabriel Dell, Harry Lewis, Murray Alper, Bernard Gorcey, Jody Gilbert, William ['Billy'] Benedict, Buddy Gorman, David Gorcey, John Harmon, Michael Ross, Lynn Davies [Davis], Beverlee [Beverly] Crane, Karen Randle, Stanley Andrews, Florence Auer, Constance Purdy, Dick Elliott, Tom Kennedy, Robert Emmett Keane.

The Bowery Boys have the run of the sweet shop when Louie Dumbrowski (Bernard Gorcey) goes on vacation. They turn it into an escort service and end up becoming patsies for bank-robbing gangsters—who distract the Boys with a group of women. Sach (Hall) ends up taking a stout, upper crust matron on an opera date. Screenplay by Charles [R.] Marion. Produced by Jan Grippo.

Songs:
"Overture" to the "The Marriage of Figaro" (K. 492) (instrumental) (Wolfgang Amadeus Mozart)

"So You're the One" (Hy Zaret; Joan Whitney; Alex Kramer)

Music by Edward J. Kay.

Released on February 12.

(66 minutes/Western Electric Recording/DVD)

Monogram

"They're cheating the cheaters…but they don't know the dice…and guns…are loaded!"

Lucky Losers (1950) D: William Beaudine.

Leo Gorcey, Huntz Hall, Hillary Brooke, Gabriel Dell, Lyle Talbot, Bernard Gorcey, William ['Billy'] Benedict, Joseph [Joe] Turkel, Harry Tyler, Buddy Gorman, David

Gorcey, Harry Cheshire, Frank Jenks, Douglas Evans, Wendy Waldron, Glen Vernon, Chester Clute, Selmer Jackson, Dick Elliott, Franklyn Farnum, Frank Hagney, Zon Murray, Mike Ragan.

The Bowery Boys go from Wall Street brokers to gambling house croupiers as a brokerage owner's suspicious death leads them to syndicate members using a casino as a front. Screenplay by Charles R. Marion, with additional dialogue by Bert Lawrence. Produced by Jan Grippo.

Music by Edward J. Kay.

Released on May 14.

(69 minutes/Western Electric Recording/DVD)

Monogram

> "If they had the wings of an angel over these prison walls they would fly! The big house becomes a fun house... when looney Leo and half-wit Huntz tangle with killer 'cons'... to prove they're as innocent as babes!"

Triple Trouble (1950) D: Jean Yarbrough.

Leo Gorcey, Huntz Hall, Gabriel Dell, Richard Benedict, [G.] Pat Collins, Lyn Thomas, Bernard Gorcey, Paul Dubov, Joseph [Joe] Turkel, William ['Billy'] Benedict, Buddy Gorman, David Gorcey, George Chandler, Eddie Gribbon, Jonathan Hale, Joseph Crehan, Effie Laird, Edward Gargan, Eddie Foster, Frank Marlowe, Tom Kennedy, Lyle Talbot, Stanley Blystone, Paul Bryar, William Haade, William Ruhl.

Slip and Sach (Leo Gorcey, Hall) try to stop a warehouse robbery, but are accused of taking part in it. The boys accept a jail term so they can follow a link between a con doing time and his short-wave messages to the gang guilty of the crime. Screenplay by Charles R. Marion, with additional dialogue by Bert Lawrence. Produced by Jan Grippo.

Music by Edward J. Kay.

Released on August 13.

(66 minutes/Western Electric Recording/DVD)

Monogram

Behind Sach: The Huntz Hall Story

"The most riotous night club kings you'll ever see!"
                                        Blues Busters (1950) D: William Beaudine.

Leo Gorcey, Huntz Hall, Adele Jergens, Gabriel Dell, Craig Stevens, Phyllis Coates, Bernard Gorcey, William ['Billy'] Benedict, Buddy Gorman, David Gorcey, Paul Bryar, Matty King, William [Sailor] Vincent, Franklyn Farnum, Bess Flowers, Frank Hagney, Hank Mann, Sam McDaniel.

A tonsillectomy turns Sach (Hall) into a singing sensation, and the Bowery Boys see a money-making proposition—until a rival night spot owner schemes to put Sach under personal contract. Hall's singing voice is dubbed by John Laurenz. Story and screenplay by Charles R. Marion, with additional dialogue by Bert Lawrence. Produced by Jan Grippo.

Songs:
"Wasn't It You?" (Ben Raleigh; Bernie Wayne) (sung by Hall/Laurenz)

"Bluebirds Keep Singin' in the Rain" (Johnny Lange; Elliott Daniel) (sung by Hall/Laurenz)

"Let's Have a Heart to Heart Talk" (Billy Austin; Edward Brandt; Paul Landers) (sung by Hall/Laurenz)

"You Walk By" (Raleigh; Wayne) (sung by Hall/Laurenz)

"Better Be Lookin' Out for Love" (Ralph Wolf; Johnny Lange)

"Joshua Fit de Battle of Jericho" (traditional, composer unknown)

"Dixie's Land" (Daniel Decatur Emmett)

"Swanee River" (instrumental) (Stephen Collins Foster)

Music by Edward J. Kay.

Released on October 29.

(67 minutes/Western Electric Recording/video/DVD)

Monogram

"They're the daffiest draftees in history!"
                                    Bowery Battalion (1951) D: William Beaudine.

Leo Gorcey, Huntz Hall, Donald MacBride, Virginia Hewitt, Russell Hicks, Bernard Gorcey, William ['Billy'] Benedict, Buddy Gorman, David Gorcey, John Bleifer, Al Eben, Frank Jenks, Selmer Jackson, Michael Ross, Emil Sitka, Harry Lauter, George Offerman Jr., William Ruhl.

The Bowery Boys are army privates who are assigned to protect Louie Dumbrowski (Bernard Gorcey) during a mission to net foreign spies. Sach (Hall) ends up in the mud during maneuvers. Screenplay by Charles R. Marion, with additional dialogue by Bert Lawrence. Produced by Jan Grippo.

Music by Edward J. Kay.

Released on January 24.

(69 minutes/Western Electric Recording/DVD)

Monogram

"They've got ants in their trance at a séance!"
                                    Ghost Chasers (1951) D: William Beaudine.

Leo Gorcey, Huntz Hall, Lloyd Corrigan, Lela Bliss, Philip Van Zandt, Bernard Gorcey, [William] Billy Benedict, Robert Coogan, Buddy Gorman, David Gorcey, Jan Kayne, Argentina Brunetti, Marshall Bradford, Michael Ross, Donald Lawton, Hal Gerard, Doris Kemper, Belle Mitchell, Paul Bryar, Pat Gleason, Bob Peoples, Bess Flowers, Maudie Prickett.

The Boys attempt to expose phony spiritualists, resulting in a ghost (Corrigan) helping Sach (Hall) when trouble looms. Screenplay by Charles R. Marion, with additional dialogue by Bert Lawrence. Produced by Jan Grippo.

Music by Edward J. Kay.

Released on April 29.

(69 minutes/video/DVD)

Monogram

> "The fleet's all fouled up... because of their sea going shenanigans and hilarious hi-jinks!"
>
> *Let's Go Navy!* (1951) D: William Beaudine.

Leo Gorcey, Huntz Hall, Allen Jenkins, Tom Neal, Charlita, Richard Benedict, Paul Harvey, Jonathan Hale, William ['Billy'] Benedict, Bernard Gorcey, Buddy Gorman, David Gorcey, Emory Parnell, Douglas Evans, Frank Jenks, Dave Willock, Ray Walker, Tom Kennedy, Murray Alper, Dorothy Ford, Harry Lauter, Peter Mamakos, Paul Bryar, Richard Monahan, Billy Lechner, George Offerman Jr., Mike Lally, Russ Conway, Harry Strang, Sailor Vincent, Lee Graham, Pat Gleason, George Eldredge, William Hudson, Bob Peoples, John Close, Emil Sitka, Ray Dawe, Jimmy Cross, Bill Chandler, Don Gordon, Neyle Morrow, Joey Ray.

When two sailors steal a charity fund, the Bowery Boys join the navy to find the thieves. Sach (Hall) wins $2000 with the help of a parrot; he also hides in a cannon barrel just prior to its firing. Screenplay by Max Adams, with additional dialogue by Bert Lawrence. Produced by Jan Grippo.

Music by Edward J. Kay.

Released on July 29.

(68 minutes/Western Electric Recording/DVD)

Monogram

> "It's hee-hawlarious! Nutty nags take to their heels, when the boys start horsin' around!"
>
> *Crazy Over Horses* (1951) D: William Beaudine.

Leo Gorcey, Huntz Hall, Ted de Corsia, Allen Jenkins, Gloria Saunders, Tim Ryan, William ['Billy'] Benedict, Bernard Gorcey, David Condon [Gorcey], Bennie

[Benny] Bartlett, Mike [Michael] Ross, Russell Hicks, Peggy Wynne, Sam Balter, Leo 'Ukie' Sherin, Bob Peoples, Ray Page, Darr Smith, Smoki Whitfield, Perc Launders, Wilbur Mack, Gertrude Astor, Bill Cartledge, Whitey Hughes, Delmar Thomas, Bernard Pludow, Ben Frommer.

The Bowery Boys end up with a stake in a racehorse, but crooked gamblers want the animal for their own scheme. During an argument, Slip (Leo Gorcey) dismisses Sach (Hall) with the latter replying "When you get in trouble, don't call on me for more." Screenplay by Tim Ryan. Produced by Jerry Thomas. Portions filmed at Hollywood Racetrack, Inglewood, California.

Song:
"William Tell Overture" (instrumental) (Gioachino Rossini)

Music by Edward J. Kay.

Released on November 18.

(65 minutes/Western Electric Recording/DVD)

Monogram

> *"They're a razzle dazzle riot as collegiate cut-ups!"*
> Hold That Line (1952) D: William Beaudine.

Leo Gorcey, Huntz Hall, John Bromfield, Veda Ann Borg, Mona Knox, Gloria Winters, Taylor Holmes, Bernard Gorcey, Gil Stratton Jr., David Conden [Gorcey], David [Benny] Bartlett, Francis Pierlot, Pierre Watkin, Bob [Robert] Nichols, Paul Bryar, Bob Peoples, George [J.] Lewis, Al Eben, Tom Hanlon, Byron Foulger, Ted Stanhope, Percival Vivian, Tom Kennedy, Bert Davidson, Marjorie Eaton, Jean Dean, Steve Wayne, Ted Jordan, George Sanders, Marvelle Andre, Franklyn Farnum.

Sach (Hall) develops a vitamin in a college chemistry class that gives him an athletic edge on the football field. Unfortunately, he is kidnapped before the big game. Screenplay by Tim Ryan and Charles R. Marion, with additional dialogue by Bert Lawrence. Produced by Jerry Thomas. Portions filmed at Los Angeles City College, California.

Music by Edward J. Kay.

Released on March 23.

(64 minutes/DVD)

Monogram

> *"They're loaded for laughs… with bombs and blondes!"*
> Here Comes The Marines (1952) D: William Beaudine.

Leo Gorcey, Huntz Hall, Hanley Stafford, Myrna Dell, Murray Alper, Arthur Space, Tim Ryan, Bernard Gorcey, Gil Stratton Jr., David Condon [Gorcey], Bennie [Benny] Bartlett, Paul Maxey, William Newell, Lisa Wilson, Riley Hill, James Flavin, Robert Coogan, Leo 'Ukie' Sherin, Bob Peoples, Sammy Finn, Buck Russell, Stanley Blystone, Wayne Mallory, Perc Launders, Alan Jeffrey, Bob Cudlip, Sailor Vincent, Jack Wilson, Dick Paxton, Court Shepard, William Bailey, Paul Bradley.

The Bowery Boys are drafted into the military, but it isn't long before they find a murdered soldier and a playing card clue that leads them to a suspect gambling house. Sach (Hall) becomes a sergeant because his father's old army buddy is in his unit. Screenplay by Tim Ryan, Charles R. Marion, and Jack Crutcher. Produced by Jerry Thomas. Music by Edward J. Kay.

Released on June 29.

(66 minutes/DVD)

Monogram

Feudin' Fools (1952) D: William Beaudine.

Leo Gorcey, Huntz Hall, Dorothy Ford, Lyle Talbot, Benny Baker, Anne Kimbell, Oliver Blake, Bernard Gorcey, David Condon [Gorcey], Bennie [Benny] Bartlett, Fuzzy Knight, Robert Easton, O.Z. Whitehead, Paul Wexler, Russell Simpson, Leo 'Ukie' Sherin, Arthur Space, Bob [Robert] Bray, Bob [Robert] Keyes, Stanley Blystone, Elizabeth Russell.

The Bowery Boys follow Sach (Hall) to Kentucky when he inherits a farm—which is smack-dab in the middle of a shooting feud between the Smiths and Jones clans. Screenplay by Bert Lawrence and Tim Ryan. Produced by Jerry Thomas.

Music by Edward J. Kay.

Released on September 21.

(63 minutes/Western Electric Sound/DVD)

Monogram

No Holds Barred (1952) D: William Beaudine.

Leo Gorcey, Huntz Hall, Marjorie Reynolds, Bernard Gorcey, Leonard Penn, Henry Kulky, Hombre Montana, David Condon [Gorcey], Bennie [Benny] Bartlett, Sandra Gould, Tim Ryan, Lisa Wilson, Murray Alper, Barbara Grey, Leo 'Ukie' Sherin, Ray Walker, Nick Stewart, Mike Ruby, John Indrisano, 'Brother' Frank Jares, Ted Christy, John Smith, Pat Fraley, Bob Cudlip, Mort Mills, William Page, John Eldredge, Meyer Grace, Jimmy Cross, Beverly Michaels.

The Bowery Boys grapple with the wrestling world when Sach (Hall) discovers he has the ability to take down any opponent. Screenplay by Tim Ryan, Jack Crutcher, and Bert Lawrence. Produced by Jerry Thomas.

Music by Edward J. Kay.

Released on November 23.

(65 minutes/DVD)

Monogram

"You'll blow your gasket howling at these dizzy whizzes of the racing world!"
Jalopy (1953) D: William Beaudine.

Leo Gorcey, Huntz Hall, Bernard Gorcey, Bob Lowry [Robert Lowery], Leon Belasco, Richard Benedict, Jane Easton, Murray Alper, David Condon [Gorcey], Bennie [Benny] Bartlett, Tom Hanlon, Mona Knox, Conrad Brooks, Bob Rose, George Dockstader, George Barrows, Fred Lamont, Teddy Mangean, Bud Wolfe, Carey Loftin, Louis Tomei, Dude Criswell, Dick Crockett, Pete Kellett, Carl Saxe.

The Bowery Boys get into the auto racing game thanks to a fuel formula Sach (Hall) develops—which speeds up a car's performance. Screenplay by Tim Ryan, Jack Crutcher, and Edmond Seward Jr., from a story by Ryan and Crutcher. Additional dialogue provided by Bert Lawrence. Produced by Ben Schwalb. Portions filmed at Culver City Speedway, California.

Song:
"(Hail, Hail) The Gang's All Here" (instrumental) (Theodore F.

Morse; Theodora Morse; Dolly Morse)

Music by (Marlin Skiles).

Released on February 15.

(62 minutes/Western Electric Recording/DVD)

Allied Artists

> "They're panics in Piccadilly!...making merrie with the shapeliest plum in the royal pudding!"
>
> Loose in London (1953) D: Edward Bernds.

Leo Gorcey, Huntz Hall, Bernard Gorcey, Angela Greene, Walter Kingsford, Norma Varden, John Dodsworth, William Cottrell, David Gorcey, Benny Bartlett, Rex Evans, James Logan, Alex Fraser, Charles Keane, Clyde Cook, Joan Shawlee, James Fairfax, Wilbur Mack, Teddy Mangean, Gertrude Astor, Matthew Boulton, Charles Wagenheim, Bess Flowers.

The Bowery Boys go across the pond to merry olde England when Sach (Hall) learns he is the heir to a dying earl. After they arrive, the Boys discover the earl is a victim of his relatives' scheme to do away with him. Screenplay by Elwood Ullman and Edward Bernds. Produced by Ben Schwalb.

Music by (Marlin Skiles).

Released on May 24.

(63 minutes/DVD)

Allied Artists

> *"A jet-propelled joyride of laughs, WAFs and daffy thrills!"*
> Clipped Wings (1953) D: Edward Bernds.

Leo Gorcey, Huntz Hall, Bernard Gorcey, Renie Riano, Todd Karns, June Vincent, Fay Roope, Mary Treen, Anne Kimbell, David Condon [Gorcey], Bennie [Benny] Bartlett, Elaine Riley, Lou Nova, Philip Van Zandt, Lyle Talbot, Ray Walker, Frank Richards, Michael Ross, Jean Dean, Henry Kulky, Arthur Space, Conrad Brooks, Tristram Coffin, Tommy Cook, William Tannen.

Slip and Sach (Leo Gorcey, Hall) mistakenly join the air force, but manage to round up some enemy agents while helping a friend. Screenplay by Charles R. Marion and Elwood Ullman, from a story by Marion. Produced by Ben Schwalb.

Music by (Marlin Skiles).

Released on August 14.

(65 minutes/video/DVD)

Allied Artists

> *"You'll yock and yowl... as those half-wit hawkshaws go on the prowl for a missing blonde minx in a mink!"*
> Private Eyes (1953) D: Edward Bernds.

Leo Gorcey, Huntz Hall, Bernard Gorcey, Robert Osterloh, Joyce Holden, William ['Bill'] Phillips, Rudy Lee, William Forrest, Chick Chandler, David Condon [Gorcey], Bennie [Benny] Bartlett, Lou Lubin, Tim Ryan, Peter Mamakos, Edith Leslie, Myron Healey, Emil Sitka, Gil Perkins.

A belt in the nose turns Sach (Hall) into a mind reader, a skill he uses to aid him and Slip (Leo Gorcey) set up a detective agency. They quickly get a client who is blonde, beautiful, and neck-deep in underworld intrigue. Screenplay by Elwood Ullman and Edward Bernds. Produced by Ben Schwalb.

Music by (Marlin Skiles).

Released on December 6.

(64 minutes/DVD)

Allied Artists

> *"A zany laff spree in gay Paree!"*
>
> *Paris Playboys* (1954) D: William Beaudine.

Leo Gorcey, Huntz Hall, Bernard Gorcey, Veola Vonn, Steven Geray, John E. Wengraf, Marianna [Mari] Lynn, David Condon [Gorcey], Bennie [Benny] Bartlett, Gordon B. Clark, Alphonse Martell, Fritz Feld, Jack Chefe, Bess Flowers, Robin Hughes, Charles La Torre, Roy Gordon, Cosmo Sardo.

Hall plays a dual role as Sach is mistaken for a look-alike French scientist who disappeared while working on a rocket formula. The Boys discover that spies are eager to get their hands on the valuable papers. Screenplay by Elwood Ullman and Edward Bernds. Produced by Ben Schwalb.

Music by (Marlin Skiles, Arthur Morton).

Released on March 7.

(62 minutes/DVD)

Allied Artists

> *"The scariest, screwiest laugh riot since Frankenstein gave up the ghost!"*
>
> *The Bowery Boys Meet The Monsters* (1954) D: Edward Bernds.

Leo Gorcey, Huntz Hall, Bernard Gorcey, Lloyd Corrigan, Ellen Corby, John Dehner, Laura Mason, Paul Wexler, David Condon [Gorcey], Bennie [Benny] Bartlett, Norman Bishop, Steve Calvert, Rudy Lee, Paul Bryar.

Slip and Sach (Leo Gorcey, Hall) become fodder for experiments conducted by a family of mad scientists, which include a gorilla, a robot, a cleaver-wielding butler, and a lady vampire. Screenplay by Elwood Ullman and Edward Bernds. Produced by Ben Schwalb.

Music by (Marlin Skiles).

Released on June 6.

(65 minutes/DVD)

Allied Artists

> "You'll go wild with laffs!...as the boys go native and cut-up monkeyshines on a wacky safari!"
>
> Jungle Gents (1954) D: Edward Bernds.

Leo Gorcey, Huntz Hall, Bernard Gorcey, Laurette Luez, Patrick O'Moore, Rudolph Anders, Harry Cording, David Condon [Gorcey], Bennie [Benny] Bartlett, Eric Snowden, Woody Strode, Joel Fluellen, Murray Alper, Emory Parnell, Jett Norman [Clint Walker], Emil Sitka, Roy Glenn, John Harmon, Pat Flaherty.

The Bowery Boys take an expedition to Africa, where Sach (Hall) demonstrates he can use his sense of smell (heightened by some sinus medication) to detect valuable diamonds. The gang also exposes a "spirit" fakir who is scaring the superstitious natives. Screenplay by Elwood Ullman and Edward Bernds. Produced by Ben Schwalb.

Music by (Marlin Skiles).

Released on September 5.

(64 minutes/Western Electric Recording/DVD)

Allied Artists

> "The Bowery Boys run riot as harem hot-shots with Babylonian babes in the land of enchantment and dancing girls!"
>
> Bowery to Bagdad (1955) D: Edward Bernds.

Leo Gorcey, Huntz Hall, Bernard Gorcey, Joan Shawlee, Eric Blore, Jean Willes, Robert Bice, Richard [Dick] Wessel, Michael Ross, Rayford Barnes, Rick Vallin, Paul Marion, David Condon [Gorcey], Bennie [Benny] Bartlett, Charles Lung, Leon Burbank.

Sach (Hall) buys an ancient lamp and releases a genie who grants Sach and Slip a bevy of wishes—which come in handy when crooks set out to steal the magic curio. Story and screenplay by Elwood Ullman and Edward Bernds. Produced by Ben Schwalb.

Music by (Marlin Skiles).

Released on January 2.

(64 minutes/Western Electric Recording/DVD)

Allied Artists

> "What a ball! What a brawl! Those half-baked lowbrows crash the upper crust!"
>
> *High Society* (1955) D: William Beaudine.

Leo Gorcey, Huntz Hall, Bernard Gorcey, Amanda Blake, David Condon [Gorcey], Addison Richards, Paul Harvey, Dayton Lummis, Ronald Keith, Gavin Gordon, Dave Barry, Bennie [Benny] Bartlett, Kem Dibbs, James Conaty.

Slip and Sach (Leo Gorcey, Hall) side with a young heir who is threatened with the loss of his wealthy inheritance due to the machinations of his scheming relatives. Screenplay by Bert Lawrence and Jerome S. Gottler, from a story by Elwood Ullman and Edward Bernds. Produced by Ben Schwalb.

Academy Award Nomination*
(Writing—Motion Picture Story) Edward Bernds, Elwood Ullman.

> *Withdrawn from the final Academy Award ballot due to the assumed confusion with the 1956 film High Society, which starred Bing Crosby, Grace Kelly, and Frank Sinatra.*

Music by (Marlin Skiles, Arthur Morton).

Released on April 17.

Credits

(61 minutes/DVD)

Allied Artists

> "The Iron Curtain is cracked with laughter!"
>
> *Spy Chasers* (1955) D: Edward Bernds.

Leo Gorcey, Huntz Hall, Bernard Gorcey, Leon Askin, Sig Ruman, Veola Vonn, Lisa Davis, David Condon [Gorcey], Bennie [Benny] Bartlett, Richard Benedict, Frank Richards, Linda Bennett, Paul Burke, Mel Welles, John Bleifer.

The Bowery Boys aid an exiled king and his daughter from being usurped by traitors. Unfortunately, Sach (Hall) falls under the hypnotic influence of the princess' lady-in-waiting. Story and screenplay by Bert Lawrence and Jerome S. Gottler. Produced by Ben Schwalb.

Music by Marlin Skiles.

Released on July 31.

(66 minutes/DVD)

Allied Artists

> "It's real crazy, stir-crazy fun!"
>
> *Jail Busters* (1955) D: William Beaudine.

Leo Gorcey, Huntz Hall, Bernard Gorcey, Barton MacLane, Anthony Caruso, Percy Helton, David Condon [Gorcey], Bennie [Benny] Bartlett, Lyle Talbot, Michael Ross, John Harmon, Murray Alper, Fritz Feld, Henry Kulky, Emil Sitka, Harry Tyler, Ray Walker.

Slip and Sach (Leo Gorcey, Hall) help their reporter-friend Chuck (Condon) expose prison corruption by having themselves jailed on a phony robbery charge. Screenplay by Edward Bernds and Elwood Ullman. Produced by Ben Schwalb.

Music by Marlin Skiles.

Released on September 18.

(61 minutes/Western Electric Recording/DVD)

Allied Artists

"They're on the trail of those crazy hot rocks!"
Dig That Uranium (1955) D: Edward Bernds.

Leo Gorcey, Huntz Hall, Bernard Gorcey, Mary Beth Hughes, Raymond Hatton, Harry Lauter, Myron Healey, Richard Powers [Tom Keene], Paul Fierro, David Condon [Gorcey], Bennie [Benny] Bartlett, Francis McDonald, Frank Jenks, Don C. Harvey, Carl "Alfalfa" Switzer.

Some nasty varmints set their sights on the uranium mine that the Bowery Boys have purchased. Sach (Hall) dreams that he and Slip (Leo Gorcey) are two tough western hombres. Screenplay by Elwood Ullman and Bert Lawrence. Produced by Ben Schwalb.

Music by Marlin Skiles.

Released on December 25.

(61 minutes/Western Electric Recording/DVD)

Allied Artists

"The jokers were never wilder! They're breaking the laff bank!"
Crashing Las Vegas (1956) D: Jean Yarbrough.

Leo Gorcey, Huntz Hall, Mary Castle, Don Haggerty, David Condon [Gorcey], Terry Frost, Jimmy Murphy, Mort Mills, Jack Rice, Nicky Blair, Doris Kemper, Bob Hopkins, John Bleifer, Emil Sitka, Dick Foote, Don Marlowe, Jack Grinnage, Minerva Urecal, Frank J. Scannell, Joey Ray, Jack Chefe, Frank Hagney, Speer Martin, Jim Brandt, Cosmo Sardo, Alfred Tonkel.

Sach (Hall) suffers an electric shock and becomes a whiz at predicting numbers, so the Bowery Boys are off to Las Vegas to win big. A batch of crooks are also along, and they gain influence over Sach when they convince him he killed a man. Story and screenplay by Jack Townley. Produced by Ben Schwalb. Portions filmed on location.

Music by Marlin Skiles.

Released on April 22.

(62 minutes/Western Electric Recording/DVD)

Allied Artists

> "Those cool kids you love get the goods on the town's hottest hoods... with their super-duper crime camera!"
>
> *Fighting Trouble* (1956) D: George Blair.

Huntz Hall, Stanley Clements, Adele Jergens, Queenie Smith, Thomas B. Henry, Tim Ryan, Joseph [Joe] Downing, Laurie Mitchell, David Condon [Gorcey], Danny Welton, John Bleifer, Charles Williams, Clegg Hoyt, Michael Ross, Benny Burt, Rick Vallin, Ann Griffith, Paul Brinegar.

Sach and Duke (Hall, Clements) are out for a newspaper photo scoop on a notorious gangster, leading Sach to pose as a hood from Chicago called Handsome Hal. Screenplay by Elwood Ullman. Produced by Ben Schwalb.

Music by Buddy Bregman, Jill Campbell.

Released on September 16.

(61 minutes/Westrex Recording/DVD)

Allied Artists

> "Coast to coast hiccup on a nutwork of fun!"
>
> *Hot Shots* (1956) D: Jean Yarbrough.

Huntz Hall, Stanley Clements, Joi Lansing, Phil [Philip] Phillips, David Condon [Gorcey], Jimmy Murphy, Queenie Smith, Robert Shayne, Mark Dana, Henry Rowland, Isabel Randolph, Dennis Moore, Frank Marlowe, Joe Kirk, Ray Walker, Bess Flowers, Gloria Pall, Emory Parnell, Evelyn Rudie.

Sach and Duke (Hall, Clements) become the de facto guardians of an eight-year-old television star after the boy tries to steal their car. They are also on hand to thwart a kidnapping plot hatched by the lad's uncle and manager. Screenplay by Jack Townley and Elwood Ullman, from a story by Townley. Produced by Ben Schwalb.

Music by Marlin Skiles, (Arthur Morton).

Released on December 23.

(61 minutes/DVD)

Allied Artists

> "Going… going… gone… on a hypnutical joy ride!"

Hold That Hypnotist (1957) D: Austen Jewell.

Huntz Hall, Stanley Clements, Jane Nigh, Robert Foulk, James Flavin, Queenie Smith, David Condon [Gorcey], Jimmy Murphy, Murray Alper, Dick Elliott, Mel Welles, Mary Treen, George Barrows, Robert Bice, Frank Orth.

Sach (Hall) becomes the pawn of a hypnotist who is after a treasure hidden by a tax collector in 1682—said tax man being Sach as he lived in a previous life. Screenplay by Dan Pepper. Produced by Ben Schwalb.

Music by Marlin Skiles.

Released on February 24.

(61 minutes/DVD)

Allied Artists

Credits

"It's a howl of a prowl...as a-hauntin' they go for cool ghouls and hot gals!"
Spook Chasers (1957) D: George Blair.

Huntz Hall, Stanley Clements, Darlene Fields, David Gorcey, Jimmy Murphy, Eddie LeRoy, Percy Helton, Peter Mamakos, Ben Welden, Robert Shayne, Bill [William] Henry, Robert Christopher, Pierre Watkin, Audrey Conti, Anne Fleming, Bill Cassidy.

Sach (Hall) and the Bowery Boys find a cache of money hidden away in a house purchased by their friend Mike Clancy (Helton). This draws the attention of crooks and the real estate agent. The latter and a female assistant "haunts" the house so they can chase away Clancy and the Boys. Screenplay by Elwood Ullman. Produced by Ben Schwalb.

Music by Marlin Skiles, Eve Newman.

Released on June 2.

(62 minutes/Westrex Recording/DVD)

Allied Artists

"Ah...what sights!...in the land of Arabian nights!"
Looking For Danger (1957) D: Austen Jewell.

Huntz Hall, Stanley Clements, Lili Kardell, David Gorcey, Jimmy Murphy, Richard Avonde, Eddie LeRoy, Otto Reichow, Michael Granger, Peter Mamakos, Dick Elliott, Joan Bradshaw, George Khoury, Henry Rowland, Harry Strang, Paul Bryar, Jane Burgess, John Harmon, Michael Vallon.

Duke (Clements) tells of a wartime exploit of the Bowery Boys wherein they used Nazi disguises to help the Allies locate a North African underground leader named the Hawk. Sach (Hall) wields a sword to fight a pro-Nazi sultan. Screenplay by Elwood Ullman, from a story by Ullman and Edward Bernds. Produced by Ben Schwalb.

Music by Marlin Skiles.

Released on October 6.

(62 minutes/DVD)

Allied Artists

"They're off... in the world's craziest horse race with daffy devils, talking monkeys, screwy skeletons and beautiful blondes!"
                                                       Up in Smoke (1957) D: William Beaudine.

Huntz Hall, Stanley Clements, David Gorcey, Eddie LeRoy, Dick Elliott, Judy Bamber, Byron Foulger, Ralph Sanford, Ric Roman, Joe Devlin, Fritz Feld, Benny Rubin, James Flavin, Earle Hodgins, John Mitchum, Jack Mulhall, Wilbur Mack.

A touch of fantasy pervades this Bowery Boys entry as Sach (Hall) sells his soul to the Devil in order to recoup some charity money he lost at the horse races. Screenplay by Jack Townley, from a story by Elwood Ullman and Bert Lawrence. Produced by Richard Heermance.

Music by Marlin Skiles.

Released on December 22.

(64 minutes/DVD)

Allied Artists

"Nutnicks on the loose in old London!"
                                                      In the Money (1958) D: William Beaudine.

Huntz Hall, Stanley Clements, Patricia Donahue, Paul Cavanagh, David Gorcey, Eddie LeRoy, Leonard Penn, John Dodsworth, Leslie Denison, Dick Elliott, Owen McGiveney, Norma Varden, Ashley Cowan, Ralph Gamble, Patrick O'Moore, Pamela Light, 'Snub' Pollard, Gloria (a dog).

Sach (Hall) is retained to escort a poodle on an ocean liner to London, unaware that the pooch is carrying smuggled diamonds. The final Bowery Boys film. Screenplay by Al Martin and Elwood Ullman, from a story by Martin. Produced by Richard Heermance.

Music by Marlin Skiles.

Released on February 16.

(61 minutes/Westrex Recording/DVD)

Allied Artists

Credits

Second Fiddle to a Steel Guitar (1966) D: Victor Duncan.

Pamela Hayes, Leo Gorcey, Huntz Hall, Arnold Stang, Homer & Jethro, Kitty Wells, Webb Pierce, Faron Young, Minnie Pearl, Lefty Frizzell, Sonny James, Bill Monroe, George Hamilton IV, Del Reeves, Carl Butler, Pearl Butler, Merle Kilgore, Little Jimmy Dickens, Johnnie Wright, Dottie West, Billy Walker, Connie Smith, Old Joe Clark, Delores Smiley, Marilyn Gallo, Pete Drake, Bill Phillips, Buddy Spicher, Murv Shiner, Curly Fox, Clyde Smith, Lamar Morris, Dave Lewis, Bob Perry.

Musical-comedy about a benefit performance which has to switch from opera to country music. Hall plays Huntz, a stagehand. Screenplay by Seymour D. Rothman. No producer credited.

Music by Audrey Williams.

Released on December 29.

(107 minutes/Eastmancolor)

Marathon

"A wisp of a boy... a ton of bear... and a whole angry town trying to tear them apart."
Gentle Giant (1967) D: James Neilson.

Dennis Weaver, Vera Miles, Ralph Meeker, Clint Howard, Huntz Hall, Charles Martin, Rance Howard, Frank Schuller, Robertson White, Ric O'Feldman [Richard O'Barry], James Riddle, Jerry Newby, Frank Logan, Alfred Metz, Levirne DeBord.

A young boy (Clint Howard) bonds with a baby bear cub, which grows into a 650-pound grizzly. Hall plays Dink Smith in this adventure drama that became the basis for TV's *Gentle Ben* series. Screenplay by Edward J. Lakso and Andy White, from the novel *Gentle Ben* by Walt Morey. Produced by Ivan Tors. Filmed in Florida.

Music by Samuel Matlovsky.

Released on October 25.

(93 minutes/Eastmancolor/video/DVD)

Ivan Tors Productions/Paramount

Behind Sach: The Huntz Hall Story

"Of all the American heroes who served their country in it's hour of need—only one had a great rock sound…"

The Phynx (1970) D: Lee H. Katzin.

A. Michael Miller, Ray Chippeway, Dennis Larden, Lonnie [Lonny] Stevens, Lou Antonio, Mike Kellin, Michael Ansara, George Tobias, Joan Blondell, Martha Raye, Larry Hankin, Ted Eccles, Ultra Violet, Pat McCormick, Joseph Gazal, Robert Williams, Barbara Noonan, Rich Little, Sue Bernard, Ann Morell, Sherry Miles, Patty Andrews, Busby Berkeley, Xavier Cugat, Fritz Feld, John Hart, Ruby Keeler, Joe Louis, Marilyn Maxwell, Maureen O'Sullivan, Harold Sakata, Ed Sullivan, Rona Barrett, James Brown, Cass Daley, Leo Gorcey, Louis Hayward, Patsy Kelly, Guy Lombardo, Butterfly McQueen, Richard Pryor, Colonel Harland Sanders, Rudy Vallee, Johnny Weissmuller, Edgar Bergen, Dick Clark, Andy Devine, Huntz Hall, George Jessel, Dorothy Lamour, Trini Lopez, Pat O'Brien, Jay Silverheels, Clint Walker, Sally Struthers, I. Stanford Jolley, Jack Bannon.

A plethora of popular American celebrities (including Hall, playing himself) have been kidnapped by Communists, but don't worry—a rock group (Miller, Chippeway, Larden, Stevens) has been sent behind the Iron Curtain to save them. Screenplay by Stan Cornyn, from a story by Bob Booker and George Foster. Produced by George Foster and Bob Booker. Mike Stoller and Jerry Leiber.

Songs:
"What Is Your Sign?"

"I've Got Them Feelin' Too Good Today Blues"

"Hello"

"You Know the Feeling"

"Trip with Me"

"They Say That You're Mad"

"It Nearly Blew My Mind"

Credits

"The Boys in the Band"

Music by Mike Stoller, Sonny Burke.

Released on May 6.

(92 minutes/color/Rated [M-PG]

Cinema Organization/Warner Bros.

"The loveable bug's back doin' his thing!"
  Herbie Rides Again (1974) D: Robert Stevenson.

Helen Hayes, Ken Berry, Stefanie Powers, John McIntire, Keenan Wynn, Huntz Hall, Ivor Barry, Dan Tobin, Vito Scotti, Raymond Bailey, Liam Dunn, Elaine Devry, Chuck McCann, Richard X. Slattery, Hank Jones, Rod McCary, Don Pedro Colley, Larry J. Blake, Iggie Wolfington, Jack Manning, Hal Baylor, Herb Vigran, James Almanzar, Candy Candido, Edward Ashley, Beverly Carter, Norman Grabowski, Hal Williams, Irwin Charone, Gail Bonney, Burt Mustin, John Myhers, John Stephenson, Robert S. Carson, Arthur Space, John Hubbard, Fritz Feld, Alvy Moore, Karl Lukas, Paul Micale, John Zaremba, Alan Carney, Ken Sansom, Maurice Marsac, Martin Braddock.

The little Volkswagen car that possesses a human-like personality sides with elderly Hayes when an unscrupulous developer schemes to raze her house to make room for a new high-rise building. Hall plays the car-joust judge. Screenplay by Bill Walsh, from a story by Gordon Buford. Produced by Bill Walsh. Filmed at these California locations: Castagnola's Restaurant, San Francisco; Golden Gate Bridge, San Francisco; Paramount Ranch, Agoura; Sheraton Palace, San Francisco.

Song:
"Carnival of the Animals—the Swan" (instrumental) (Camille Saint-Saens)

Golden Globe Award Nomination

(Best Motion Picture Actress—Musical/Comedy) Helen Hayes.

Box office: $38,229,000.

Music by George Bruns.

Released on June 6.

(88 minutes/RCA Photophone Sound/Technicolor/Rated [G]/video/laserdisc/DVD)

Walt Disney Productions/Buena Vista

The Manchu Eagle Murder Caper Mystery (1975) D: Dean Hargrove.

Gabriel Dell, Jackie Coogan, Huntz Hall, Joyce Van Patten, Robbi Tremaine, Helen Finley, Sorrell Booke, Dick Gautier, Nita Talbot, Nicholas Colasanto, Old Tom, Winston, Howard Storm, Vincent Gardenia, Anjanette Comer, Barbara Harris, Will Geer, Jason Fithian.

When a local milkman is murdered by an arrow, a poultry company owner-turned-private detective looks into the case and discovers the victim had a secret life. This satire of 1940s caper films casts Hall as Deputy Roy. Screenplay by Dean Hargrove and Gabriel Dell. Produced by Edward K. Dodds.

Music by Dick De Benedictus.

Released in March.

(80 minutes/color/Rated [PG])

Strathmore Productions/United Artists

> *"Introducing the dog who launched 1000 stars."*
> *Won Ton Ton, the Dog Who Saved Hollywood* (1976) D: Michael Winner.

Dennis Morgan, Shecky Greene, Phil Leeds, Cliff Norton, Madeline Kahn, Teri Garr, Romo Vincent, Bruce Dern, Sterling Holloway, William ['Billy'] Benedict, Dorothy Gulliver, William Demarest, Art Carney, Virginia Mayo, Henny Youngman, Rory Calhoun, Billy Barty, Henry Wilcoxon, Ricardo Montalban, Jackie Coogan, Aldo Ray, Ethel Merman, Yvonne De Carlo, Joan Blondell, Andy Devine, Broderick Crawford, Richard Arlen, Jack LaRue, Dorothy Lamour, Phil Silvers, Nancy Walker, Gloria De Haven, Louis Nye, Johnny Weissmuller, Stepin Fetchit, Ken Murray, Rudy Vallee, George Jessel, Rhonda Fleming, Ann Miller, Dean Stockwell, Dick Haymes, Tab Hunter, Robert Alda, Eli Mintz, Ron Leibman, Fritz Feld, Edward Ashley, Kres Mersky, Jane Connell, Janet Blair, Dennis Day, Mike Mazurki, The Ritz Brothers [Harry, Jimmy], Jesse White, Carmel Myers, Jack Carter, Jack Bernardi, Victor Mature, Barbara Nichols, Army Archerd, Fernando Lamas, Zsa Zsa Gabor, Cyd Charisse, Huntz Hall, Doodles Weaver, Pedro Gonzales-Gonzales, Eddie Le Veque, Edgar Bergen, Ronny Graham, Morey Amsterdam, Eddie Foy Jr., Peter Lawford, Patricia Morison, Guy Madison, Regis Toomey, Alice Faye, Ann Rutherford, Milton Berle, James E. Brodhead, John Carradine, Keye Luke, Walter Pidgeon, Augustus Von Schumacher (a dog), Tony Basil.

A ditzy actress adopts a German shepherd, which becomes a box office star after the dog is 'discovered' by a studio head. A send-up of 1920s Hollywood with many cameos by veteran motion picture stars (including Hall as a moving man). Screenplay by Cy Howard and Arnold Schulman. Produced by David V. Picker, Arnold Schulman, and Michael Winner. Filmed at these California locations: Arlington Theater, Santa Barbara; Carpinteria; Grauman's Chinese Theater, Hollywood; Mayan Theater, Los Angeles; Montecito.

Songs:
"To Be Loved By You" (Neal Hefti; Don Black)

"They're Playing Our Song" (Hefti; Black)

"Paramount on Parade" (Jack King; Elsie Janis)

"Love Theme from *The Godfather*" (Nino Rota)

"Happy Birthday to You" (Mildred J. and Patty S. Hill)

"Dagger-Dance from Natona" (Victor Herbert)

Music by Neal Hefti.

Released on May 26.

(92 minutes/Technicolor/Rated [PG]/DVD)

Paramount

"In life he was a movie star, in death he became a legend."
           Valentino (1977) D: Ken Russell.

Rudolf Nureyev, Leslie Caron, Michelle Phillips, Carol Kane, Felicity Kendal, Seymour Cassel, Huntz Hall, Alfred Marks, David de Keyser, Linda Thorson, Leland Palmer, Lindsay Kemp, Peter Vaughan, Anthony Dowell, Penny [Penelope] Milford, June [Emily] Bolton, Robin Brent Clarke, William Hootkins, John Justin, Anton Diffring, Nicolette Marvin, Jennie Linden, Percy Herbert, Dudley Sutton, Christine Carlson, Don Fellows, Bill McKinney, Marcella Markham, John Alderson, Elizabeth Bagley, John Ratzenberger, Ken Russell.

Screen biography of the famed silent film idol Rudolph Valentino (Nureyev) and his associations within Hollywood of the 1920s. Hall plays studio executive Jesse Lasky. Screenplay by Mardik Martin and Ken Russell, from the book *Valentino, an Intimate Expose of the Sheik* by Brad Steiger and Chaw Mank. Produced by Robert Chartoff and Irwin Winkler. Filmed at these locations in Spain: S'*Agaró*, Castell-*Platja* d'Aro, Girona, Catalonia; Barcelona; Tabernas, Almeria, Andalusia. Filmed at these locations in England: Bournemouth, Dorset; Southampton, Hampshire; Blackpool Tower Ballroom, Lancashire; Elstree Studios, Borehamwood, Hertfordshire.

Songs:
"New Star in Heaven Tonight" (Jimmy McHugh; J. Keirn Brennan; Irving Mills)

"The Sheik of Araby" (Ted Snyder; Harry B. Smith; Francis Wheeler)

"Dark Eyes" (arranged by Stanley Black)

"El Choco" (arranged by Black)

"Pink Powder Puff" (Ted Snyder)

British Academy of Film and Television Arts Award Nominations

(Best Cinematography) Peter Suschitzky.

(Best Costume Design) Shirley Russell.

(Best Production Design/Art Direction) Philip Harrison.

British Society of Cinematographers Award Nomination (Best Cinematography) Peter Suschitzky.

Music by Stanley Black, Ferde Grofe.

Released on October 5.

(127 minutes/Dolby Sound/color/Rated [R]/video/DVD)

Chartoff-Winkler Productions/United Artists

> "They give new meaning to the term 'full-service station'!"
> Gas Pump Girls (1979) D: Joel Bender.

Kirsten Baker, Linda Lawrence, Sandy Johnson, Rikki Marin, Leslie King, Demetre Phillips, Steve Bond, Ken Lerner, Dave Shelley, Huntz Hall, Joe E. Ross, Mike Mazurki, Dennis Bowen, Rob [Robert] Kenneally, Paul Tinder, Cousin Bruce Morrow, Michael Alden.

Some fetching female service station attendants become high-octane operators of a garage when the proprietor (Hall, as Uncle Joe) has a heart attack. Screenplay by David A. Davies, Joel Bender, and Isaac Blech. Produced by David Gil and David A. Davies. Filmed in Sacramento, California.

Music by Leigh Crizoe.

Released in December.

(86 minutes/color/Rated [R]/DVD)

David A. Davies Productions/American Screen Productions/Cannon

> "When you meet him, you're going to love him."
> The Escape Artist (1982) D: Caleb Deschanel.

Raul Julia, Griffin O'Neal, Desiderio [Desi] Arnaz, Teri Garr, Joan Hackett, Gabriel Dell, John P. Ryan, Elizabeth Daily, M. Emmet Walsh, Jackie Coogan, Hal Williams, Helen Page Camp, David Clennon, Harry Caesar, Huntz Hall, Harry Anderson, Carlin Glynn, Margaret Ladd.

A teenager becomes a magician, joining his aunt and uncle's entertainment act. Along the way he falls in with the corrupt son of the local mayor and comes to terms with the death of his father—a legendary escape artist in his own right. Hall plays Turnkey. Screenplay by Melissa Mathison and Stephen Zito, from the novel by David Wagoner. Produced by Francis [Ford] Coppola, Fred Roos, Doug Claybourne, and Buck Houghton. Portions filmed in Cleveland, Ohio.

Music by Georges Delerue.

Released on May 28.

(96 minutes/Dolby Sound/Technicolor/Rated [PG]/video/DVD)

Zoetrope/Orion/Warner Bros.

> *"The ultimate team of woman and machine."*
>
> *Cyclone* (1987) D: Fred Olen Ray.

Heather Thomas, Jeffrey Combs, Ashley Ferrare, Dar Robinson, Martine Beswicke, Robert Quarry, Martin Landau, Huntz Hall, Troy Donahue, Michael Reagan, Tim Conway Jr., Dawn Wildsmith, Bruce Fairbairn, Sam Hiona, John Stewart, Russ Tamblyn, Fred Olen Ray.

After her scientist-boyfriend is murdered, a young woman (Thomas) takes it upon herself to deliver his futuristic motorcycle prototype to the government—and keep it out of the hands of corrupt elements. Hall is seen as Long John. Screenplay by Paul Garson (with additional material from T.L. Lankford), taken from the story by Fred Olen Ray. Produced by Paul Hertzberg and Neil Lundell.

Songs:
"Sputnik Liks" (Shawna Wright; Anthony Riparetti; James Sadd)

"Riding on the Edge of Night" (David A. Jackson; Jill S. Gaynes)

"Are You Too Tough" (Jackson; Gaynes)

"Devil Metal" (Michael Sonye; Tim Henderson)

"Blackufunkture" (Sonye; Henderson)

Music by David A. Jackson, Haunted Garage, James Sadd, (Michael Sonye).

Released on June 5.

(83 minutes/stereo sound/color/Rated [R]/video/laserdisc/DVD)]

Cinetel

> *"How do you handle a hungry man? They have him for dinner!"*
> Auntie Lee's Meat Pies (1992) D: Joseph F. Robertson.

Karen Black, Pat Morita, Kristine Anne Rose, Michael Berryman, Pat Paulsen, Huntz Hall, Ava Fabian, Richard Vidan, David Parry, Teri Weigel, Stephen Quadros, Pia Reyes, Louie Bonanno, Walter [Lex] Lang, Grant Cramer.

A woman and her nieces are in the pie-making business, but have to murder a series of men to obtain their secret ingredient. Hall plays a farmer in this horror-comedy. Screenplay by Joseph F. Robertson and Gerald M. Steiner [Gerald Stein]. Produced by Gerald M. Steiner [Gerald Stein] and Nicholas Stamos.

Songs:
"I Saw Your Mommy" (Mike Muir)
"Young, Fresh, Tight, Sweet Stuff" (The Mentors)
"Hail, Hail, Hail to Drunken Women" (The Mentors)

Music by Scott Bromberg, Michael Licari.

Released on October 21.

(100 minutes/Dolby Sound/color/Rated [R]/video)

Steiner Films/Trans World Entertainment

Short Subjects:

Swingtime In The Movies (1938) D: Crane Wilbur.

Fritz Feld, Katherine [Kathryn] Kane, John Carroll, Charley Foy, Jerry Colonna, Helen Lynd, Irene Franklin, Humphrey Bogart, George Brent, Pat O'Brien, John Garfield, Leo Gorcey, Huntz Hall, Billy Halop, Stuart Holmes, Bobby Jordan, Eddie Kane, Priscilla Lane, Rosemary Lane, Frank Mayo, Fay McKenzie, Kansas Moehring, Jack Perrin, Marie Wilson.

Movie director Feld is trying to find an actress who can do a flawless Southern accent for his latest western. Besieged by a bevy of hopeful starlets, he spots a waitress who comes from the South. Hall is seen as a "Crime School Kid" being made to toe the line by Bogart. Written by Crane Wilbur. Choreography by William O'Donnell.

Songs:
"You Oughta Be in Pictures" (instrumental) (Dana Suesse)
"Swingin' Through the Kitchen Door" (M.K. Jerome; Jack Scholl)
"Drifting on the Rio Grande" (Jerome; Scholl)
"The Toast of the Texas Frontier" (Jerome; Scholl)
"Look Out for Love" (Jerome; Scholl)
Academy Award Nomination: Best Short Subject—Two Reel
20 minutes/Vitaphone Sound/Technicolor
Vitaphone/Warner Bros.

Don't Kill Your Friends (1943) D: No director credited.

Huntz Hall.

Hall plays Ensign Dilbert, a Navy pilot learning aerial gunnery, but his dangerous ineptitude causes deadly havoc with fellow soldiers and civilians. Military documentary short stressing the need for full attentiveness and serious attitude when firing aerial guns.

Also identified as Training Film MN-84d.

(13 minutes)

Bureau of Aeronautics/United States Navy

Stage Appearances:

Dead End (1935-37) D: Sidney Kingsley.

Elspeth Eric, Joseph Downing, Margaret Mullen, Sheila Trent, Martin Gabel, Marjorie Main, Billy Halop, Huntz Hall, Bobby Jordan, Leo Gorcey, Gabriel Dell, Bernard Punsly, Charles Bellin, Carroll Ashburn, Robert J. Mulligan, George Cotton, Sidonie Espero, Philip Bourneuf, Marc Daniels, Francis De Sales, Dan Duryea, David Gorcey, Sidney Lumet, Elizabeth [Betty] Wragge, Bernard Zanville [Dane Clark].

A gang of kids grow up on the streets of a slum as a notorious gangster returns to take up with his former girlfriend. Written by Sidney Kingsley. Produced by Norman Bel Geddes.

Run: October 28, 1935 to June 12, 1937 (687 performances)

Belasco Theatre, New York City

The Odd Couple (1967)

Huntz Hall, E.G. Marshall.

Overly neat and fastidious Felix Ungar (Hall) is thrown out by his wife and finds refuge with his friend Oscar Madison. Oscar is the exact opposite of Felix: slovenly, loose with money, and a gambler. However, Oscar is able to enjoy life—something that Felix is somehow unable to do. Written by Neil Simon.

Southern road company production

The Odd Couple (1974).

Huntz Hall, Gabriel Dell.

Run: July 7 to 14, 1974.

Oaks Playhouse, Ojai, California

A production of this play also featured Shelley Berman alongside Huntz Hall, dates undetermined.

The Quadrangle (1977) D: Gabriel Dell.

Play with Huntz Hall in the cast.

Beverly Hills Playhouse, California

The Sunshine Boys (1979).

Huntz Hall, Marvin Kaplan.

A pair of old-time vaudevillians are asked to re-create their comedy act for a television special, but the two men have nursed a decades-old resentment for each other that may doom the project. Written by Neil Simon.

Run: April 24 to May 27, 1979

Harlequin Dinner Playhouse, Santa Ana, California

Luv (1979).

Huntz Hall, Gabriel Dell, Carole Goldman.

Milt Manville (Hall) saves his old college buddy Harry (Dell) from jumping off a bridge and they trade their stories of woe. Milt concocts a plan to have Harry take his wife off his hands, leaving Milt free to pursue his mistress. Written by Murray Schisgal.

Run: July 8 to August 5, 1979.

Queen Mary Dinner Playhouse, Long Beach, California

The Sunshine Boys (1982) D: Gary Davis.

Huntz Hall (as Willie Clark), Tom Pedi.

Run: September 28 to October 17, 1982.

Lawrence Welk Village Theater, Escondido, California

Arsenic and Old Lace (1988) D: Elliot Woodruff.

Dody Goodman, Edie Adams, James MacArthur, Jonathan Frid, Huntz Hall.

Wacky tale of the Brewster sisters, two eccentric matrons who pick off lonely gentlemen with arsenic-laced elderberry wine. Hall played Dr. Einstein. Written by Joseph Kesselring.

Run: February 16 through March 1, 1988.

Royal Poinciana Theater, Palm Beach, Florida

Radio Appearances:

The Lady Next Door (NBC) circa 1930-35.

Dramatized stories for children hosted, written, and directed by Madge Tucker. The cast included Huntz Hall, Celia Babcock, Florence Baker, Vivian Block, Billy & Bobby Mauch, Jimmy [James] McCallion, Howard Merrill, Laddie Seaman, Winifred Toomey, the Vass Family, Eddie & Elizabeth [Betty] Wragge.

Betty and Bob (Blue/CBS) circa 1932-36.

A young married couple, from two divergent backgrounds, strives for happiness in spite of jealousy, schemes and tragedy. Huntz Hall played a supporting role.

Bobby Benson (CBS) (Series) 1933-36.

The serialized adventures of a teen cowboy and his friends on the H-Bar-O ranch. Billy Halop stars as Bobby; Huntz Hall plays in a supporting role.

Coast to Coast on a Bus (Blue) (Series) circa 1935-36.

Children ride the White Rabbit Line hearing stories and songs.

Conductor: Milton J. Cross

Driver: Jimmy [James] McCallion

Porter: Art Scanlon

The Lady Next Door: Madge Tucker

Mumsy Pig: Audrey Egan

Various Roles: Billy Halop, Florence Halop, Huntz Hall, Jackie Kelk, Estelle Levy [Gwen Davies], Vivian Smolen, Eddie Wragge, et.al.

Orchestra: Walter Fleischer.

The Fleischmann Yeast Hour (NBC) March 5, 1936.

Star: Rudy Vallee. Announcer: Graham McNamee. The Connecticut Yankees Orchestra.

Tonight's guests are Freddie Bartholomew and Huntz Hall; comedians Frank Fay, Eddie Green, and Helen Lynd. Bartholomew and Hall co-star in the dramatic sketch "Rich Kid." written by Arch Oboler—a wealthy youngster learns for the first time the horror and misery of want.

Elza Schallert Interviews (Blue) May 26, 1938.

Elza reviews the film *Alexander's Ragtime Band* and interviews the Dead End Kids (Billy Halop, Leo Gorcey, Huntz Hall, Bobby Jordan, Gabriel Dell, Bernard Punsly).

The Kate Smith Hour (CBS) October 20, 1938.

Host: Ted Collins. Star: Kate Smith. Regulars: Bud Abbott & Lou Costello, Parker Fennelly & Arthur Allen. Vocalists: The Kate Smith Singers. Announcer: Andre Baruch. The Jack Miller Orchestra.

The Dead End Kids perform in an original radio drama written by Norman Corwin. Leo Gorcey, Huntz Hall, Gabriel Dell, Bernard Punsly.

How To (CBS) November 8, 1951.

Host: Roger Price. Announcer: Bob LeMond.

Today's celebrity panel consists of Huntz Hall, Art Linkletter, and Anita Martell. Contestants ask the panel's advice on a variety of subjects. A dentist in Hollywood wants to know how he can eliminate the fear of a dental visit from patients.

Television Appearances:

(*Note: Hall reportedly appeared in a 1932 experimental television broadcast, but no details are available.*)

Texaco Star Theater (NBC) October 28, 1952.

Stars: Milton Berle, Ruth Gilbert, Bobby Sherwood. The Alan Roth Orchestra. Uncle Miltie entertains film lovely Paulette Goddard; movie, radio and TV personality Don Ameche; and 'Bowery Boy' Huntz Hall. Jimmy Nelson and 'Danny O'Day' for Texaco gas and oil.

Saints and Sinners Milkathon (KHJ-channel 9, Los Angeles, California) December 20, 1952.

Fund appeal special to provide milk for hundreds of undernourished schoolchildren in Los Angeles. Directed by Jackie Coogan.

Denise Darcel, Herb Jeffries, [Charles] Buddy Rogers, John Carroll, Sidney Miller, Ziggy Elman, Rose Marie, Vince Barnett, Jack LaRue, Wally [Wallace] Ford, David Street, Huntz Hall, Harvey Stone, the Four Jokers.

The Red Buttons Show (CBS) March 29, 1954.

Stars: Red Buttons, Joe Silver, Betty Ann Grove. The Elliot Lawrence Orchestra.

Sketches and songs with Frank McHugh, Betty Garde, Lynn Loring, and Huntz Hall.

The Red Buttons Show (CBS) April 26, 1954.

Stars: Red Buttons, Joe Silver, Betty Ann Grove. The Elliot Lawrence Orchestra. Red provides his comedy characters in sketches and songs. Also appearing are Frank McHugh, Betty Garde, Lynn Loring, and Huntz Hall.

The Eddie Fisher Show (NBC) Huntz Hall reportedly appeared on this program, dates unknown. *Coke Time with Eddie Fisher* ran from 1953 to 1957; and *The Eddie Fisher Show* ran from 1957 to 1959.

Musical Chairs (KRCA-Channel 4, Los Angeles, California) January 18, 1955.

Host: Bill Leyden. Panel: Mel Blanc, Johnny Mercer, Bobby Troup. The Troup Group Band. The panel's knowledge of musical matters is tested by questions submitted from home viewers. Huntz Hall served as the guest panelist for this session.

The Tonight Show Starring Johnny Carson (NBC) February 5, 1963.

Host: Johnny Carson. Regular: Ed McMahon. The Skitch Henderson Orchestra.

Late-night talk and variety with guest Huntz Hall.

The Jerry Lester Show (Canadian Television Network) February 16, 1963.

Host: Jerry Lester.

Variety with guests Morey Amsterdam of TV's *The Dick Van Dyke Show*; rock-and-roll concert singer Lillian Briggs; and actor Huntz Hall.

Flipper (NBC) "Disaster in the Everglades" Part 1. September 24, 1966.

Stars: Brian Kelly, Luke Halpin, Tommy Norden, Suzy (a dolphin).

Park Ranger Porter Ricks (Kelly) is captured by an alligator trapper who is poaching in the Everglades. Barney: Huntz Hall

Flipper (NBC) "Disaster in the Everglades" Part 2. October 1, 1966.

Stars: Brian Kelly, Luke Halpin, Tommy Norden, Suzy (a dolphin).

Sandy and Bud (Halpin, Norden) still have not heard from their father, who set out on a flight over the Everglades twenty-four hours earlier. Barney: Huntz Hall. Mrs. Tremaine: Dolores Kirby

The Tonight Show Starring Johnny Carson (NBC) December, 1967 (day unknown).

Host: Johnny Carson. Regular: Ed McMahon. The Doc Severinsen Orchestra. Guests include comedian Buddy Hackett and actor Huntz Hall.

The Merv Griffin Show (Syndicated) December 29, 1967.

Host: Merv Griffin. Regular: Arthur Treacher, The Mort Lindsey Orchestra.

Talk and variety with guests singer-actor Tony Martin; Huntz Hall; rock and roll singer/trombonist Lillian Briggs; mentalist the Amazing Kreskin; and actress Ultra Violet (appears in Andy Warhol's underground films).

The Merv Griffin Show (Syndicated) January 31, 1968.

Host: Merv Griffin. Regular: Arthur Treacher. The Mort Lindsey Orchestra.

Guests: comedian Jack Carter; actress-dancer Ann Miller; former 'Dead End Kids' Gabriel Dell and Huntz Hall; actress Maureen Arthur; Boston Celtics basketball player Bill Russell; singer Lee Meza; comedy team Jerry Stiller and Anne Meara.

The Mike Douglas Show (Syndicated) circa late 1960s.

Host: Mike Douglas. Guest: Huntz Hall.

The Lohman and Barkley Show (KNBC-Los Angeles, California) October 17, 1970.

Hosts: Al Lohman, Roger Barkley.

Mostly unscripted zany humor and interviews. Guest Huntz Hall joins in the fun.

Barefoot in the Park (ABC) "Disorder in the Court" December 3, 1970.

Stars: Scoey Mitchill, Tracy Reed, Thelma Carpenter, Nipsey Russell, Harry Holcombe, Vito Scotti.

Paul's first court case is cause for celebration until fate decrees that his debut will be as mother-in-law Mabel's defense attorney.

Walding: Jackie Coogan

Fellows: Huntz Hall

Judge: Tol Avery

Lost Island (TV-Movie) 1971.

(*According to David Hayes and Brent Walker in their book The Films of the Bowery Boys, Huntz Hall was a dialogue coach for this telefilm. However, various sources—including the comprehensive six-volume set Movies Made for Television by Alvin H. Marill—make no mention of this movie.*)

Movie of the Week (ABC) *Escape* April 6, 1971.

Escape artist Cameron Steele (Christopher George) uses his unique death-defying talents to help others. Case in point: a kidnapped biologist who may hold the key to synthesized life. Directed by John Llewellyn Moxey for Paramount Network Television. *An unsuccessful pilot for a proposed adventure series to star George and Avery Schreiber (who plays Nicholas Slye).*

Dr. Henry Walding: William Windom

Susan Walding: Marlyn Mason

Charles Walding: John Vernon

Evelyn Harrison: Gloria Grahame

Lewis Harrison: William Schallert

Gilbert: Huntz Hall

Dan: Mark Tapscott

Roger: George Clifton

Trudy: Lucille Benson

Vicki: Lisa Bronwyn Moore

Carter: Chuck Hicks

Customer: Edward Call

Designer: Lester Fletcher

Model: Merriana Henrig

Photographer: Caroline Ross

The Merv Griffin Show (CBS) June 2, 1971.

Host: Merv Griffin. Regular: Arthur Treacher, The Mort Lindsey Orchestra.

Merv gathers together a group of former child stars as his guests: Jane Withers, Margaret O'Brien, Gloria Jean, Brandon de Wilde, and Huntz Hall.

The Chicago Teddy Bears (CBS) (Series) September 17 to December 17, 1971.

During the 1920s in the Windy City, speakeasy owner Linc McCray continually outwits his mobster-cousin—Big Nick Marr—who wants to 'muscle in' on Linc's action.

Linc McCray: Dean Jones

Big Nick Marr: Art Metrano

Marvin: Marvin Kaplan

Duke: Mickey Shaughnessy

Lefty: Jamie Farr

Julius: Mike Mazurki

Dutch: Huntz Hall

Uncle Latzi: John Banner

Produced by Hy Averback and Jerry Thorpe (Dean Jones Productions/Warner Bros. Television) 13 episodes

The Corner Bar (ABC) "The Navy Reunion" August 16, 1972.

Stars: Gabriel Dell, J.J. Barry, Bill Fiore, Joe Keyes, Vincent Schiavelli, Shimen Ruskin, Langhorn Scruggs.

Harry's old sailor buddy (Huntz Hall) swindles Harry and the bar regulars in a fraudulent real estate deal.

The Wonderful World of Disney (NBC) "The Sky's the Limit" Part 1. January 19, 1975.

Announcer: Dick Wesson.

Young Abner Therman III (Ike Eisenmann), boarded at an English school, spends his summer vacation with his grandfather in California. They get to know each other better as they fix an old airplane together.

Abner Therman I: Pat O'Brien

Cornwall: Lloyd Nolan

Gertie: Jeanette Nolan

Ben: Ben Blue

Cholly: Alan Hale

Grimes: Richard Arlen

Abner Therman II: Robert Sampson

Hitchhiker: Huntz Hall

FAA Representative: Ben Cooper

Police Chief: Bill [William] Zuckert

Captain Willoughby: Norman Bartold

Credits

The Wonderful World of Disney (NBC) "The Sky's the Limit" Part 2. January 26, 1975.

The restoration of the old airplane by Abner III and his grandfather leads to the boy's hope that he can learn to fly—but his father has objections. *The cast is the same as part one.*

The Ghost Busters (CBS) "Which Witch Is Which?" October 25, 1975.

Stars: Forrest Tucker, Larry Storch, Bob Burns, Lou Scheimer (voice).

The spirit of a witch from the 17th century desires revenge on Eddie (Storch) because he is the descendant of the man who thwarted her at the Salem witch trials.

Gronk: Huntz Hall

The Witch: Ann Morgan Guilbert

Salem: Lee Christian

The Ghost Busters (CBS) "Merlin, the Magician" December 6, 1975.

Stars: Forrest Tucker, Larry Storch, Bob Burns, Lou Scheimer (voice).

Jake and Eddie (Tucker, Storch) side with an ancient mage when the sorcerer and his jester (Huntz Hall as Gronk) are pursued through time by Morgan Le Fay.

Merlin: Carl Ballantine

Morgan: Ina Balin

Matt Helm (ABC) "Die Once, Die Twice" January 3, 1976.

Stars: Anthony Franciosa, Laraine Stephens, Gene Evans, Jeff Donnell.

Claire Kronski (Stephens) looks into the case of a murder victim who was once thought to be already dead; now her client is suspected of the crime.

Ellen Tanner: Susan Dey

Dan Mallory: Howard Duff

Mr. Simmons: Charles Drake

Mrs. Simmons: Audrey Totter

Willy: Huntz Hall

Griff Tanner: Robert Ginty

Mrs. Lake: Holly [Hollis] Irving

Paul Tyler: Fred Lerner

Jean: Eileen Chesis

Good Heavens (ABC) "Good Neighbor Maxine" March 15, 1976.

Star: Carl Reiner

Mr. Angel (Reiner), an agent from the afterlife, is sent to help people who are deserving of divine intervention. Maxine (Loretta Swit) tells him that she wants a more adventurous life.

Jim Pearson: Clu Gulagher

Buck: Ron Masak

Rocky: Michael Gregory

Barney: Huntz Hall

Blanca: Karmin Marcelo

Ray Sherwood: Michael Pataki

State Trooper: R.B. [Ari] Soko-Ram

Gas Station Attendant: Robert B. Williams

CHiPs (NBC) "Crack-Up" March 9, 1978.

Stars: Larry Wilcox, Erik Estrada, Robert Pine.

Jon (Wilcox) is taken off duty due to an injury, leaving Sgt. Getraer (Pine) to fill in as Ponch's (Erik Estrada) partner. A vengeful tow-truck driver who is targeting highway officers threatens them and the rest of the unit.

Wanda: Phyllis Diller

Niles: Joey Aresco

Ray: Gary Sandy

Armored Car Driver: Huntz Hall

Father: Harry [Hari] Rhodes

Armored Car Co-Driver: Marc Lawrence

Dr. Ansgar: Phillip Pine

Officer Arthur Grossman: Paul Linke

Officer Barry Baricza: Brodie Greer

Dr. Bosca: Danny Goldman

Nurse Chrissy: Linda Thompson

Little Girl: Pamela Sye

The Tomorrow Show (NBC) March 19, 1979.

Host: Tom Snyder.

Former 'Dead End Kids' Huntz Hall and Gabriel Dell guest with their fan club president Richard Roat. Franklin McNulty appears to discuss his refusal to pay US income tax on his Irish Sweepstakes winnings.

Channel Zero (Made for Cable) 1982.

Chevy Chase, Laraine Newman, and Martin Mull. Further details unknown, except that Huntz Hall spoofed a long distance telephone commercial.

Diff'rent Strokes (NBC) "Big Brother" October 23, 1982.

Stars: Conrad Bain, Gary Coleman, Todd Bridges, Dana Plato.

Arnold (Coleman) feels rejected by the whole family when Willis (Bridges) becomes a 'big brother' to a lonely boy.

Pearl Gallagher: Mary Jo Catlett

Joey: Joey Lawrence

Happy Wanderer: Huntz Hall

Late Night with David Letterman (NBC) February 22, 1983.

Host: David Letterman. Regular: Calvert DeForest. The Paul Shaffer Orchestra.

Dave presents a February 22 'Reunion Day' show, with guests from February 22, 1982 (not detailed here for that date) making repeat appearances: newswoman Jessica Savitch; Simon Bond, author of the book *101 Uses for a Dead Cat*; and students from P.S. 84. Also, actor Huntz Hall appears.

"The Ratings Game" (Movie Channel) (TV-Movie) December 15, 1984.

A trucking executive dabbles in the television industry and manages to make a megahit with one of the worst ideas for a TV show ever to be created. Directed by Danny DeVito for Imagination/New Street Productions.

Vic DeSalvo: Danny DeVito

Francine Kester: Rhea Perlman

Parker Braithwaite: Gerrit Graham

Mrs. Sweeney: Bernadette Birkett

Colonel: Barry Corbin

Goody DeSalvo: Louis Giambalvo

Cap'n Andy: Ronny Graham

Benny Bentson: Huntz Hall

Wes Vandergelder: Kevin McCarthy

Sal: Michael Richards

Television Director: Ron Rifkin

Tony: Joe Santos

Mr. Sweeney: George Wendt

Himself: Steve Allen

Herself: Jayne Meadows

Teresa: Randi Brooks

Bambi: Candy Brough

Stacy: Randi Brough

Himself: Army Archerd

Paisan Receptionist: Allyce Beasley

Vic's Tailor: Peter Brocco

Nunzio: Robert Costanzo

Voice of Francine's Mother: Selma Diamond

Le Boeuf Maitre'd: Michael Ensign.

Network Spokesman: Kenneth Kimmins.

First Network Representative: Jerry Seinfeld.

Robert Klein Time (USA) February 15, 1987.

Host: Robert Klein. The Bob Stein Orchestra.

Two of the original Dead End Kids, Huntz Hall and Gabe [Gabriel] Dell now doing stand-up comedy, sit down to talk with Robert.

Night Heat (CBS) "Bless Me Father" September 29, 1988.

Stars: Scott Hylands, Allan Royal, Jeff Wincott, Susan Hogan.

A priest (Huntz Hall as Father O'Malley) helps Kevin and Frank (Hylands, Wincott) locate the hit-and-run driver who killed a woman in front of a church. They find she was connected to a gang called the Terminators.

Lt. Jim Hogan: Sean McCann

Detective Colby Burns: Eugene Clark

Detective Freddie Carson: Stephen Mandel

Prosecutor Elaine Jeffers: Deborah Grover

Detective Christine Meadows: Laura Robinson

Ellen: Maxine Miller

Simone: Isabelle Mejias

Emilio Sarda: Joseph Griffin

Rico: Damon D'Oliveira

Fleming: Anthony Sherwood.

Daddy Dearest (FOX) "American We" November 7, 1993.

Stars: Richard Lewis, Don Rickles, Renee Taylor, Sydney Walsh, Barney Martin.

Steven (Lewis) tries to get back at a guy he thinks mugged him, but his misguided action—robbing the so-called mugger—lands him and his father Al (Rickles) in jail.

Pretzel Man: Huntz Hall

Stan: Garrett Morris

Cop #1: Bubba Smith

Cop #2: Marion Ramsey

Inmate #1: Rosey Brown

Inmate #2: Donald Gibb

The Aspiring Author Sach:

Sach: "Anyone that doesn't adore me, I write 'em right out of my book."

Sach: "You know something, Chief? I think I'll write a book, *How to Become a Millionaire in Three Easy Lessons.*"

Slip: "You gonna write a book? Write a book. You couldn't even read one."

Sach (taking out a comic book): "Oh yeah! What's this, chopped liver? How do you like that, *Dumbo Gets Drafted?*"

(*Crashing Las Vegas*, Allied Artists, 1956)

I imagined Sach could have responded:

"Ohp! Ohp! Ohp!"

I insist: LONG LIVE SACH!

www.ingramcontent.com/pod-product-compliance
Lightning Source LLC
Chambersburg PA
CBHW052048230426
43671CB00011B/1832